MISSISSIPPI

Picture Research by Patti Carr Black

Produced in Cooperation with the Mississippi Historical Society

American Historical Press
Sun Valley, California

MISSISSIPPI

An Illustrated History

Edward N. Akin and Charles C. Bolton

© 2002 American Historical Press
All Rights Reserved
Published 2002
Printed in the United States of America

Library of Congress Catalogue Card Number: 2002094842

ISBN: 1-892724-33-2

Bibliography: p. 236
Includes Index

CONTENTS

For Leslie, Laura, and Ben

Looking east on Capitol Street in downtown Jackson. The building on the right with the clock tower is the Lamar Life Insurance Building, built in 1925, and at ten stories, by far the tallest building in the city at the time. At the end of the street is the Old Capitol Building. Courtesy, Mississippi Development Authority

The automobile began to change Mississippi in the 1920s and continues to shape the landscape today. A continually growing system of roads made Mississippians mobile. Business districts in small towns and downtown urban areas began to be abandoned as people drove to larger town centers to shop and work. Courtesy, Mississippi Department of Archives and History

INTRODUCTION

There are thousands of stories that comprise the tapestry of Mississippi's past, from accounts of the earliest native inhabitants to descriptions of the French and Spanish colonies to chronicles of the days of King Cotton and civil war to the memories of the civil rights movement of the twentieth century. The narrative presented here attempts to capture something of both the richness and complexity of Mississippi history, though interested readers will also want to consult the numerous studies of Mississippi's past that historians and others have conducted over the years for a more detailed rendering of the Mississippi story. A sampling of these works appears at the end of this book in the bibliography. The text here is accompanied by an array of photographs and illustrations that bear out the old saying that "a picture is worth a thousand words." The images themselves speak volumes to the triumphs and tragedies of Mississippi and her people.

An earlier version of this work, published in 1987, was sponsored by the Mississippi Historical Society and authored by Edward N. Akin, with editorial assistance from Elbert Hillard, Chrissy Wilson, and Ray Skates. The original author and editors are to be commended for a job well done. And in large part, the original text has been retained, though it has been updated in places to reflect the insights of recent scholarship on Mississippi history. A new chapter, "Modern Mississippi," details the developments in Mississippi political, economic, and social life over the last thirty years. Another new feature of the book is the chronology, which outlines some of the key events of Mississippi's past.

Most of the photographs and illustrations for this book were identified by Patti Carr Black, former director of the Old Capitol State Historical Museum. She is the most knowledgeable person in the state of Mississippi concerning the state's photographic archives, and she uncovered images that vividly depict the history of Mississippi. I managed to locate a few more historic images to illustrate the chronology, some new color photographs, and the pictures that accompany the "Modern Mississippi" chapter.

In closing, I would like to thank a few people who assisted me in my efforts. Photo research was a new job description for me, and the task was made easier by the assistance of Hank Holmes of the Mississippi Department of Archives and History; Janet Martin of the Mississippi Development Authority; Yvonne Arnold of the McCain Library and Archives at the University of Southern Mississippi; and Diana and Stephen Young, formerly of Hattiesburg, now living in France. I also benefitted from the editorial suggestions of my wife, Leslie Bloch, and my colleague and friend, Bradley Bond. Finally, my editor at American Historical Press, Carolyn Martin, patiently answered all my questions and skillfully helped move this project along to completion.

Charles C. Bolton
Hattiesburg, Mississippi

Mississippi adopted the magnolia as its state tree in 1938. The evergreen tree's fragrant white flowers are most abundant in late spring and early summer. Courtesy, Mississippi Development Authority/Division of Tourism

CHAPTER I
GEOGRAPHY AND PREHISTORY

Centuries ago, the Indians, impressed with the majesty of the Mississippi River, called the river *Messippi,* "Father of Waters." When French explorers arrived in the Mississippi area, they adopted the Indians' term for the vast river that links the Gulf of Mexico to the heartland of what is now the United States. It is fitting that the state of Mississippi also bears the name, as an acknowledgment of the river's influence, both actual and symbolic, on the area.

Geography plays a central role in the history of a people. Availability of water, terrain and soil types, as well as climate determine both where people settle and the shape of their daily existence.

The state of Mississippi is located in the geographic center of the Gulf South and is bounded by the Mississippi and Pearl rivers on the west, the state of Alabama on the east, the state of Tennessee on the north, and Louisiana and the Gulf of Mexico on the south.

Mississippi's climate has been both its blessing and its curse. It has mild winters, with an average January temperature of almost forty-eight degrees. Winter is relatively short, giving the state a long growing season for crops. During summer in Mississippi, humidity often reaches 90 percent. Although the summers can be quite hot, with the thermometer reading into the nineties in July and August, the average July temperature is only eighty-one

degrees. Of course, the temperatures have not been consistent through history. When the Europeans first arrived, the climate was far different, for the North American continent had experienced the "Little Ice Age" of the fifteenth and sixteenth centuries. Although this era produced no glaciers, it was characterized by lower temperatures and shorter growing seasons.

The state of Mississippi can be divided into ten geographic regions. The Yazoo River Basin, bordering the Mississippi River, is located in the northwestern section of the state. Between the Yazoo River and the Mississippi lies one of the most notable regions of the state, the Delta. With its tributaries, the Yazoo drains the area, emptying into the Mississippi just above Vicksburg. Because of the frequent floods over the centuries by both the Yazoo and Mississippi rivers across this level delta area, the soil is a very fertile, black alluvial loam. A narrow belt of this rich soil extends along the Mississippi River as far south as Natchez and a little beyond.

Just to the east of the black-loam Delta region is the area of Bluff Hills. This ridge divides the rest of the state from the Delta along a line that runs northward from Natchez through Vicksburg and Yazoo City. The brown loam (or loess) of the bluff region is rich, but differs greatly from the even richer bottomlands of the Delta. The loess, which was blown into the area over the centuries from the river floodplain, is loose and erodes easily.

To the east of the Bluff Hills, Mississippi has three geographic regions. From north to south, they are the North Central Hills (Red Clay Hills), which are traversed by the headwaters of the Pearl River; the Jackson Prairie; and the Pine Hills (known locally as the Piney Woods). In the North Central Hills, river bottomlands provide a sandy loam, the best soil for agriculture in the area. The southern end of the North Central Hills is a rough line from just north of Jackson to just south of Meridian. The Jackson Prairie was originally woodlands. However, the Indian practice of burning forest undergrowth to aid in hunting helped to create the open savannahs of the prairie and the longleaf-pine belt across the southeast Pine Hills region.

The Pontotoc Ridge in northeast Mississippi separates the Flatwoods, a heavily forested band just east of the North Central Hills, from the Black Prairie. Persons familiar with fertile seaboard areas elsewhere in the South often have difficulty understanding that Mississippi's two richest agricultural areas, the Delta and the Black Prairie, are in the northern portion of the state, rather than next to the coastal plain, or tidewater. The Black Prairie, stretching from Corinth near the Tennessee line beyond Macon, is approximately twenty to twenty-five miles in width. The area of Mississippi most at odds with the prevailing notion that the state consists only of flatlands is the Tennessee Hills region in the northeastern corner of the state. With the highest point near Iuka in Tishomingo County, these Appalachian foothills vary in height from 650 feet up to 806 feet above sea level. The soil in the area is unfertile and subject to erosion.

South of the Pine Hills, the Coastal Plain stretches along the Gulf Coast. The Coastal Plain was not heavily populated nor economically productive prior to the twentieth century. Its soil was of the poorest quality, and the area did not have good ports with excellent river connections, as did nearby New Orleans and Mobile. Since World War II, however, the Gulf Coast's contributions to the state through tourism, industry, and military bases have made it more prominent.

The river systems of the state have played important roles in its development. The Yazoo River Basin consists of the Yazoo River, running along the eastern edge of the Delta, and its tributaries. Marking the headwaters of the Yazoo River Basin near the Tennessee state line, the Coldwater River

Above: *The Mississippi Delta is a fertile wedge of alluvial soil deposited through the centuries by floods of the Yazoo and Mississippi rivers. When the interior of the Delta was opened up around the turn of the century, cotton production moved up the river from the old Natchez District to the Delta, which became "The New Cotton Kingdom." Courtesy, Mississippi Department of Economic Development*

Top: *The Mississippi River was first an avenue of settlement by Indian tribes, and later an avenue of exploration by European nations. The river has become a busy thoroughfare for the entire central portion of North America, with ports at Greenville, Vicksburg, and Natchez. The Vicksburg bridge is one of four that span the river from Mississippi into Arkansas and Louisiana. Courtesy, Mississippi Department of Economic Development*

flows into the Tallahatchie, which in turn receives the Yocona River (Panola-Quitman Floodway) in Tallahatchie County west of Charleston. At Greenwood, the Yalobusha and Tallahatchie rivers meet to form the Yazoo River. While the Yazoo and its tributaries drain the hills to the east, the Sunflower River traverses the middle of the Delta, emptying into the Yazoo River near its confluence with the Mississippi.

The Big Black River courses from the north-central portion of the state in a southwesterly direction, emptying into the Mississippi below Vicksburg. The Pearl River drains central Mississippi before emptying into the Gulf of Mexico. The

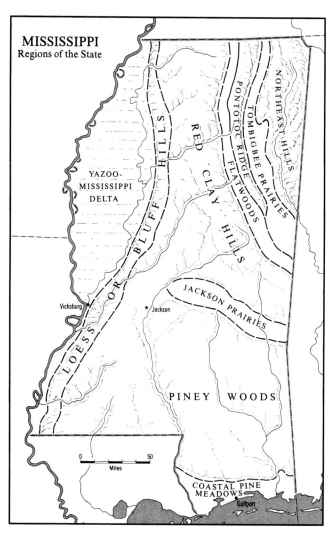

Above: *Mississippi can be easily divided into ten physiographic regions because the topography is so varied and distinctive. It ranges from flat delta to undulating prairie to steep eroded hills, and each region has its recognizable characteristics. Courtesy, American Association for State and Local History*

Above, left: *The southeastern region of Mississippi was once an immense stand of virgin long-leaf pine trees. Those forests were stripped by the lumber industries in the early part of the twentieth century. Today, short-leaf pine and reforested areas still earn it the name of "The Piney Woods." Courtesy, Forest History Society, Durham, North Carolina*

Pascagoula River, which flows into the Gulf near the eastern edge of the state, is formed by the Leaf and Chickasawhay rivers. The other major river of the state is the Tombigbee River, which has its headwaters in Mississippi but leaves the state near Columbus, entering Alabama where it unites with other rivers. In the 1980s the Tombigbee was connected with the Tennessee River at the Alabama-Mississippi state line by the Tennessee-Tombigbee Waterway. Boosters of the waterway hope that it will provide major economic benefits to the area.

Steamboats and flatboats moved people and goods on the state's rivers throughout the nineteenth and early twentieth centuries. But the rivers have been vital to people of the area from the beginning, both for transportation and as a source of life-giving water.

The earliest entry of Indians into North America cannot be precisely dated, but estimates as to when Asiatic groups first crossed the Bering Straits range from 40,000 to 25,000 years ago. Likewise, the entry date of Indians into Mississippi cannot be exactly determined, but archaeologists have found remains of prehistoric Indian cultures dating to circa 9,500 B.C., suggesting an entry date of approximately 10,000 B.C.

These Paleo-Indians were hunters and gatherers. Undoubtedly, they were attracted to the area by its abundant game and lush environment. They

probably killed such animals as mammoths and mastodons, in addition to deer, bear, rabbits, and turkeys. Following the hunt, the Indians would field-dress the animals, either eating the food immediately or drying it for winter nourishment.

Over time, the Indians also became familiar with the wild plants of the area and probably gathered berries, nuts, and other edible flora. Coastal Indians took advantage of opportunities the sea offered, collecting mussels and oysters and fishing in the rivers and Gulf.

During the Poverty Point Period (circa 2000-500 B.C.), the Indians of Mississippi participated in an extensive trade network that stretched from the Atlantic Coast to the Rocky Mountains. Soapstone was obtained from the southern Appalachians, shells from the Atlantic and Gulf coasts, obsidian from the Rockies, and copper from the Great Lakes.

The introduction of pottery was an impressive cultural development that flourished during the Woodland Period (circa 500 B.C.-800 A.D.), when an increased emphasis upon gathered foods may have

led to the beginnings of horticulture. The Woodland Period was also characterized by an apparently enhanced ceremonialism centered around the construction of conical burial mounds.

Even though little is known of the societies of these early Indians in Mississippi, we do know that they had settled into communities and established agricultural patterns by 800 A.D. The raising of crops such as corn, squash, and beans made security and permanence of settlement possible. Agricultural developments permitted larger groups of people to live together in close proximity and therefore led to new and more complex social organization.

In the Mississippian Period (circa 1050 A.D. to 1650 A.D.), social forms evolved into chiefdoms with a governmental hierarchy, led by a hereditary leader and reinforced by a specialized priesthood. The social structure was reflected in the civic architecture of the period, which included flat-topped pyramidal mounds on which stood the residence of the leader and ceremonial buildings. Some of the large mound complexes that are still extant in Mississippi are the Winterville Mounds in Washington County, the Lake George Site in Yazoo County, the Emerald Mound in Adams County, and the Grand Village of the Natchez Indians in the city of Natchez.

At the time of European exploration in Mississippi, the Choctaw and Chickasaw were the largest tribes. There were approximately 20,000 Choctaw and 8,000 Chickasaw, both of whom were Muskogean-speaking peoples. Several myths in their lore emphasized their kinship and sought to explain their presence in Mississippi. One Choctaw myth has it that the tribe emerged from a cave near the Nanih

Above, left: Flooding has always been a problem in Mississippi, which contains eleven river basins with numerous small streams. All of the state's land area drains into the Gulf of Mexico, with half draining through the Mississippi River. Spring invariably brings threatening flood waters in some areas of the state. Courtesy, Mississippi Department of Archives and History

Left: Emerald Mound dates to the Mississippian era. Courtesy, Mississippi Department of Economic Development

Waiya Mound in Neshoba County.

A myth common to both the Choctaw and Chickasaw, as recorded in the nineteenth century, tells how they came to be separate peoples. Two brothers, Chacta and Chicksa, led their people eastward across the Mississippi River, using a special pole to guide them throughout their journey. When they arrived in present-day east-central Mississippi, the people under Chicksa crossed a creek and set up camp. That night a heavy rain came; the following morning Chicksa and his followers continued on their journey. The Chacta group, however, noticed that the pole, which had always been leaning eastward each morning, was straight up, indicating that the group was to settle in that area.

Many of the customs and traditions of the Choctaw and Chickasaw were as similar as their languages. As with other Indian peoples of the area, they had no concept of private ownership of land: it was something to be held in common for the good of the group. They built houses of poles and cane in village communities, and cleared nearby areas for fields. Their religious life was an important part of their culture. The Choctaw worshiped the Great Spirit and lesser spirits. The Chickasaw worshiped an all-powerful force made up of the Sun, Clouds, Clear Sky, and "He That Lives in the Clear Sky." The details of their religious beliefs may have been confused by having been filtered through the perceptions of Christian missionaries.

The social and governmental structures of the Choctaw and Chickasaw were similar. Tribes were divided into clans, with a prohibition against persons marrying within the clan. The tribal governments did not exercise strong central control, with most decisions made at the village level. One unique provision—at least from our modern perspective—was their two-chief system of leadership, including a "peace chief" or "white chief," who served as the articulator of the tribe's wisdom at all times, and a "war chief" or "red chief," who during time of war would organize the young men for raiding parties. The governmental organization was a confederacy presided over by an annual tribal council.

The Natchez, the other major Indian group in the area, numbered about 4,500 at the time of the European intrusion. Like the Choctaw and Chickasaw, their neighbors to the north and east, they also were a Muskogean-speaking people, although their language was a remote dialect of western Muskogean. In other respects, the Natchez differed

This redware pot dates from about 1400-1541 A.D. Courtesy, The Cottonlandia Museum, Greenwood

This effigy pipe was used during the Mississippian era. Courtesy, Mississippi Department of Archives and History

from the other Mississippi Indian tribes. For example, the Natchez believed so strongly in a life after death that servants, relatives, and others accompanied a fallen leader in his afterlife pilgrimage by joining him in death. These sacrifices, although often ordered, were sometimes voluntary.

It was in social organization, however, that the Natchez differed most significantly from the Choctaw and Chickasaw. The Natchez had a highly structured society divided into two main strata, the common people and the nobility. The nobility was further divided into the Suns, Nobles, and Honored Persons. The chief, called the Great Sun, ruled the Natchez as the earthly representative of the Supreme Spirit. Unlike other societies with a caste system, such as India, the Natchez had a marital custom that provided for the continuous reintegration of the society: members of the nobility were obligated to marry persons who came from the commoner caste.

Because women did most of the work in the village, ranging from tending livestock to basket weaving, cooking, and other domestic chores, many early European accounts depicted Indian males as lazy and females as virtual slaves. The Europeans failed to recognize that they observed Indian men in "resting" periods between hunts and that social activities were interwoven with the women's work. One irony of the situation was that Indian men's greater participation in hunting rather than agri-

culture was prompted by the European encouragement of the animal skins trade.

It should be noted that all Mississippi Indian groups were matrilineal—that is, a child inherited his or her status from the mother. Within Natchez society, women could become leaders in their own right. The Indian women are credited for many of the material products, such as pottery and baskets, that remain to characterize the Indian culture.

Slavery existed among the Indians in Mississippi long before their contact with the Old World. When Indian groups captured enemies during a war, the prisoners became slaves. However, this type of slavery differed greatly from the system of chattel slavery practiced by the Europeans, in which people were treated as property. Among the Mississippi Indians, slaves often were adopted by the family that had used them as servants. The slave could marry within the tribe and even become a part of the group.

Methods of Indian warfare likewise differed from those of the Europeans. The Indians usually fought a limited engagement to avenge a wrong, such as a killing. It was the later introduction of the white man's ways and "civilized" methods of warfare that led to Indians adopting the concept of large groups fighting prolonged wars.

Other Indian groups were also present in Mississippi at the time of the European arrival. The Chakchiuma lived in the northern section of the Delta, and the Tunica inhabited the southern portion. The Natchez were located along the Mississippi River from south of what is now Vicksburg to the area below the present-day city of Natchez. The Yazoo Indians lived near Vicksburg on the Yazoo River. Along the coast were the Acolapissa, Biloxi, and Pascagoula. The Chickasaw occupied the northern section of the state east of the Mississippi River—not to mention all of present-day western Tennessee—and the remainder of what is now Mississippi was dominated by the Choctaw.

In late 1540, European explorers made the first significant penetration into Mississippi, encountering societies that had evolved over thousands of years. Within 300 years, there would be little left of these Indian cultures, and for most Mississippi Indians the end would come more quickly. Hernando De Soto's expedition was the first major intrusive force into Indian society.

De Soto was a Spanish explorer who desired fame and glory for the crown—and for himself. He

Above: The major visual information we have on early Choctaw Indians is from George Catlin, the noted American artist who devoted his life to documenting American Indians. In the 1830s he visited the Choctaw nation and sketched a Choctaw ballgame. Catlin's written description of several thousand Indians encamped at the ball playground, the torch parade and ball-play dance on the eve of the game, and the play itself, is a vivid account of a major event. Courtesy, Mississippi Department of Archives and History

Top: The Chickasaw, Choctaw, and Natchez Indian tribes were all primarily agricultural societies. Corn was their chief crop; they also planted beans, pumpkins, peas, melons, sunflowers, and tobacco, and gathered wild rice. Weeding and cultivation was done by the women and children, but the men participated in the heavy planting and the harvest. Courtesy, Mississippi Department of Archives and History

left Spain in the spring of 1538, bound for Cuba. There he outfitted his party, which included Dominican friars and priests as well as armorers and smiths. In all, 620 men made up the expedition. They brought with them 223 horses and hundreds of pigs.

Landing at Tampa Bay in the spring of 1539, De Soto took into his service Juan Ortiz, a Spaniard from an earlier expedition who had been held captive for twelve years by different Indian tribes. Ortiz, who had learned several of the Indian languages, became De Soto's interpreter. As it turned out, De Soto's treatment of the Indians did not need much interpretation. De Soto's usual method of dealing with Indians was to capture a chief and hold him as hostage while his followers served as burden bearers, until De Soto could capture another chief.

Most of the time the Indians went along with De Soto's tactics, if only to get rid of him. Their servitude worked well for De Soto as he pushed his men north of present-day Florida into the area now occupied by Georgia, South and North Carolina, Tennessee, and Alabama. Occasionally, however, the Indians resisted. In November 1540, just before De Soto entered what is now Mississippi, he was attacked by Indians at Mauvila. The tremendous advantage of Spanish military technology can be seen in a comparison of the casualties: there were only eighteen Spanish deaths, while as many as two thousand Indians were killed.

De Soto and his men spent the winter of 1540-1541 in northeast Mississippi, where they were supplied with food by the Chickasaw. When it came time to break camp in the spring, De Soto demanded that the Chickasaw provide him with more food and burden bearers. The Chickasaw

Right and below: Hernando De Soto reached the Mississippi River in May of 1541, almost five months after he entered present-day Mississippi. He had come to North America with visions of the riches and fame he had found in Peru with Pizarro. De Soto died shortly after he reached the Mississippi and his body was consigned to the river. Courtesy, The Historic New Orleans Collection

refused to furnish the burden bearers and launched a surprise night attack on the Spanish. Not only did De Soto lose ten men and fifty horses, but also a number of his pigs escaped, the descendants of which would eventually become the basis of one of the Southeast's most notable agricultural products.

On May 8, 1541, after many days of marching through relatively empty country, De Soto and his men arrived at the Mississippi and the villages of the Quiz-Quiz chiefdom, whose descendants were later known as the Tunica tribe. The members of the expedition thus probably became the first Europeans to see the "Father of Waters" from an inland vantage point. After reaching the river, De Soto's men spent a month building four barges for the crossing, which archaeologists believe was accomplished near present-day Friars Point in Coahoma County. De Soto left Mississippi and wandered about west of the river for the remainder of 1541 and into 1542. He died that year, and his body was subsequently consigned to the Mississippi River. The survivors of the expedition proceeded down the Mississippi to the Gulf and made their way westward in rough-hewn boats, finally reaching the Mexican coast at Vera Cruz in September 1543.

De Soto's intrusion into the lives of the Indians of the Southeast was relatively brief, but it was devastating. His expedition, as well as earlier and later European visits in the Southeast, brought diseases against which the Indians had no immunity. Perhaps 80 percent fewer Indians inhabited the Southeast when the French arrived in 1673 than when De Soto's men departed. De Soto came as a conquistador, but it was inglorious disease that vanquished the Indians and destroyed their culture.

*In 1698 three Jesuit priests from Canada came down the
Mississippi River and established a mission at Fort St. Pierre
at present-day Redwood, north of Vicksburg. They concentrated their efforts on Tunica Indians, the largest tribe in the
area, but abandoned the site in 1706. Courtesy, The Historic
New Orleans Collection*

EUROPEAN EXPLORATION AND SETTLEMENT

The European conquest of North America was not accomplished quickly; in fact, no Europeans traveled the Mississippi for more than a hundred years after De Soto's men left the area. Meanwhile, European settlement of the Atlantic Coast area took place in a haphazard fashion. St. Augustine, established by the Spanish in 1565, became the first permanent settlement in what is now the United States. The first permanent English settlements were Jamestown and Plymouth, founded in 1607 and 1620, respectively.

To the north of the rival Spanish and English territories, the French staked their claim to New France (Canada). In 1608 they established their first settlement at Quebec. The French came also to the islands of the Caribbean. Using its naval power effectively, France placed colonies on Santo Domingo, Martinique, Guadeloupe, and Tortuga.

French power in the New World was separated between Canada and the Caribbean, and the Mississippi River offered an attractive waterway connection between the two regions of colonization. The river could aid the French in their efforts to outmaneuver the British for control of the interior of North America. The Spanish world empire was sinking, and by the beginning of the seventeenth century that nation was no longer a contender in the struggle for the New World. The governor of New France, therefore, confidently sent a group to explore the Mississippi River, beginning at its headwaters.

Louis Joliet and Father Jacques Marquette led this venture in 1673. While exploring Illinois, Marquette and Joliet found the headwaters of the Illinois River, which led them to the Mississippi. They journeyed as far south as the large Indian village called Akansea, which was located on the eastern side of the river, probably near present-day Rosedale in Bolivar County, Mississippi. Fearing they were getting too near Spanish territory, Marquette and Joliet returned to Canada. In failing to complete their exploration of the Mississippi, Marquette and Joliet had done little to establish the French claim to the American interior, but they had forged an effective alliance with the Quapaw Indians.

The Quapaw alliance would be of great aid to the next Mississippi explorer, Robert Cavelier, Sieur de La Salle. Born in Rouen, France, in 1643 and

educated by Jesuits, La Salle went to Montreal in 1666 and opened a trading post nearby. After exploring the Great Lakes region, he decided to venture south on the Mississippi. He obtained an official commission for his exploration of the Mississippi and, in 1679, began preparations for his 1680 trip down the Father of Waters. After a return to Canada in early 1681 for supplies, he finally entered the Mississippi in February 1682. On April 9, having arrived at the Gulf of Mexico, La Salle claimed the entire Mississippi River watershed for France and named the area Louisiana in honor of Louis XIV.

The claim was not easily enforceable—as La Salle well knew. He therefore developed plans for a fort at the mouth of the Mississippi River that would control access to the vast interior from the Gulf. La Salle returned to France and equipped a new expedition. In 1684 he sailed from France with four ships and 400 men. They searched in vain for the mouth of the river and landed instead on the coast of Texas. La Salle attempted to return overland to Canada, but on the way he was killed by some of his men.

Two years later, Henri de Tonty, who had been on the first expedition with La Salle, came down the river, hoping to meet La Salle. When Tonty reached the river's mouth, he sent out search parties along the coastline but found no sign of La Salle. Insofar as France's later claim to the area is concerned, the most important thing Tonty did was to leave a letter for La Salle with a local Indian chief. Fourteen years later another French expedition, after successfully finding the river's mouth from the Gulf, would receive the letter, which served to substantiate and reinforce the French claim to the Mississippi Valley.

That later expedition was led by Pierre Le Moyne, Sieur d'Iberville, who was the third of the

Above: At the mouth of the Mississippi River, Robert Cavelier, Sieur de La Salle, claimed Louisiana for France on April 9, 1682. It had been 141 years since the last European, Hernando de Soto, touched Mississippi soil. La Salle, a French explorer, had migrated to Canada where he received a commission to travel the Mississippi River and secure lands for France in the American interior. On his descent he became friendly with the Indian tribes along the river and in early 1682 visited the Natchez chief at the Grand Village. Courtesy, The Historic New Orleans Collection

Above, left: When Father Jacques Marquette and Louis Joliet explored the Mississippi River in 1673 for New France (Canada), they saw the land that would become Mississippi. Their expedition took them as far south as the mouth of the Arkansas River near present-day Rosedale, Mississippi, but they did not land on Mississippi soil. Courtesy, The Historic New Orleans Collection

A letter written by Henri de Tonty proved the French claim to the mouth of the Mississippi River. Tonty came down the river several times searching for his lost colleague, La Salle. Failing to find him, he left a letter for La Salle at an Indian village in 1685. The letter was delivered to Iberville fourteen years later in exchange for an axe. It was proof to Pierre Le Moyne, Sieur d'Iberville, that he had found the river claimed by La Salle for France. Courtesy, The Historic New Orleans Collection

Pierre Le Moyne, Sieur d'Iberville, was the leader of the first European group to settle in Mississippi. A French-Canadian naval officer, Iberville claimed the Gulf Coast of Mississippi and solidified La Salle's claim to the Mississippi River Valley for France in 1699.

A stone, alleged to have been carved by Iberville's crew, is in the Louisiana State Historical Museum. After landing off Ship Island on February 10, 1699, the group went ashore at present-day Ocean Springs. Courtesy, Louisiana State Historical Museum

eleven sons of Charles Le Moyne, a distinguished French Canadian soldier. Iberville's younger brother, Jean-Baptiste de Bienville, would also be an important part of the French venture in the lower Mississippi Valley. Iberville had helped settle French Canadian colonies in Acadia and Cape Breton Island. During the lengthy war with England known as the War of the League of Augsburg (1688-1697), Iberville had captured several English forts in Canada's Hudson Bay region.

Iberville's Mississippi expedition left Brest in late 1698, bound for the French Caribbean island of Santo Domingo. Enlisting a former pirate as a guide, Iberville set out for the mainland. He sighted the Apalachicola River and then on January 25 reached his planned destination of Pensacola. Since the Spanish held the harbor—Iberville was under instructions not to attack Spanish positions—he continued to Mobile Bay, arriving on January 31. On February 10, 1699, Iberville first entered "Mississippi," dropping anchor on the landward side of Ship Island. Iberville led a small party ashore, where they met the Biloxi Indians. Iberville named the bay in the Indians' honor. He and his men then came across a band of Bayougoulas, who told the Frenchmen about a large river to the west where their village was located.

With that information, Iberville set out on February 28 to find the river, and Iberville successfully navigated the North Pass into the Mississippi. The party moved upriver in search of the village of the Bayougoulas. Along the way they gave gifts to Indians and marked their way with crosses. After finding the Bayougoulas, Iberville continued upriver, coming to a decorated pole, which he later learned was the boundary marker between the Bayougoulas and the Houma. The site of this marker, which the French called the *Baton Rouge*, would later become the site of the city of that name.

As Iberville returned to Biloxi Bay, he came across the Mongoulachas, allies of the Bayougoulas. They gave him Tonty's letter to La Salle, which they had held for fourteen years. The letter was used by Iberville to reaffirm the French claim to the Mississippi watershed.

Iberville took certain precautions before he returned to France with the good news. He had his men build a fort on the the eastern shore of Biloxi Bay at present-day Ocean Springs (*Vieux Biloxy*). The fort had the natural protection of deep gullies to the sides and the bay to its front. Upon the

completion of Fort Maurepas on May 4, 1699, Iberville returned to France both to report on his mission and to obtain more men and supplies.

Sauvole de la Villantry was left in charge of Fort Maurepas. Iberville's brother Bienville was second-in-command of the garrison of seventy-six men. During this short period of time Bienville demonstrated qualities that later made him such a successful and colorful leader of French Louisiana. He led small parties in explorations of the coastline and the Mississippi River. While on the Mississippi in September 1699, Bienville came across an English ship, the *Carolina Galley*. He warned the captain of the English ship that the French had already established a permanent settlement on the river. The English left the river, and the incident was passed down in French explorers' lore as the *Detour des Anglais* (the English Bend).

Some major decisions had to be made when Iberville returned to Biloxi in January 1700. A permanent site had not been selected for the settlers he had brought from France. His top priority, however, was the fortification of the Mississippi River in case the English should return. Henri de Tonty arrived at Biloxi from upriver on January 16, 1700, to help in the building of the settlements and fortifications. With his arrival, the two French colonies on the North American continent were thus linked for the first time. The French now had a solid claim to the Mississippi Valley in an era in which territorial claims were usually not so clear-cut.

After another trip back to France in May 1700, Iberville returned to *Vieux Biloxy* in December 1701 with new colonists and supplies, only to inform the men who had been left behind that the colony had to be relocated to Mobile Bay. French authorities wanted the settlement to be near their new Spanish allies at Pensacola for their anticipated war with England. Bienville, therefore, went to Mobile Bay to oversee the building of Fort Louis. Soon thereafter,

the fort became the site of an alliance struck between the French and the Choctaw and Chickasaw nations. Tonty used threats and bribes to induce the chiefs, who represented 6,000 braves, to unite against the English.

On April 22, 1702, Iberville left for France, never to return to Louisiana. Despite his intentions to return, illness and military obligations delayed the trip for four years. Then, when he did make it as far as Cuba, he died of yellow fever on a ship in the Havana harbor in July 1706. During the period of his leadership, Iberville had solidified the French claims to the Mississippi River watershed and had established French settlements at *Vieux Biloxy* and Mobile as well as a small fort on the Mississippi. Now it was time for his brother, Bienville, to dominate the history of the French colony.

Bienville, only twenty-two years old when Iberville left the colony for the last time in 1702, was to be active in the affairs of the colony for the next forty years. As acting governor during what was assumed to be his brother's temporary absence, Bienville faced problems that multiplied quickly. He had difficulty recruiting and retaining settlers for the struggling colony; disease was ever-present, and the desertion rate of the military garrison was high. Most of the settlers were French Canadians who wanted to live among the Indians and become traders and trappers. They were not so interested in helping Bienville create a series of settlements.

The most critical problem Bienville encountered was the colony's lack of an economic base upon which to build. The settlers' efforts to grow European foodstuffs usually failed; most food either had to come from France or from nearby Indians. Even furs, which were the major product Louisiana had to offer France at that time, were of poor quality when compared to Canadian pelts.

Added to these internal problems was the renewed warfare of Europe, which once again

Above: *John Law, a Scottish entrepreneur, got permission from Louis XV of France to organize the Mississippi Company to settle and develop Louisiana. He controlled Louisiana, which included the Natchez District, for more than a dozen years, bringing in thousands of settlers. Courtesy, The Historic New Orleans Collection*

Facing page, left: *Jean Baptiste de Bienville, younger brother of Pierre Le Moyne, Sieur d'Iberville, had a far-reaching effect on Mississippi's history. Guiding French activities in Mississippi and Louisiana for forty years, he was responsible for the French settlements of Old Biloxi, Natchez, and New Biloxi. He presided over the expulsion of the Natchez Indians from their homeland in 1732 and forced a peace treaty with the Chickasaws in 1739.*

Facing page, right: *Bienville forced the Natchez Indians to provide lumber and labor for the construction of Fort Rosalie in 1716. After the 1729 attack by the Natchez Indians, the fort was rebuilt, from 1730 to 1734, but remained sparsely inhabited until the British took over in 1766. Courtesy, Mississippi Department of Archives and History*

spilled over into the New World. Bienville attempted to preserve the French alliances with the Indians amidst the War of the Spanish Succession (known in North America as Queen Anne's War), which reached Louisiana in 1702. From 1702 until 1712, when the English threat to Louisiana finally died away, Bienville struggled to keep the Chickasaw from allying with the English. The only military action actually affecting the French in Louisiana came when the English took the undefended Dauphin Island in Mobile Bay in 1710.

With the English threat to his colony removed after 1712, King Louis XIV decided that a change was in order. He gave a fifteen-year charter to businessman Antoine Crozat for the exploitation of Louisiana. With this economic monopoly, there also came a change in government. The crown appointed Antoine de la Mothe Cadillac, who had served for twenty-seven years in Canada and was at the time its lieutenant governor, as the new governor of Louisiana. In what would later prove to have been an unwise move, Bienville remained in Louisiana as its lieutenant governor. Cadillac, a rather quarrelsome fellow and, at the age of fifty-two, near the end of a long career of government service, was not excited about his "promotion." After unsuccessfully fighting the change, Cadillac arrived in Louisiana in May 1713 for what would become four years of political and economic turmoil.

The personal relationship of the governor and lieutenant governor was a source of much of the trouble. One dispute led Cadillac to place Bienville under house arrest, though it only lasted twenty-four hours. A much more serious situation arose when Bienville refused to marry Cadillac's daughter. Shortly thereafter Cadillac ordered Bienville to go into hostile Indian territory to oversee the construction of a fort—with half the number of men recommended for the mission. Despite his handicap, Bienville made the mission a success. He and forty-five men went to the site of present-day Natchez and, after De Soto's example, captured several Natchez chiefs. Bienville demanded that the Indians who had recently killed four Canadians be punished; the Natchez complied and, in addition, agreed to assist the French in building a fort on the bluff near their villages which, when completed in August 1716, was named Fort Rosalie, in honor of the wife of the Comte de Pontchartrain, the French Minister of Marine and Colonies.

Soon afterwards, Cadillac was recalled to France. In 1717 Crozat, having failed to make the

Slave ships destined for Mississippi began arriving during the era of French dominion. Large numbers of slaves were brought in from Africa and the French West Indies by John Law's Mississippi Company between 1719 and 1730. Great Britain and Spain continued the slave trade and by the time Mississippi became a United States territory, slavery was a deeply ingrained institution. Courtesy, The Historic New Orleans Collection

colony profitable, surrendered his charter to the crown. King Louis XIV promptly awarded the charter to a Scotsman named John Law, founder of the Bank of France and a presumed financial genius. Law established the Mississippi Company, actually a subsidiary of the Company of the Indies, to manage the colony. Law received almost dictatorial powers: the Mississippi Company could appoint its own governor and other officials, make land grants, and exercise other powers that ordinarily only a king would have. In return, the Mississippi Company was to transport 6,000 Europeans and 3,000 slaves to the colony during the twenty-five-year term of the charter. In promoting the colony, the Mississippi Company quickly overextended itself, creating the infamous speculative boom known as the "Mississippi Bubble." French investors became greedy with the promise of quick wealth, only to be caught up in an exercise in fraud and corruption. When the bubble burst, many Frenchmen lost fortunes, and Louisiana's reputation suffered to the extent that settlers lost interest in coming to the area.

Under John Law's leadership, Bienville was appointed Louisiana's governor. For a few years the colony was relatively peaceful and its economy was expanding. There was some warfare: Bienville twice captured Pensacola from the Spanish, but each time he quickly returned the port city. Such exercises indicated to the Spanish that the French were firmly in control of Louisiana and its borders.

During the period of the Mississippi Company charter, Biloxi once again became the capital of the territory, replacing the Mobile Bay settlement established during the alliance with Spain. The primary reason for the move was to have the capital more centrally located, since New Orleans (founded in 1718 by Bienville) was thriving on the Mississippi River. The capital was established in 1720 at "New Biloxi," and a new fort was built on the peninsula separating Biloxi Bay from the Gulf.

New Biloxi enjoyed its status for only a short time, for in 1722 the rapidly growing New Orleans became the permanent capital of the territory. By 1724 the colony's population was at 5,000, more than ten times what it had been ten years earlier; the New Orleans area had a population of 1,600. In keeping with Louisiana's new status, its territorial government was made completely independent of Canada.

Slavery was the cornerstone of the economy of the Louisiana territory. At first, the French attempted to make slaves of local Indians, but it proved too easy for the Indians to escape and disappear into the forests they knew so well. In 1719 the first significant number of blacks were brought to the territory. By 1731 there were almost 3,400 black slaves in Louisiana, with the number mushrooming to approximately 6,000 by the end of French control in 1763. The slaves harvested silk, rice, and indigo, as well as forest products such as pitch and lumber for shipment to Europe. However,

The Natchez Indians re-sisted French attempts to appropriate their lands, finally resorting to an attack on Fort Rosalie in November 1729. They killed approximately 236 Frenchmen and took wo-men, children, and slaves captive. In 1732 the French retaliated; many of the Natchez Indians were killed, some 400 were sold into slavery to Santo Domingo, and a few es-caped to other tribes. Courtesy, The St. Louis Art Museum, Eliza McMillan Fund

the colony depended most heavily on the export of tobacco for its economic survival.

To deal with the large slave population in the colony, Bienville instituted a Black Code in 1724 to regulate the institution. A slave had to gain his master's permission for a wide range of activities, from owning firearms to marrying. But the code also required masters to exercise certain care of the slaves by meeting minimal needs for clothing and shelter. Personal rights of slaves were somewhat protected: for example, a husband and wife could not be sold separately, and, if a slave were freed by his master, he had full citizenship rights. Over time, this last provision resulted in a significant population of free blacks, especially in New Orleans, where they frequently became small businessmen.

Bienville was forced to leave the colony for a time in the mid-1720s, when charges of corruption were brought against him by a subordinate with connections in Paris. In 1725 he went to France to confront the charges, lost, and was pensioned off for past services. While he was gone, the Mississippi Company's new appointee, Governor Perier, found it impossible to control the Indians, a problem that led to the Second Natchez Revolt.

In 1729 Perier had appointed Sieur de Chepart to the command of Fort Rosalie. Chepart was so high-handed in his attitude toward the Natchez that they rebelled, attacking the French settlers at Fort Rosalie on November 28, 1729. The fort was burned, and the Natchez killed 138 men, 35 women, and 56 children. The revolt spread throughout the Yazoo basin. Indians killed most of the garrison at Fort St. Pierre, which overlooked the Yazoo River near present-day Redwood. Following these attacks, the French brought in reinforcements from New Orleans and drove the Natchez out of the Grand Village. Within two years, the Natchez were virtually destroyed as a nation. Though driven from their homeland, remnants of the Natchez settled with the Chickasaw, who refused to turn them over to the French.

Bienville, on being reinstated as governor of Louisiana, decided that the Chickasaw must be brought to submission and planned a two-front attack in 1736. A French force, marching from the Illinois country to the north under the command of Pierre d'Artaguette, suffered a crushing defeat on March 25, 1736, at the hands of the Chickasaw at the Battle of Ougoula Tchetoka. Some twenty Frenchmen were captured and burned to death. Shortly thereafter, the French were also soundly repulsed at the Battle of Ackia near the site of present-day Tupelo.

In 1739, a major force of 3,700 under Bienville's command marched against the Chickasaw, but the French army, struck down by a fever, was reduced to a fighting force of only 200 men. As in 1736, a French force from the north came to join in the expedition. This one was more successful. Led by Celeron, this group engaged the Chickasaw, who then agreed to a token peace. Following this success,

Bienville, who was in poor health, returned home to France, having placed his permanent mark on Louisiana.

Bienville was replaced by a vigorous and effective administrator, Philippe de Rigaud, Marquis de Vaudreuil, son of a former governor of Canada. In 1744 war with Britain broke out in Europe, and it was reflected in the New World by a blockade of French supply ships. By now the French colony could provide for itself if necessary, but the blockade meant that the colonists could not import the manufactured trade goods that were crucial to their Indian alliances. The Choctaw invited English traders in to supply the goods they had come to depend on. The French pressured their most loyal

chiefs to resist this move, while the British tempted the younger leaders to gain power through control over the only available European trade.

In this time of tension, a single incident was enough to precipitate serious consequences. A young French officer and two traders were killed by the Choctaw in 1746 (the reasons were never entirely clear but may have included improper attentions to the wife of the pro-English war chief Red Shoe). The French demanded that their Choctaw allies obtain retribution for these deaths, but because such punishment risked a blood feud, the Choctaw hesitated, undertaking instead to kill English traders. The pro-British faction responded with attacks on French settlements, an action that

Esteban Miro governed the Natchez area as part of West Florida from 1786 to 1792. He set up a government for the Natchez District with regulations based on Spanish law, modified by frontier and English common law traditions of the Natchez settlers. Courtesy, The Historic New Orleans Collection

Natchez, the most illustrious city in Mississippi, was the center of the Natchez District under all three foreign dominions. It was to become the first capital of the Mississippi Territory, the first capital of the state, and as center of Mississippi's first cotton kingdom, the financial and cultural hub of the state. Courtesy, The Historic New Orleans Collection

in turn escalated French demands. Finally, a civil war of Choctaw against Choctaw broke out when Red Shoe was killed. The war pitted Red Shoe's pro-British allies against the pro-French side led by Alibamon Mingo. In the end, French blockade-running succeeded, and the long British line of supply from Carolina failed. The British allies were reduced to firing acorns and pine knots from their guns, and in 1750 the Grandpré treaty settled the war in favor of the French allies.

In 1753 Vaudreuil moved on to bigger things: the governorship of Canada. His replacement was a Breton naval officer, Louis Billouart de Kerlerec. Like other governors before him, Kerlerec engaged in some rather questionable private trading practices on the side, but from his arrival in the colony he concentrated on the vital Indian alliances. By the outbreak of the French and Indian War in 1754, he had reestablished the Choctaw alliance on a firm footing and had begun serious overtures to the

Upper Creeks in what is now north central Alabama.

In 1755 Kerlerec saw an opportunity to extend his Indian alliances even further. Antoine Lantagnac, a nephew of Vaudreuil who had wandered away from Fort Toulouse on the Alabama River in 1745 and ended up as a Cherokee trader, returned to the French colony, leaving a Cherokee wife and numerous adopted relatives behind. Instead of subjecting him to a court-martial, Kerlerec was shrewd enough to turn Lantagnac into an *agent provacateur.* Working through Montaut de Monberaut, commandant of Fort Toulouse, and Lantagnac, using promises and a trickle of trade goods, Kerlerec welded a chain of Indian alliances from the Smokies to the Mississippi. Kerlerec, now prepared for a major push against the British in Georgia and the Carolinas, suddenly found himself without an ally when France signed the Peace of Paris with Britain in 1763.

As a result of the treaty that ended the French and Indian War, France turned over to Britain all of Canada and all her territory east of the Mississippi, except New Orleans. The remainder of French territory on the North American continent, including New Orleans, went to Spain.

Another important development at this time was King George III's Proclamation of 1763, which reserved the area north of the thirty-first parallel and west of the Appalachian Mountains for the Indians and specified that settlers were not to enter this territory. This decision on the part of the British government infuriated the colonists and contributed to the deterioration of relations between the English colonies and the mother country which, twelve years later, would culminate in the American Revolution.

British rule of present-day Mississippi, a part of what was then referred to as British West Florida, was for the most part uneventful until the American Revolution. The seat of government for British West Florida was established at Pensacola, and British troops were dispatched to various points, including Natchez, where they occupied and repaired Fort Rosalie, renamed Fort Panmure. Many of the French settlers, who had been advised by the British government that they would have eighteen months to dispose of their property and leave the colony, elected to transfer their allegiance to the British king. On the other hand, it appears that practically all of the Spanish living in Pensacola left the colony when the British came in.

West Florida was a frontier province with conditions very similar to those in Georgia a generation earlier and in the Carolinas during the first part of the eighteenth century. Although there were occasional exceptions, the cultural refinements and niceties of life found in the older colonies were generally lacking. Representative government was attempted, as in the other British colonies, but the Board of Trade exercised veto power over the assembly's bills. In the meantime, the British were having major Indian problems.

The most effective governor of British West Florida was Peter Chester, a veteran of twenty years' army service when he became governor in 1770. Through a series of negotiations in 1771-1772, he maintained peaceful relations with Indian groups in the area, although some outbreaks still occurred. Thomas Hutchins, an engineer and cartographer for the British army, reported that the settlers on the east side of the Pascagoula River, along with those at Biloxi and points further west, were harassed by the Indians, especially the Choctaw, who occasionally killed the settlers' cattle.

During its first years British West Florida was sparsely populated. In 1774, Lieutenant Governor Elias estimated the colony's population to be 4,900 (3,700 whites and 1,200 slaves). During the next five years, the population increased rapidly due to the heavy influx of Loyalists, who sought freedom from persecution in the older colonies.

Because of a combination of circumstances, among which were the short term of British control and the sparsity of settlement, British West Florida did not join the 1776 rebellion of the original thirteen colonies against the mother country. The American Revolution did not directly affect the "fifteenth colony" (East Florida often called the "fourteenth") in any way until several years after the fighting had begun.

In 1778 James Willing, who had once lived in Natchez, led an American raid on pro-British settlements along the Mississippi. Hoping to get supplies into the New Orleans area for American forces, Willing, under the authorization of the Continental Congress, attacked Natchez. Willing's raid on William Dunbar's plantation at Manchac was so destructive that Dunbar, who would later become prominent in Mississippi history, was forced to leave the area to rebuild his life and fortune in New Orleans. Willing attempted to win British settlers in the area over to the cause of the American Revolution, but found only Loyalists.

In 1779 the Spanish joined the French in

Soon after Eli Whitney's invention became known, Daniel Clark, a Natchez planter, gave a crude sketch of the cotton gin to his master-mechanic slave, Barcley, who then designed and built Mississippi's first cotton gin in August 1795. Courtesy, Mississippi Department of Archives and History

As this early illustration emphasizes, the steamboat revolutionized commerce on the Mississippi River. Nicholas Roosevelt built the first successful steamboat on the Mississippi River and put it into service between New Orleans and Natchez in 1812. Steamboat traffic and Mississippi River trade boomed in the 1820s and remained important until railroads supplanted them after the Civil War. Courtesy, The Historic New Orleans Collection

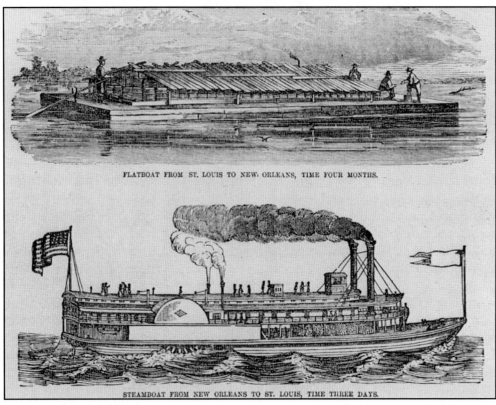

FLATBOAT FROM ST. LOUIS TO NEW ORLEANS, TIME FOUR MONTHS.

STEAMBOAT FROM NEW ORLEANS TO ST. LOUIS, TIME THREE DAYS.

opposition to Britain during the American Revolution. This event caused the Spanish to move against the British, defeating them at Baton Rouge on September 21. On the same date, the Spanish took control of the British post at Natchez. These actions were the first of a series that strengthened Spanish post-war claims to its former Florida possessions. Spain followed the victories at Baton Rouge and Natchez with the capture of Mobile in 1780 and Pensacola the following year.

Under the Treaty of Paris of 1783, which ended the American Revolution, Spain was given its old Florida territories plus the territory of British West Florida. Although Spanish control over the Natchez area was briefer than that of the British, Spain had

a greater impact. It had already been an established presence in surrounding areas for many years. With its Louisiana capital at New Orleans, Spain made effective use of its administrative foothold in the area.

The Spanish authorities promoted American settlement in the Natchez District, a rather ill-defined area along the Mississippi River with Natchez as its commercial center.

The Spanish governor-general of Louisiana, Esteban Miro, drew up new regulations in 1787 that gave the Natchez District its own government within Spanish Louisiana. Miro promoted American settlement in other ways. Spanish colonial law stated that only Spanish was to be spoken in court and religious gatherings. Also, in order to become a citizen and hold property, a person had to be a member of the state-sanctioned Catholic Church. Since most settlers in the Natchez area were English-speaking Protestant Americans, Miro tried to make it easy for the would-be citizens to become Catholics by recruiting English-speaking priests from Ireland who had been trained in Spanish at the University of Salamanca.

The Americans refused to convert to Catholicism and found that it really did not make any difference; the Spanish authorities were so desperate for settlers that they ignored the old rules. Protestants were allowed to continue their own religious practices, as long as it was done in the privacy of their homes. Jews also found the Natchez area to be religiously tolerant and a good place to begin businesses. The Spanish code was even somewhat modified to blend with English common law tradition.

Friction continued between Spanish Natchez and the United States. In 1785 the Georgia state assembly created the County of Bourbon, which ran across present-day Alabama and Mississippi. Land speculators came to the Natchez area hoping to use this Georgia legislation to establish land claims. The scheme was blocked when both the Spanish and American governments stood together against such moves.

Spanish authorities were aware of the fragile nature of their control of the area. In 1784 they were able to obtain peace with the various Indian groups. In order to strengthen their position, in 1791 the Spanish built Fort Nogales at Walnut Hills on the site of present-day Vicksburg. In 1793 the Spanish formalized their peaceful relations with the Indians of the Southeast with the Treaty of Nogales.

Meanwhile, Natchez thrived. Planters took out large loans, increasing their acreage to take full advantage of the rich soil in the area. Tobacco could be produced at the rate of a ton an acre. In 1789 the Natchez District produced about 1.5 million pounds of tobacco, although the quality of the product was not as high as that of Virginia and other areas.

During the 1790s the price of tobacco dropped, and Natchez planters searched for another money crop. They tried indigo but rejected it because of stiff foreign competition and because it rapidly drained the soil's fertility. Finally, in 1795, "King Cotton" came to the area. Local inventors, including David Greenleaf and John Barcley, contributed to the expanding local economy with their own versions of cotton gins. Using horses for power, these gins could clear the seeds and produce 500 pounds of lint cotton a day. William Dunbar, who had recouped his fortune in New Orleans and returned to the Natchez area, invented a screw press for the baling of cotton and began manufacturing and selling the machine throughout the region.

With the booming economy came the beginnings of "Natchez Society," though the Natchez District was still a rough agricultural frontier. In 1785 the settlement along St. Catherine's Creek, which consisted of about 180 families, became the core of Natchez. The Natchez District at that time had a population of 1,100 whites and 900 slaves. By the time the United States officially took over the area in 1798, the population figures stood at 4,500 and 2,400, respectively.

Governor Manuel Gayoso was an excellent administrator of the Natchez District. He gave permanence to the Natchez settlement with the building of six streets at right angles to the Mississippi River, with seven intersecting streets running parallel with the river. Although most residents of Natchez built wood frame houses, the richer planters built fine homes and ordered their furniture from Europe, thereby setting the standards for the antebellum Natchez tradition. The transition from Spanish to American authority came peacefully. In 1795 the United States and Spain signed the Treaty of San Lorenzo, known in American history as Pinckney's Treaty. In the treaty the conflicting claims over the Natchez District were settled in the United States' favor, with the permanent boundary line set at the thirty-first parallel. The transition occurred slowly; it was not until 1798 that the American flag officially flew over Natchez.

As the period of European colonial rule came to an end, there was some uneasiness among the settlers. Many had enjoyed the economic stability the Spanish had given Natchez. For example, creditors appreciated the general Spanish attitude that debts must be paid in a timely fashion. Others, however, wondered what the change in government would do to land claims. Finally, there was the constant threat of Indian uprisings. Could the Americans keep peace with the Indians as well as the Spanish had? Only the Americans—white, black, and red—would be able to answer these questions during the ensuing two decades, which made up the territorial period of Mississippi's history.

Winthrop Sargent of Massachusetts was the first governor of the Mississippi Territory. Appointed by President John Adams, he arrived in Natchez in 1798. The settlers perceived him as haughty and dictatorial and succeeded in ousting him in 1801. Remaining in Natchez, Sargent married a wealthy Natchez widow and built a palatial house, Gloucester. He later served as president of the Bank of Mississippi. Courtesy, Mississippi Department of Archives and History

FROM TERRITORY TO STATEHOOD

In the Treaty of San Lorenzo, signed on October 27, 1795, Spain officially turned over to the United States the area between the thirty-first parallel and the Yazoo River, commonly referred to as the Yazoo Strip. This treaty, also called the Pinckney Treaty, was one of the most successful treaties the United States negotiated during its early history. In addition to obtaining the Yazoo Strip, the United States gained the free navigation of the Mississippi River through Spanish territory and "the right of deposit" at New Orleans, which meant Spain could not limit American use of the port. In spite of the ease with which the United States gained these important diplomatic points, it would be almost three years before the transfer of power over the Yazoo Strip actually occurred.

After the treaty was signed, American and Spanish officials began to argue over the exact boundary. In the spring of 1796 Andrew Ellicott became the United States boundary commissioner. Ellicott's task was to work with the Spanish commissioner, William Dunbar, to ensure an accurate thirty-first parallel border between American and Spanish territory. Another personality closely involved in the transfer was Stephen Minor, a large plantation owner and holder of a number of slaves. When Governor Gayoso left Natchez for New Orleans to become governor-general of Louisiana, Minor became the last Spanish governor of the Natchez District.

Both Natchez debtors and the Indians of the area did their part to cause problems between Spanish and American authorities. Debtors anticipated that American rule would be more understanding of their inability to pay than the more authoritarian Spanish regime. The Indians felt that the Spanish had undercut them after promising to protect them from the British and Americans.

On April 7, 1798, the United States Congress created the Territory of Mississippi. The original boundaries of the territory were the Chattahoochee River to the east, the Mississippi River to the west, Spanish Florida to the south, and on the north, a line drawn east from 32°28', a point near the mouth of the Yazoo River. In 1804, the northern boundary was extended to the 35th parallel, the southern border of Tennessee. The Mississippi Territory was mostly Indian country and, except for the settlements of Natchez and St. Stephens (located on the Tombigbee River in what is now Alabama), there were few whites in the area. A dominant theme in Mississippi for the next forty years would be the removal of Indians from the path of white settlement.

For such a frontier environment, President John Adams' selection of Winthrop Sargent, a Massachusetts blue blood as territorial governor, was a major tactical blunder. The Puritan ideals that had

Manuel de Gayoso, the first Spanish governor of Natchez, had a British education and an American wife and governed with great tolerance for local customs. It was his duty to surrender the Natchez District to the United States in 1798 and oversee the removal of the Spanish authorities from the area. He then returned to New Orleans and became governor of Louisiana. Courtesy, The Historic New Orleans Collection, original in the Louisiana State Museum

been in Sargent's family for generations did not square with the realities of a raw frontier.

The government of the territory got off to a rocky start. Sargent, having served as secretary of the Northwest Territory for ten years, was the only official with previous experience in territorial government. Only Peter Bruin of Bruinsburg, Mississippi, one of the two territorial judges appointed to assist Sargent, had any acquaintance with the area. None of the territorial officials, Bruin and Sargent included, had enough knowledge of the law to provide a just and fair administration.

Nevertheless, Sargent had to begin the process of American governance of the area. Arriving in Natchez in August 1798, he began to issue executive orders and decrees that from his perspective were needed to ensure an orderly transition. Many local

citizens, however, saw them as arbitrary and abusive, and Sargent quickly gained a reputation as a dictator.

The arrival of a second judge in January 1799 gave Bruin and Sargent the opportunity to draw up a territorial code. They turned to the code of the Northwest Territory as their guide, though it did not fit the local situation. Even Sargent himself admitted that the code was only a patchwork arrangement.

Settlers in the Natchez area were concerned about the legality of land claims. Since the area had undergone so many changes in sovereignty during the 1700s, there were all kinds of conflicting titles and grants. As if that were not enough, the earlier claims by the state of Georgia had not entirely disappeared. As late as 1795 the Georgia legislature made grants in the Yazoo Strip.

In 1798 Zachariah Cox came to Mississippi. He was a land promoter and head of the Tennessee Yazoo Company. What most concerned Governor Sargent was Cox's band of almost a hundred armed men. Cox was fairly careful in his activities, but he did nothing to dismiss rumors that he had come to assume control under the authority of the State of Georgia. Taking no chances, Sargent placed Cox under house confinement at the old fort in Natchez. About a month later, Cox escaped to New Orleans, where Spanish governor Gayoso gave him protection.

During the Sargent administration, factions that had surfaced during the 1795-1798 transition began to take more visible form. Persons in Natchez who had earlier supported Andrew Ellicott became partisans in Sargent's camp. These included William Dunbar; George Cochran, a successful Natchez merchant; Captain John Girault, a veteran of George Rogers Clark's Illinois expedition; and Lewis Evans, a man who transformed his Natchez blacksmithing profits into a plantation that made him one of the largest landholders in Adams County.

Early in his administration, Sargent had shown a preference for the Ellicott group in his political appointments. For example, former Spanish boundary commissioner William Dunbar (having switched his allegiance and remade his fortune in New Orleans) became a probate judge—a critical position in an era of questionable land titles. However, in an effort to promote harmony with the anti-Ellicott faction, Sargent made the mistake of attempting to compromise with its leaders, Anthony Hutchins and Thomas Green. Although Hutchins had been very pro-British during the American

Revolution, he was powerful due to his large landholdings in the Natchez District. Governor Gayoso had banished Colonel Thomas Green from the Natchez area because of his resistance to Spanish rule.

Sargent gave critical militia appointments to members of this opposing faction, including one to Hutchins' son and another to the son-in-law of Thomas Green, Cato West, who became one of the new territory's leaders. The Green-West faction, as it was later known, moved on several fronts to undercut Sargent's administration. They went to Philadelphia, the nation's capital, to lobby Jeffersonian Republicans for relief from Sargent, who was an appointee of Adams' Federalists. Meanwhile, in 1799, they gained control of the only grand juries in Mississippi at the time, those of Adams and Pickering counties. These grand juries drew up long lists of objections to Sargent's administration of the territory, especially what they termed "Sargent's Codes."

The Green-West forces did not merely complain; they hired Narsworthy Hunter to lobby for their cause in the nation's capital. He gained the confidence and support of two western congressmen, W.C.C. Claiborne of Tennessee and Thomas Davis of Kentucky. Claiborne initiated congressional consideration for the Green-West proposal that the Mississippi Territory be allowed to enter the second stage in the process toward statehood by electing a legislature. While this legislation was being debated,

Mississippi's first printing press was brought into the state by Andrew Marschalk, an officer stationed at Walnut Hills (Vicksburg). In 1799 he moved to Natchez to set up a print shop, where his first job was to publish Sargent's Codes. In 1802 he began publication of the **Mississippi Herald.** *Courtesy, Mississippi Department of Archives and History*

Natchez-Under-the-Hill was a celebrated haven for the flatboatmen called "Kentuckians" who brought produce down the Mississippi River from the Ohio Valley to Natchez and New Orleans. Saloons, gambling houses, and brothels provided entertainment for the men before they started their journeys home up the Natchez Trace. The traditions of Natchez-Under-the-Hill continued through the steamboat era. Courtesy, The Historic New Orleans Collection

Congress began an investigation of the Sargent administration.

Sargent was in trouble. The second stage toward statehood passed Congress. Sargent now had the embarrassing task of supervising elections in Mississippi that were obviously going to be controlled by his opponents, while, at the same time, answering the charges of a congressional investigation. As a result of the election, eight of Sargent's most vocal critics, including West, Green, and Hutchins, took their seats in the Mississippi assembly.

While Sargent's supporters fruitlessly challenged the election, the governor rapidly lost his power. The newly convened assembly elected Narsworthy Hunter as the territory's congressional delegate and drew up a list of ten anti-Sargent nominees for the governor's council. The 1800 presidential election results finally sealed Sargent's fate. With Thomas Jefferson as president, Federalist appointees, especially ones so despised locally as Sargent, were replaced by Jeffersonian Republicans.

Jefferson's 1801 appointment of W.C.C. Claiborne, at the time only twenty-six years old, as governor of Mississippi was a good one, although Claiborne's tenure as territorial governor was brief. In 1803, when Jefferson engineered the purchase of Louisiana from the French, Claiborne left Mississippi for the more critical governorship of the Louisiana Territory.

During Claiborne's tenure as governor of Mississippi, the assembly began to assert its power. It performed both substantive and symbolic acts, ranging from repealing "Sargent's Codes" to changing the name of Pickering County to Jefferson in the president's honor. In dealing with Mississippi's rapid population growth, the assembly divided the counties of Adams and Jefferson, forming the new counties of Wilkinson and Claiborne.

Finally the thorny subject of land titles was settled, as the United States government awarded the state of Georgia $1,250,000 in 1802 in return for dropping its Mississippi claims. With that settlement, the following year Congress passed a comprehensive land act that addressed the remaining problems of land titles in the Mississippi Territory. Claimants who had settled in Mississippi prior to the Spanish evacuation were allowed 640 acres, whether they could establish a valid land title or not.

The Federalist element in Adams County did not allow the Claiborne forces to dominate the scene completely. In 1802 William Dunbar came out of a

William C.C. Claiborne came to Mississippi from Tennessee, committed to Republican ideals and frontier democracy. He had to tackle the problems of pacifying the Indians, organizing a militia, reorganizing Sargent's code of laws, and settling land claims. When he was sent by the president to New Orleans to accept the city from France after the Louisiana Purchase, he remained to become the first governor of the Orleans Territory. Courtesy, The Historic New Orleans Collection

brief political retirement to run for and win a seat in the territorial assembly. For the remainder of his life Dunbar dominated that body, serving as its Speaker until his death in 1810.

Often referred to as the Thomas Jefferson of the West, Dunbar dominated the entire territorial scene in Mississippi with his vast knowledge and wide-ranging interests. Born in Scotland in 1751, Dunbar came to America with a small inheritance at his father's death in 1769. After becoming a successful fur trader in the area of Pittsburgh, Pennsylvania, in the early 1770s, he settled in Mississippi in 1773. A politician, inventor, and man of wealth, Dunbar was trained as a naturalist at King's College in Aberdeen, Scotland; he developed three varieties of cotton and wrote articles on a wide range of scientific topics.

Dunbar led one of the expeditions into the Louisiana Purchase area, though it was overshadowed by Lewis and Clark's much longer journey to the Pacific coast. Dunbar also was a strong supporter of Jefferson College, the territory's first institution of higher education, which was established at Washington, the territorial capital located six miles east of Natchez. In honor of his accomplishments, Dunbar was elected to the American Philosophical Society in 1803.

During Claiborne's 1803 absence from Mississippi, which was initially to be temporary, Cato West assumed the executive duties of the territory. The ambitious West thought he would become the permanent governor of Mississippi should Claiborne not return. West's tenure, however, proved to be brief and chaotic. In the 1804 assembly elections the Green-West faction lost power, and Thomas Jefferson appointed Robert Williams, one of the United States land commissioners in Mississippi, as governor in 1806.

During the Williams administration, two incidents illustrated the frontier character of Mississippi. First, West took the official papers of the territory to his Greenville home in Jefferson County and refused to release them. Williams had the assembly threaten West with a fine before he finally turned over the papers. The second incident, the Aaron Burr affair, was a bit more serious.

After killing Alexander Hamilton in a duel, Burr's political fortunes on the national scene plummeted. Against this backdrop of disappointed ambition, Burr next came to public notice when, accompanied by a small flotilla, he visited Judge Bruin in Bruinsburg during 1807. Rumors began to fly. Some thought Burr was leading a conspiracy for the separation of the Southwest from the United States. Others felt General James Wilkinson, who had returned to military service after having been accused of a similar plot in the 1790s, was at the center of this one, also. Still others thought there might be an attempt to take Texas from the Spanish. In the absence of Governor Williams, who was in his native North Carolina recuperating from an illness, territorial secretary Cowles Mead ordered military preparations.

When Burr heard that General Wilkinson had ordered his arrest, he surrendered to Mississippi authorities, upon the assurance that he would be tried in territorial courts rather than being turned over to Wilkinson. In its findings, a grand jury refused to bring an indictment against Burr. Burr

Sir William Dunbar of Natchez was Mississippi's "Renaissance Man." Born into nobility in Scotland, he came to Mississippi in 1792 to make his own fortune. He was a planter, explorer, judge, and member of the territorial legislature, but his greatest fame was as a scientist and inventor. He developed a cotton press, cotton seed, and a method for processing cottonseed oil. He studied astronomy and biology, and kept records of the weather and the rise and fall of the Mississippi River. Courtesy, Mississippi Department of Archives and History

was later arrested again near Mobile, returned to Richmond for trial, and cleared in a precedent-setting decision declaring that actual treasonous activity must be proven for one to be convicted of treason.

With the end of the Burr episode, the territory returned to its usual quarrelsome ways. Territorial secretary Mead joined the Green-West faction in its opposition to Governor Williams. Thomas Jefferson, upon Williams' resignation in 1809, appointed his fellow Virginian David Holmes as territorial governor. Holmes would serve not only as governor during the remainder of the territorial period but also as president of the 1817 constitutional convention and first governor of the state of Mississippi.

Mississippians knew Holmes to have Jefferson's confidence and support, which made it easier for Holmes to govern the territory without the usual strife. Holmes had been a congressman from the Shenandoah Valley for twelve years before his Mississippi appointment. Therefore, he understood both the frontier world-view and the workings of government. Although he was not a brilliant legislator, he had earned the Mississippi post through hard work and his administrative talent.

The older generation, which had created factions thriving on disharmony, was passing from the scene. Most importantly, Mississippians were most interested in promoting their common desire for statehood. Being on one's best behavior and in the good graces of Governor Holmes were seen as important elements in such a movement.

After 1810, the dominance of the river counties gave way to the new settlements to the east. For example, Madison County, which was located in the eastern Alabama section of the territory, had a population of 14,000 by 1816. An unexpected outcome of this growth was that towns in the river counties, such as old Greenville in Jefferson County and Natchez, put aside their local rivalries in favor of concerted action to protect their power.

Many Mississippians favored a challenge to Spanish rule of Florida. This matter became more pressing in 1809 when French Emperor Napoleon Bonaparte placed his brother on the Spanish throne. With the possibility that Florida would become part of Napoleon's empire, Mississippians sought to protect their southern border.

The first move came in 1810 when Mississippians assisted Americans living in the Baton Rouge area in a revolt against Spanish rule. In September 1810 the Spanish subjects requested that their area be annexed into the United States; President James Madison immediately complied. The United States officially annexed all of the area from the Mississippi to the Perdido River at Pensacola and assigned administration of the area to Louisiana and its territorial governor, W.C.C. Claiborne.

As it turned out, the United States had the military strength only to control the area west of the Pearl River. The Spanish military officer in charge of the Gulf Coast refused to surrender Mobile, declaring that Spain would not cede any of its coastal territory to the United States. During the War of 1812 the argument was settled by force when General James Wilkinson occupied Mobile for the Americans. Congress agreed with the Mississippi

delegate George Poindexter that the Mississippi Territory should receive the area between the Perdido and Pearl rivers, thereby allowing the Baton Rouge area to become part of the state of Louisiana.

After the War of 1812 ended, Mississippi's political factionalism reemerged. The political strife of this era was epitomized by a continuing feud between Congressman George Poindexter and Andrew Marschalk. Poindexter, a native Virginian, had come to the territory in 1802, embarking on a law practice and political career. He became, in rapid succession, attorney general, state legislator, and territorial delegate to Congress. As he rose in his political career, Poindexter collected enemies as well as friends. An incident early in his political career that dogged him for the rest of his controversial life was a duel with Abijah Hunt. Poindexter killed Hunt, and rumors circulated that the congressman had fired prematurely.

Andrew Marschalk was a partisan newspaperman who never tired of baiting and harassing Poindexter. Due primarily to Marschalk's attacks, Poindexter refused to run for reelection as the territorial delegate to Congress in 1813; instead, he received a territorial judgeship. If Poindexter thought that would relieve him of Marschalk's attacks, he was wrong. Writing under the pen-name Castigator, Marschalk continued to print every anti-Poindexter rumor he found. Judge Poindexter jailed him on a contempt charge, only to have Marschalk, once freed, renew the attacks.

During the War of 1812 Poindexter secured a military commission and left the area, hoping he could escape Marschalk's pen. However, when a pro-Poindexter newspaper printed a glowing account of his wartime heroics, Marschalk printed an account that had Poindexter actually fleeing the field in cowardice. Upon a chance meeting with Marschalk on the streets of the territorial capital, the politician threw a brickbat at the newsman. Marschalk responded by having a peace bond issued against Judge Poindexter. Poindexter continued the feud, first by issuing a writ of habeas corpus for himself and later by having Marschalk arrested on a charge of libel.

The Poindexter-Marschalk affair is illustrative of the intensity of politics in territorial Mississippi. These personal confrontations were reflected again in the appearance of a "city ticket," with Poindexter and others calling for the return of the territorial capital to Natchez; Marschalk and the "county ticket" wanted the capital to remain in the village

One of the sensational events in territorial Mississippi was the arrest of Aaron Burr in 1807. He was suspected of treason and surrendered himself into custody at Washington, Mississippi, where he was arraigned and released on bail. During his weeks in Natchez, he was lavishly entertained by old friends and Federalists. After he left Natchez he was again arrested in the Tombigbee area and sent back to Richmond to stand trial, but charges of treason were dropped. Courtesy, The Historic New Orleans Collection

of Washington. The 1815 election results were mixed. Although the seat of government did return to Natchez, William Lattimore for the second time defeated Poindexter's ally, Cowles Mead, to become the territory's delegate to Congress.

In the midst of this internal bickering, the territory continued to press its cause to become a state. In 1810 George Poindexter, as the territorial delegate to Congress at that time, called for the immediate admission of the entire territory as a state. The eastern (Alabama) half of the territory fought this approach, fearing the political power of Natchez. Poindexter then changed his strategy and called for the southern half of the territory to come in as a state; this 1811 proposal also got nowhere.

William Lattimore, Poindexter's successor as territorial delegate to Congress, pressed Mississippi's cause in Washington. He called for legislation that would allow the territory to begin drawing up a constitution in preparation for statehood. The proposal not only failed but caused a strong reaction back home. Mississippians from the western portion of the territory let him know that they did not wish to be a part of a single state with the eastern half.

In October 1815 a group met at what was termed the Pearl River Convention to call for the admission of the territory as a single state. In 1816 the territorial assembly endorsed this plan. With such confusion reigning in Mississippi, Lattimore followed the counsel of Southerners in the United States Senate. These senators called for admission under a two-state plan, which would give the South four additional Senate seats rather than two.

The path was now clear. The enabling bill, although opposed by some members of Congress from the Northeast, passed the Congress and was signed by President James Madison on March 1, 1817. A separate bill divided the new state of Mississippi and new territory of Alabama along the present-day boundary: an angular line was drawn from a point east of Pascagoula to the point where Bear Creek emptied into the Tennessee River, with the river as the boundary for the short distance to the Tennessee state line.

Not everyone in the former Mississippi Territory was pleased with the division. On the one hand, people in the Alabama section—their area being the more populous of the two sections—felt they should also be granted statehood. They blamed the dominance of Natchez in political affairs of the territory for the slight. On the other hand, Natchez politicians such as Poindexter and Mead were upset that Mobile was not within Mississippi's boundaries.

The Mississippi Constitutional Convention convened in July and August of 1817 at the territorial capital of Washington. Experienced politicians dominated the proceedings. Territorial governor David Holmes became president of the convention. Other territorial officials were delegates: former secretaries Cowles Mead, Cato West, and John Steele; former territorial delegates to Congress Poindexter and Lattimore; and three territorial judges. On August 17, 1817, the final document was approved, with only Cato West refusing to sign.

Since the most powerful branch of the new government was to be the legislature, the convention delegates carefully determined its composition. The interior counties wanted each county to have equal representation in the state senate, with the house of representatives apportioned according to the free white population. The river counties wanted slaves included in the population count to determine representation. The final compromise was that the house would be apportioned on the basis of free white population, with every county guaranteed at least one seat. The senate would also be divided according to population but with free white taxable inhabitants used as the basis for its apportionment.

The 1817 Mississippi constitution restricted the right to vote and hold office. One had to either be a taxpayer or have served in the militia in order to vote. To hold office, one had to possess taxable property and meet a religious test. The voters could elect only two statewide officials, the governor and lieutenant governor. The legislature appointed all other state officeholders. The constitution was for the most part conservative, tending not to give the people direct power over government. It was

adopted without being submitted to the voters for ratification. When President James Monroe approved the constitution on December 10, 1817, Mississippi became the nation's twentieth state.

Mississippi's territorial history was one of transition. Within a single generation, Mississippi evolved from being the possession of a declining European power to full partnership in the United States. Conflicts that were to mark the antebellum period were already apparent. The older areas of the state would fight to maintain the status quo against the frontiersmen of new settlements. The towns would sometimes have differing goals from the countryside. Colorful individuals, their lives shaped by the area, would in turn shape the history of the developing state.

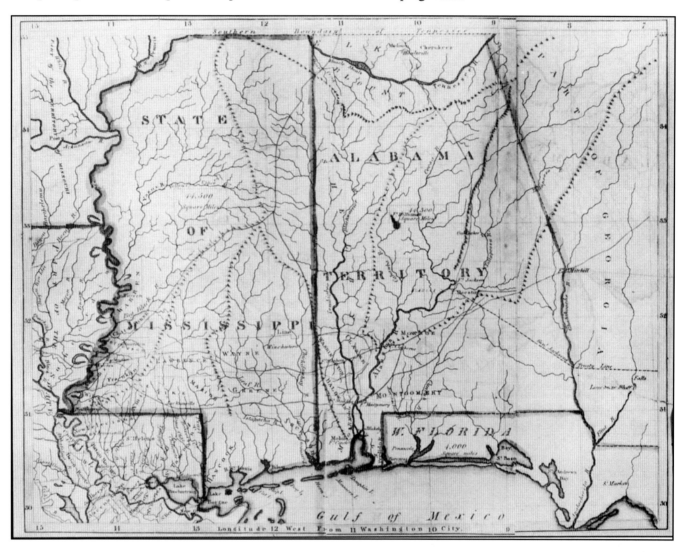

Facing page, top: *One of the most important figures in early Mississippi was George Poindexter, a Virginian who migrated to Natchez at the age of twenty-three. He was appointed attorney general of the Mississippi Territory and later served as judge, congressman, governor, and United States senator. He was the primary author of Mississippi's first constitution in 1817. Courtesy, Mississippi Department of Archives and History*

Facing page, bottom: *In 1815 the "backwoods" people of east Mississippi met at John Ford's house on the lower Pearl River to adopt a petition to Congress asking that the entire Mississippi Territory, which included Alabama, be admitted as a single state. Called the Pearl River Convention, the group sent Judge Harry Toulmin to plead its cause. Toulmin was unsuccessful and the Pearl River people were added to the Natchez District to become citizens of the new state of Mississippi. Courtesy, Mississippi Department of Archives and History*

Above: *This 1817 map shows the boundaries of the new state of Mississippi as defined in the enabling act of March 1, 1817, which granted statehood. The Alabama Territory became a state in 1819. Courtesy, Mississippi Department of Archives and History*

The slave trade was a corporate enterprise, and the largest domestic slave-trading firm in the nation, Franklin and Armfield, operated a major selling depot at Natchez. Smaller slave markets existed in Vicksburg, Woodville, Aberdeen, and Crystal Springs. An estimated 217,329 blacks were brought into Mississippi during the period between 1830 and 1860. Courtesy, The Historic New Orleans Collection

OLD SOUTHWEST TO OLD SOUTH

When Mississippi became a state, approximately two-thirds of the land area was in Indian hands. During European dominance, the Indian issue had not been crucial, since the Europeans wished only to take advantage of easily obtainable resources, such as could be gained by trading with the Indians. They did not wish to push the Indians aside, but merely wanted them to cooperate in the exploitation of the environment. American settlers, however, viewed Indian lands differently: as hindrances to American expansion.

Winthrop Sargent, the first governor of the Mississippi Territory, had as part of his assignment the "Indian Problem." He confronted the problem of Indian theft of food and livestock from outlying settlements and isolated farms. The Choctaw came to Sargent to talk about matters from their perspective, and he hired one of Stephen Minor's Choctaw-speaking slaves as an interpreter. However, relations with the Indians never improved during the Sargent years. The governor was unable to get cooperation from the local militia or United States Indian agents, and people in isolated settlements resorted to bribery to keep down Indian theft and violence.

Although Governor W.C.C. Claiborne got high marks for his patience and understanding of Indian problems—especially considering the fact that he was a frontier politician—he could not gain the cooperation of whites in improving relations with Indians. For example, he failed to halt liquor sales to Indians because many whites profited from the trade. Even Claiborne was not above manipulation in order to have his way with the Indians. On at least one occasion, he ruled that whites had the right to seize Indian lands for satisfaction of debts.

Andrew Jackson's war against the Creek Indians during the War of 1812 was a critical phase in white-Indian relations. The Creek War gave whites an opportunity to vent their accumulated hostility toward Indians through "civilized" warfare in the Battle of Horseshoe Bend and other major confrontations. Ferdinand Claiborne, the governor's brother, commanded the Mississippi forces against the Creek Indians. Although the field of battle produced glorious victory, Claiborne had to mortgage his Mississippi holdings to outfit and feed his men. He returned to Natchez in 1814 with a wound that caused his death the following year.

The War of 1812 and the Creek War had a tremendous combined effect on settlement in the Mississippi Territory. The provisions of the treaty ending the Creek War allotted twenty million acres of Creek lands between the Coosa and Tombigbee rivers to the United States. These newly available lands in the Alabama portion of the Mississippi Territory attracted thousands of settlers.

When James Monroe became president in 1817,

Above: *Among settlers with modest means, a plain two-story house was a favored style. A porch was almost obligatory, usually only over the first story. The style is typified by the J. P. Smith house at Old Hebron, built in the 1830s by Cabe Weathersby. Courtesy, Patti Carr Black*

Top: *One of the earliest extant log houses is the Sullivan home in Sullivan's Hollow, Smith County. Tom Sullivan built his one-room cabin in Choctaw Indian country and added the second "pen" around 1820. His descendants have lived in the house since and have made very few alterations. Courtesy, Patti Carr Black*

he carefully recast government policy toward the Indians. Whereas earlier administrations had simply worked to gain Indian lands, Monroe pursued a two-fold policy of "civilizing" the Indians while at the same time continuing to negotiate treaties for land. From Monroe's point of view, the land deals would be practical: the United States would obtain land for white settlement that the Indians did not need for the cultivation of food. Secretary of War John C. Calhoun was in charge of implementing the Indian policies. Although Calhoun personally felt that Indians should agree to removal west of the Mississippi River for their own safety, he actively supported Monroe's policy of indoctrinating the Indians in such ideas as individual land ownership and education.

Mississippi settlers did not agree with the Monroe-Calhoun policies. The settlers had been pleased with the grants of Choctaw lands between 1805 and 1820. These transfers had opened up much of the piney woods section of the state east of Natchez for settlement. However, white Mississippians wished to see a more rapid transfer of Indian lands and the actual removal of Indians from areas east of the Mississippi. The settlers exerted constant pressure on federal officials to force additional cessions from the Indians.

Early in 1820 Governor George Poindexter requested that the federal government push for a large Choctaw cession. President Monroe, acting on the request, appointed Andrew Jackson to head the negotiating team. Although reluctant to bargain, the Choctaw finally agreed to meet Jackson at Doak's Stand on the Natchez Trace (in the southeastern corner of present-day Madison County).

Jackson and Thomas Hinds, his assistant in the negotiations and fellow hero at the Battle of New Orleans, bargained hard with the two Choctaw chiefs, Pushmataha and Mushulatubbee. Pushmataha, born in 1764, was a strong and respected leader and had at various times been both an opponent and ally of the United States. His knowledge of the French, Spanish, and English languages, in addition to his familiarity with geography, helped protect the Choctaw interests during the Doak's Stand negotiations.

In the final agreement, the Treaty of Doak's Stand promised the Choctaw thirteen million acres between the Arkansas and Red rivers in return for about five million acres in Mississippi (approximately a third of Choctaw holdings in the state). The treaty also stated that funds from Choctaw cession land sales would provide the financial means for an education for Choctaws who wished to pursue such a goal. Also, the treaty provided that each Choctaw family would receive enough corn for a year, a blanket, kettle, rifle, bullet molds, and a year's supply of ammunition for hunting and defense.

Problems with the Choctaw were not really resolved by the treaty. On the one hand, the area of the Choctaw cession became the most rapidly developed area of the state, thereby putting additional pressure on government officials for more lands. On the other hand, the Indians felt they had been shortchanged. Pushmataha and Mushulatubbee went to Washington in 1824 to present their case.

In their Washington conferences, Pushmataha and Mushulatubbee argued that whites had already begun encroaching on Arkansas land that had been given to the Choctaw. They were able to make the best of a difficult situation, as federal officials more clearly defined the boundaries of new Choctaw trans-Mississippi territory. However, the Choctaw lost a strong leader when Pushmataha died while still in Washington on Christmas Eve, 1824. He was buried in the Congressional Cemetery with full military honors.

The Choctaw resisted removal to their new lands in the west. Only fifty Choctaws had gone to

Homes belonging to subsistence farmers in rural areas were usually simple and rustic. The dominant style in Mississippi was the dogtrot or double-pen house. Usually built of logs with stick and mud chimneys and clapboard roofs, the houses were built as one-room cabins. The second "pen" was added later and shed rooms were attached as needed. Farmer Jonathan Ainsworth built this log house in north Simpson County around 1860. Courtesy, Patti Carr Black

As Indian lands were acquired, towns in the northern part of the state developed. Holly Springs, twenty miles from the Tennessee line, was settled in 1836 and had begun to acquire impressive homes and buildings when the Civil War broke out. Holly Springs was the scene of more than fifty different engagements during the war. Courtesy, Mississippi Department of Archives and History

Left: *General Andrew Jackson first won the hearts of Mississippians in the War of 1812. Less than a decade later, the new capital city of the state, located on the Pearl River, was named for him. Courtesy, The Historic New Orleans Collection*

Facing page, top: *Two of the leading Choctaw chiefs were sketched by George Catlin in the 1830s. Mushulatubbee (left) and Pushmataha represented the Choctaws at the Treaty of Doak's Stand in 1820. Hahchootuck (right) was the Choctaw name for Peter Pitchlyn, the mixed-blood son of a white government interpreter. Pitchlyn played an important role in the 1830 treaty negotiations and went on to become a prominent leader in establishing Choctaw society west of the Mississippi and building a national tribal government. Courtesy, Mississippi Department of Archives and History*

Below: *Organized gambling was outlawed from the earliest days of Natchez and Vicksburg, but it continued to be a problem. In 1835 tensions between citizens and gamblers led to bloodshed and the peremptory hanging of five gamblers in Vicksburg, with the expulsion of the rest. Courtesy, Mississippi Department of Archives and History*

Above: When Labon Bacot was elected the first sheriff of Pike County in 1817, he had to provide his own office. For that purpose he built this log cabin on his farm near McComb. The structure remains intact today. Courtesy, Patti Carr Black

Above, right: Greenwood LeFlore, Choctaw chief, was principal negotiator at the Treaty of Dancing Rabbit Creek in 1830. Son of Louis LeFleur, a French-Canadian trader, and Rebecca Cravat, a French-Choctaw woman, he married an English woman and became a symbol and advocate of acculturation. After the Choctaw removal, LeFlore elected to remain in Mississippi. He became a large landowner, Delta planter, and a member of the Mississippi senate. Courtesy, Mississippi Department of Archives and History

Arkansas by 1829 since, under the provisions of the Treaty of Doak's Stand, such a move was encouraged but not required. The year 1829 was critical for the Choctaw because Andrew Jackson, the old Indian fighter, was now president. He took a personal interest in gaining additional concessions from the Indians of the southeast and driving them beyond the Mississippi. His "advice" to the Indians was simple: either submit to United States laws or move west of the Mississippi. He did not believe in the "nation within a nation" doctrine, which recognized American Indians as sovereign peoples within the boundaries of the United States. This legal concept had until then helped protect Indian cultures and rights.

Jackson rapidly implemented his philosophy. He first had Congress pass an act supporting his policies for the removal of the Southeastern Indian tribes. He then set about to gain further land exchanges from the Choctaw. Negotiating for the Choctaw was Greenwood LeFlore, the son of Louis LeFleur, a French trader, and a French-Choctaw woman of the Cravat family.

In September 1830 LeFlore and other Choctaw leaders met with Secretary of War John Eaton and

John Coffee, another of Jackson's Indian-fighting friends, at Dancing Rabbit Creek in present-day Noxubee County. The Treaty of Dancing Rabbit Creek, signed by 172 Choctaw leaders and Eaton and Coffee, provided that the Choctaw would receive land west of the Mississippi in exchange for the remaining Choctaw lands in Mississippi. This time the Choctaw were unable to bargain successfully. They received less compensatory land west of the Mississippi than in the Doak's Stand treaty in spite of the fact that they were giving up twice as much as in the earlier negotiation. The Choctaw were given three years to leave Mississippi. If any Choctaw chose to remain he could receive 640 acres but with the stipulation that he submit to the white man's law.

Chief LeFlore received 2,500 acres for his role in representing Choctaw interests; other Indian negotiators were similarly rewarded. LeFlore not only remained in Mississippi, but became a wealthy plantation owner and built Malmaison, a beautiful antebellum mansion, near Greenwood. He served as a member of the Mississippi legislature and was such an American patriot that he refused to use Confederate currency during the Civil War. When he died in 1865, his casket was draped with an American flag.

Other Indians did not enjoy such success. The Chickasaw followed the path of their Choctaw cousins when Jackson invited them to meet for discussions with him at Franklin, Tennessee. The eventual outcome of that meeting was the 1832 Treaty of Pontotoc, once again negotiated by John Coffee. The Chickasaw gave up all their six million acres east of the Mississippi. They were allowed some role in the selection of the area west of the Mississippi they wished to have as their cession. The Choctaw and Chickasaw thereby joined other Indians of the Southeast in the infamous trek of the 1830s, the Trail of Tears.

At the same time Indians were being pushed out of Mississippi, whites were becoming familiar with the politics of statehood. In September 1817, with the Mississippi constitution in place, David Holmes became the first governor of the state. Other major leaders elected at the time were Cowles Mead as lieutenant governor and George Poindexter as congressman. When the legislature met, it quickly elected Walter Leake and Thomas Williams to the United States Senate.

The old rivalries between richer, more settled areas and the new, emerging counties continued.

Above: *The Mississippi Governor's Mansion was completed in 1842 to serve as the official residence of the state's chief executive. It is the second oldest continuously occupied executive residence in the United States. Architect William Nichols designed the classic Greek Revival building "to avoid a profusion of ornament, and to adhere to a plain republican simplicity, as best comporting with the dignity of the State." Since Henry Clay was entertained at the mansion in 1843, many other distinguished guests have visited there, from Theodore Roosevelt to Jimmy Carter. Courtesy, Mississippi Department of Archives and History*

Top: *The old courthouse at Jacinto was saved from destruction by the Jacinto Foundation, established in 1964. As the seat of government for Old Tishomingo County, the courthouse was built in 1854 and abandoned in 1870 when Old Tishomingo was divided into several new counties. Courtesy, Mississippi Department of Economic Development*

Tilghman Tucker, a former blacksmith, was the first governor of Mississippi to occupy the Governor's Mansion. With no formal eduction, Tucker became a lawyer in Columbus and rose to the top of Mississippi politics. After serving as governor from 1842 to 1844, he was elected to the United States Congress. Courtesy, Mississippi Department of Archives and History

Public buildings erected before the Civil War reflect the aspirations and pride of the citizens for the new state of Mississippi. The most historic building in the state is the Old Capitol. The handsome Greek Revival building must have seemed incongruous with the boardwalks of the main street of a frontier town. Jackson, in the wilderness of Indian country recently secured by the state, had been settled only sixteen years when construction of the new statehouse was begun. Designed by William Nichols of England, the building was completed in 1841 at a cost of $400,000. It is now the State Historical Museum, administered by the Mississippi Department of Archives and History. Courtesy, Mississippi Department of Archives and History

Old Natchez District residents, with over three-quarters of the property wealth of Mississippi, thought they had a right to rule the state. With the Indian cessions of the 1820s, however, they began to lose their political power to the emerging majority of the state's citizens, the people living in the piney woods and New Purchase (as the Choctaw cession area was called).

Mississippi's government officials were most concerned with setting good precedents. During Holmes' administration, the state legislature organized a court system, created a militia, and reorganized the Bank of Mississippi. The bank, first chartered in 1809, now had its capital stock enlarged and received a legislative guarantee that it would have a monopoly. The changes continued during the administration of George Poindexter, who was elected governor in 1819. Poindexter was to make his greatest contribution to the development of the state after he left office by supervising a revision of the legal code. The revision, adopted in 1822, was commonly referred to as Poindexter's Code.

During the early 1820s—with all politicians claiming to be Jacksonian in their political persuasion—personalities rather than issues dominated the scene. Walter Leake succeeded Poindexter as governor in 1822. Leake had served as a member of the territorial assembly for ten years, as a member of the constitutional convention, and as a United States senator. He was reelected governor in 1823. He was governor when the Revolutionary War hero, the Marquis de Lafayette, visited Natchez in 1825 during his tour of America.

The major political event during Leake's tenure in office was the selection of a site for the permanent state capital. The legislature appointed a committee composed of Thomas Hinds, James Patton, and William Lattimore to recommend a site located on a navigable river and located within twenty miles of the center of the state. The committee selected LeFleur's Bluff, named for Louis LeFlore, who had earlier operated a trading post on the Pearl River. This site became Jackson, named in honor of the frontier hero even before his election as president. The legislature had its first meeting in Jackson in December 1822.

By the late 1820s, the dominant theme in state politics was the sectional split between the river counties and the frontier areas. By the time of the United States Census of 1830, the New Purchase region had population figures rivaling those of the Old Natchez District. In spite of the trend, an Adams

The Natchez-to-Jackson railroad line was intended to provide access to the capital city. The city contributed $200,000 in Planters' Bank stock in 1839 for its construction, but the line ended at Hamburg, far short of its goal. Courtesy, Mississippi Department of Archives and History

County native, Gerard C. Brandon, was able to defeat his interior county opponents for governor in 1827 and again in 1829 because they split the frontier vote. In 1831 Abram Scott, a resident of Wilkinson County, became governor in a similar fashion. The most important issue on the 1831 ballot, however, was whether or not to call a constitutional convention. The frontier forces led in the overwhelming support of the call.

After the election of delegates in late 1831, the constitutional convention met in Jackson in the fall of 1832. Since the convention was apportioned in the same manner as the seats of the legislature, the river counties had more power than was proportional to their population. In spite of this allocation of delegates to the convention, the document that emerged from the 1832 meeting was a constitution squarely within the tradition of Jacksonian democracy.

Among the changes reflecting Jacksonian attitudes were those involving executive offices. The two-year term for governor was retained, thereby requiring that official to stay closely attuned to the people's desires. A governor was limited to two terms in succession. Property qualifications for holding office were abolished. Also, all statewide offices were made elective. In addition to the governor, the people would now choose the secretary of state, treasurer, and auditor. The lieutenant governorship, largely a ceremonial position, was eliminated.

Since the legislature remained strong, apportionment and voting qualifications were sensitive topics. The basis for the apportionment of the senate

Slaves of Jefferson Davis, assembled for a wedding on the grounds of a plantation in Warren County, were photographed before the Civil War. The photographer is believed to have been H.J. Herrick of Vicksburg, who left his photography business in Vicksburg to join the Confederate cavalry. Courtesy, Old Courthouse Museum, Vicksburg

seats was changed from taxable white males to all white males, and all property qualifications for voting were abolished.

The most controversial issue before the convention concerned the judiciary. Pure Jacksonian Democrats believed that all judges should be answerable to the people; therefore, they wanted judges to be elected by the voters. This group became known as "whole hogs." The more conservative element of the convention wanted the membership of the state supreme court, at least, to be appointive. The "whole hogs" won the battle, with all judges, from the supreme court down to county probate courts, made elective. The principle that emerged from the 1832 constitution was that no person would hold an office without the people's approval.

The 1832 Mississippi constitution, which had widened the suffrage and abolished life-tenure offices, was the perfect model of a Jacksonian democratic constitution. Mississippi was then the only state in the Union requiring the election of all its judges. The capstone of the document was a relatively easy procedure for amending the document should the *people* wish to change it.

The 1832 constitution was a reflection of a rapidly changing Mississippi. The state's population during this period of "flush times" increased dramatically. The 1830 population of 132,621 grew to 375,621 in the 1840 census. Much of the new growth, of course, was due to the opening of former Indian lands for white settlement.

The population expansion that had begun during the 1820s was having its effect in the legislature. The Old Natchez District had been able to hold off the creation of new counties during the 1820s, but during the 1830s the Jacksonians established thirty new counties. Added to the twenty-six counties of 1832 were seventeen counties created in 1833 and thirteen in 1836 (the Chickasaw Cession counties). By 1852 Mississippi had a total of seventy counties.

During the 1830s, national issues began to play a greater role in Mississippi politics. The fight between Andrew Jackson and the Whigs over the Bank of the United States was an issue that directly affected the state. After Jackson's veto of the bank re-charter bill in 1832, he removed government funds from the Bank of the United States, including its branch in Natchez. He then placed the money in the banks of his supporters, with the Planters' Bank becoming his Mississippi depository.

During the 1830s financial speculation created great excitement among Mississippians. Railroad companies were popular capital ventures. The first railroad to operate in the state was the West Feliciana Railroad. Chartered in 1831, it began service in 1836, connecting Woodville with St. Francisville, Louisiana. In 1840 the Vicksburg and Clinton Railroad Company began service between those two towns. However, real speculation was not in the few railroads being built but rather in railroads that were never intended to be built. In 1831 the legislature passed a law allowing railroads to provide banking services, and the speculative fever rose. Although twenty-three railroads were chartered during the 1830s, the real purpose of most of these organizations was to avoid the difficulties

Plantation slaves performed many jobs. In addition to being field hands, slaves served as mechanics, operated the gins, and worked as carpenters, blacksmiths, wagon drivers, and sometimes overseers. During the off-season, they repaired fences, cleared new ground, cut wood, and crafted items such as cotton baskets, tools, and furniture. Courtesy, The Historic New Orleans Collection

of establishing chartered banking operations.

Speculation in land was the most common way to get ahead on the Mississippi frontier. At the beginning of the 1830s, there were only three United States land offices in Mississippi; this number increased to five in 1833. In the next five years, the land offices sold seven million acres of land in Mississippi, the single year of 1835 accounting for over a third of that amount. The major problem was not that people were speculating, but that they were purchasing the property on credit. Therefore, in the Panic of 1837 Mississippi was one of the hardest-hit states. Why had Mississippians been so foolhardy? "King Cotton" and his handmaiden, slavery, were to blame. Mississippians had come to believe that cotton was immune to normal economic cycles. Not even the 1837 panic deterred Mississippians from their faith in cotton. In spite of advice from Dr. Rush Nutt, an experimenter in agricultural techniques, and others calling for crop diversification, Mississippians became more and more dependent on cotton.

Although planters had grown cotton in Mississippi since the 1790s, it was not until after the War of 1812 that it came to dominate the economy of the state. The cotton grown before the war had been Creole, a long-staple, black-seed variety that was very difficult to pick. When bacterial disease began to destroy Creole cotton, Mississippians were forced to look for an alternative. They finally discovered a Mexican variety that had large wide-open bolls and could be easily grown in the upland areas as well as the more fertile lowlands.

It did not require great skill to grow the cotton, but a large labor force was needed, especially at planting and harvesting times. Therefore, the growth of cotton plantations and slavery went hand-in-hand. During the 1820s, the number of slaves in the state increased by over 100 percent. This was followed by an astonishing increase of almost 200 percent during the 1830s. The 1840 census revealed that Mississippi had a white population of 179,074 and a black population of 195,211. For the first time, blacks outnumbered whites in the state, and blacks remained the majority well into the twentieth century.

With such a large black population, the laws of Mississippi sought to control not only slaves and free blacks but also whites in their dealings with slaves. For example, one early law stated that it was illegal for a white to teach a black person how to read and write. Two events in 1831 caused white Mississip-

pians to enact even more stringent laws: Nat Turner's slave revolt in Virginia and William Lloyd Garrison's founding of a radical abolitionist newspaper, *The Liberator.*

As a direct result of the activities of abolitionists, Mississippi whites felt their institutions under attack. A siege mentality began to develop. New state laws required all free black males between the ages of sixteen and fifty to leave the state. No white could free his own slaves without the permission of the legislature. The Mississippi Colonization Society was active during this period, promoting the relocation of free blacks to Africa. By 1860 Mississippi had only 773 free blacks, the fewest of any Southern state.

Despite the general guidelines provided by law, day-to-day life for blacks and whites in Mississippi was determined by its economy, not its legal system. The agrarian life of Mississippi conformed to the rhythm of the seasons. During spring planting and fall harvesting, work was from sunup to sundown. At other times, the needs of farm and plantation did not always demand this back-breaking pace.

One of the most persistent stereotypes of antebellum Mississippi is that of whites living in Greek Revival mansions with blacks working in gangs of one hundred or more, tending plantations of thousands of acres. The truth is that the majority of white Mississippians owned *no* slaves; and less than 6 percent owned more than fifty slaves. Most slave owners had fewer than ten slaves. The overwhelming majority of white Mississippians were working in the fields themselves, either independently or alongside their slaves, or supervising the

Above: *The most renowned preacher of the Mississippi Territory was Lorenzo Dow, who gained fame as a rough-and-tumble Methodist circuit rider ministering to frontier areas. Dow founded some of the earliest churches in Mississippi. Missionaries kept coming to the new state, and by 1820 Presbyterian, Methodist, and Baptist missionaries, as well as Catholic priests, were working among Mississippi Indians and settlers. Courtesy, Mississippi Department of Archives and History*

Facing page: *The University of Mississippi was chartered in 1844. The Lyceum building, a three-story brick structure in the popular Greek Revival style of the period, was completed in 1848 in time for the first session of classes. It contained lecture rooms, a chemistry laboratory, and a library. It is still the focal point of the campus today, serving as the administrative offices of the university.*

labor of blacks. The large planter, whether an absentee landlord or someone simply removed from the day-to-day workings of agriculture, was not typical of antebellum farmers.

The social ladder of white society in Mississippi had four rungs. At the top were the large planters (those having fifty or more slaves) and their close allies in the towns and cities, such as lawyers and other professionals. Next came small planters, managers of large plantations, and merchants. Below them came yeoman farmers, that majority of whites who either worked alongside their few slaves or owned no slaves at all. At the bottom was a class of poor whites. They generally owned no land and little personal property, and they survived by working for others as tenant farmers or laborers.

Slave society, naturally, was different from that of whites. To begin with, while most whites lived on small farms, most slaves lived on plantations having twenty or more slaves. At the time of the Civil War, the largest slave owner in Mississippi was Levin R. Marshall of Adams County. He had 1,058 slaves, with his total property valued at amost $1.5 million.

Slaves on smaller land holdings might be called upon for various tasks, but once on the large plantations they had specialized tasks. Most were field hands, working in gangs with a driver over them. Over the slave drivers was an overseer, usually a white man in his twenties from a yeoman farming family. Above those slaves who worked in the fields came the artisans, who had perfected skills ranging from blacksmithing to carpentry. House slaves, usually the favorites of the owner's family, attended to such tasks as cooking, washing, assisting in child-rearing, and performing as personal servants of the owner's family on trips away from the plantation. Religion among slaves tended to combine the oft-required Sunday services at the master's church with evening meetings in brush arbors near the slave quarters, where they adapted Christianity to their own needs.

Beyond the economic realities of the cotton economy, life in Mississippi from the 1820s through the 1840s was full of contradictions. The evangelical churches, especially the Baptists and Methodists, were becoming well-established critics of the many sins of the frontier, but drinking, gambling, and dueling nevertheless continued to thrive.

Education was not a high priority for most Mississippians in the frontier state. However, higher education was actively promoted in some circles. Religious groups, especially, were able to provide

more financially stable schools than the struggling Jefferson College, a college-preparatory academy, and the oldest educational institution in the state. Mississippi College emerged as the largest ante-bellum institution of higher education in Mississippi. Established at Clinton in 1826, it became a Baptist institution in 1850. The legislature chartered the University of Mississippi in 1844, with its first classes beginning at Oxford in 1848.

The major problem with education was the absence of strong public elementary and secondary schools. During the 1820s and 1830s, private academies and tutors served those able to pay. By the mid-1840s, a public system of education was technically in place, but it suffered from inattention and insufficient funding throughout the remainder of the antebellum period.

In many ways the state remained a frontier area until the late nineteenth century. That is not to say that cultural elements were not present in the Old Natchez District or emerging in other places. It is fair to say, however, that many men took a far greater interest in drinking, horse racing, and dueling than they did in religion and education. Mississippi was reaching maturity, marking the transformation from the Old Southwest to the Old South. Meanwhile, the nation was beginning to witness the storm clouds of secession and war.

Left: *Cedarhurst in Holly Springs is a fine example of the Gothic design popular in the 1850s when the house was built. It is often referred to as the home of Sherwood Bonner, a writer and secretary to Henry Wadsworth Longfellow. Bonner's father, Dr. Charles Bonner, built the house from a design promoted by A.J. Downing, an influential architect. Courtesy, Mississippi Department of Economic Development*

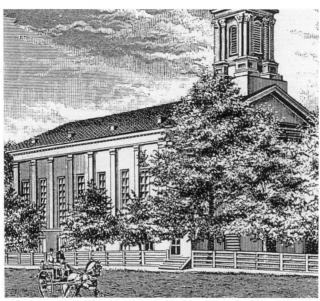

Above: *Mississippi College, the state's oldest college, was first organized in 1826 as Hampstead Academy. It became Mississippi College in 1830 and in 1850 became the property of the State Baptist Convention, which still operates it today. Courtesy, Mississippi Department of Archives and History*

Facing page, top: *Shadowlawn in Columbus combines Italianate features with Greek Revival form. It was constructed by a Columbus merchant in 1860. Courtesy, Mississippi Department of Economic Development*

Facing page, middle: *A plantation house with an unusual design is Waverly, built near Columbus in 1852. The dominant feature of the house, an octagonal dome with sixteen windows, lights the floor fifty-two feet below. Abandoned from 1913 to 1962, it is now restored and as a private home is open to the public during the Columbus pilgrimage. Courtesy, Mississippi Department of Economic Development*

Above: *Antebellum houses, exhibiting a variety of architectural styles, are in evidence throughout the state, most prominently in Natchez, Vicksburg, Columbus, and Holly Springs. The majestic Dunleith in Natchez was built in 1856 by Charles G. Dahlgren for his large family, which included his stepdaughter, Sarah Ann Ellis, a writer who later owned Beauvoir in Biloxi. Dunleith, a National Historic Landmark, is encircled by a colonnade. It sits on a hill surrounded by forty acres and has several Gothic style outbuildings. Courtesy, Mississippi Department of Economic Development*

Facing page, bottom: *Beauvoir in Biloxi is a "raised cottage" typical of coastal architecture. Built in 1852 by a Madison County planter, it became famous as the last home of Jefferson Davis. Courtesy, Mississippi Department of Economic Development*

Combat at Vicksburg grew too close for cannons to be used. On the night of June 13, as General Sherman's corps pushed up to a Confederate stronghold, the rebels threw lighted shells over the parapet, and the Federals in return lobbed hand grenades into the Confederate line. Courtesy, Mississippi Department of Archives and History

CHAPTER V

SECESSION AND CIVIL WAR

The Civil War, variously referred to as the War for the Union, the War of Rebellion, the War Between the States, and the War for Southern Independence, is surrounded with numerous historical myths. First, the Civil War did not begin suddenly with the election of Abraham Lincoln in 1860; rather, the forces that led to war had developed over a period of four decades. Also, the war was waged primarily over the *expansion* of slavery—at least to begin with—not the *abolition* of slavery.

To illustrate the deep roots of the secession crisis, we might well consider the political career of Mississippi's John Anthony Quitman. Quitman, supporting South Carolina's John C. Calhoun in opposition to Andrew Jackson's presidency, was an early advocate of the state rights position. The issue came into focus during the South Carolina Nullification Crisis of 1828-1832, in which Quitman and others worked to affirm the right of South Carolina to declare "King Andrew's" tariff policies null and void within its own borders.

Quitman's politics and subsequent adventures could not have been predicted at his birth. Born in New York in 1799, he studied for the ministry before going to Ohio for a career in the law. In 1822 Quitman finally arrived in Natchez; four years later he bought the beautiful mansion Monmouth for $12,000. He quickly adapted to the politics of Mississippi and was elected to the legislature in 1827.

He was a delegate to the 1832 state constitutional convention and was even acting governor of the state for a brief period when Hiram Runnels died in 1835.

In addition to being an active participant in the State Rights Association, he joined many causes considered proper for a Mississippi gentleman. He was a member of the Anti-Dueling and Anti-Gambling societies. Most of all, Quitman was an ardent expansionist who wished to see Southerners have unlimited opportunities to enlarge the cotton belt—as was their "Manifest Destiny."

Always available for foreign ventures, Quitman, in 1836, organized a company of volunteers to go to Texas and assist in its war of independence, personally financing the mission with $10,000. In 1846, during the Mexican War, Quitman achieved the status of Mississippi hero as a result of his valiant service during the battle for Mexico City. He was critical of the treaty terms ending the war—he thought the United States had missed a golden opportunity to annex additional Mexican territory.

Quitman, promoted to general in 1847, capitalized on his Mexican War experience to build a successful political career back home. He was honorably discharged in July 1848, just in time for the national Democratic convention, where his name was placed in nomination for the vice presidency. Although he did not secure the

nomination, the strength of Quitman's candidacy was an early indication of the dissension within the Democratic party. The fact that Quitman, an avowed anti-Jacksonian, could do so well within a dozen years after Old Hickory left office demonstrated that the frontier South had given way to the plantation South.

Quitman was a part of the Young America movement of the 1850s and believed that America's vision should go beyond its borders. Elected governor of Mississippi in 1849, he continued his foreign exploits, becoming involved in a conspiracy of Cuban planters to liberate Cuba from Spain. He resigned the governorship before the end of his term in order to go to federal court in New Orleans and defend himself against charges arising from the Cuban activities. Although the charges against him were subsequently dropped, Quitman could not relinquish his Young America hopes for making

Cuba an ally of the slave South, if not an American possession.

In 1853 Quitman became actively involved in another Cuban venture. This time he signed a written agreement with a Cuban group to become virtual dictator of the island should a revolution be successful. In 1854, he again found himself in a New Orleans court. He refused to testify about his role in the affair; however, he did argue the case for the defense when the judge implied that the jury could use rumor in lieu of evidence to come to its decision. Quitman avoided a jail term by posting a bond and promising to abstain from future filibusters (illegal military expeditions).

The Cuban activities certainly did not harm the political career of Quitman. Upon being elected to Congress in 1855, he continued to speak out for state rights. In 1856 he was again nominated for vice president at the national Democratic convention in Cincinnati. On the first vote, Quitman led in the count. When the balloting was over, however, John C. Breckinridge of Kentucky won the position. During the remainder of his career in Congress, Quitman vocally argued against Northern opinion on the Kansas question. He died in July 1858, before the Civil War that his career had foreshadowed.

Politics in Mississippi during the 1850s underwent significant changes. All successful politicians supported slavery; however, there was a continuing debate as to how best to continue the system within the context of American politics. Some leaders, like

Several Mississippians were launched into their political and military careers by the Mexican War. Jefferson Davis, John A. Quitman, Earl Van Dorn, and Charles Clark were among those who served in Mississippi regiments during the 1848 war. This 1922 painting by Alexander Alaux depicts Jefferson Davis at the Battle of Buena Vista. Courtesy, Mississippi Department of Archives and History

Albert G. Brown was the first governor to advocate public education. In 1846 he succeeded in getting a special school tax authorized by the state legislature, but local communities failed to implement it. Courtesy, Mississippi Department of Archives and History

Henry S. Foote, considered one of the greatest orators of his day, also participated in one of the most famous duels in Mississippi history. Foote and fellow Vicksburg attorney Seargent S. Prentiss met each other on the field of honor three times. Foote was twice wounded in the shoulder before they settled their differences. Courtesy, Mississippi Department of Archives and History

Albert Gallatin Brown, allied with Quitman's strong state rights position. Others, most prominently Henry Foote, pursued a more moderate unionist course.

The 1851 gubernatorial election was the first major test between the two forces. Quitman, wishing to be vindicated by the voters after his New Orleans court appearance, won the right to run for governor on the Democratic State Rights party ticket. Henry Foote, who had become a United States senator when Robert Walker became James K. Polk's secretary of the treasury in 1847, led the Union party ticket, designed to appeal to both Whigs and Unionist Democrats. The contest was to determine the position of Mississippi in its relationship with the national government. Early in the campaign Foote's rhetorical power gave him an advantage over Quitman. State Rights leaders convinced Quitman to move aside in favor of Mississippi's other United States senator, Jefferson Davis, who resigned his Senate seat in order to run for governor.

On the heels of the Compromise of 1850, Mississippians were simply not willing to give up on the Union. The compromise, including a provision to admit California as a free state, had given some people hope that the nation would overcome its

Born in Kentucky, Jefferson Davis moved with his family to Wilkinson County at the age of four. He attended Wilkinson Academy and Jefferson College in Adams County. After graduating from West Point, Davis had a brief military career before he returned to Mississippi to become a cotton planter in Warren County in 1836. His distinguished political career began in 1845 and culminated with his election as president of the Confederacy. After the war he was president of an insurance company in Memphis. Courtesy, Mississippi Department of Archives and History

Varina Howell was the daughter of plantation owners Margaret and William B. Howell of Natchez. She married the young widower Jefferson Davis in 1845. As a prominent politician's wife, she became known in Washington circles as a vivacious and intelligent part of the social life in the capital. Courtesy, National Portrait Gallery, Smithsonian Institution

divisions. The Unionists dominated the 1851 elections in Mississippi. Although the governor's election was close, with Foote defeating Davis by fewer than a thousand votes, the Union party dominated the legislative contests. The Unionists also won all the congressional races, except for Albert G. Brown's seat, which he retained. The defeated Davis was subsequently appointed secretary of war by President Franklin Pierce.

Henry Foote took the opportunity of a special legislative session to present his platform. Foote persuaded the legislature to adopt resolutions stating that the people of Mississippi were willing to support the Compromise of 1850. (Ironically, this special session had been called by Quitman, while he was still governor, for the state to consider secession.) Foote enjoyed little success in Mississippi after that. He became so frustrated, blaming his lack of success on Secretary of War Jefferson Davis' control of federal patronage, that he resigned before his term expired and left the state for California. Although he would never again be directly associated with Mississippi politics, Foote continued to hound Davis for the remainder of their political careers.

The 1851 election of Foote as governor was the high-water mark for Unionist sentiment in Mississippi. During the remainder of the 1850s, State Rights Democrats were firmly in control of the Mississippi governorship, electing John J. McRae (1853 and 1855), William McWillie (1857), and John Jones Pettus (1859). The Democratic State Rights party was so strong after 1857 that its political enemies were simply referred to as the "opposition party" in subsequent elections. One 1857 contest, important primarily as the major initiation of two future leaders of Mississippi, featured Democrat L.Q.C. Lamar's defeat of Whig James L. Alcorn for a congressional seat.

Leading the loose coalition of State Rights Democrats during this period was Jefferson Davis. He was born in Kentucky on June 3, 1808. Following a brief sojourn in Louisiana, his family moved to Woodville, in Wilkinson County, Mississippi, where Davis grew to adulthood. He received a brief portion of his college-preparatory training at Jefferson College before journeying to Kentucky, where he attended Transylvania College. At the age of sixteen he entered West Point, where he graduated in 1828.

For the next seven years, Davis served in various army posts in the West. He saw his most notable service during the Black Hawk War. In 1835 he

EVA'S FORBODINGS,

retired from the army and married Sara Knox Taylor, the daughter of General Zachary Taylor. Davis returned to Warren County, Mississippi, to engage in the life of a cotton planter on the Brierfield Plantation given to him by his eldest brother, Joseph. Tragically, his wife died of a fever three months later. In 1845 he married Varina Howell at the Briars, her family home in Natchez. The Davises would have six children, but only the oldest daughter would live to adulthood.

A year following his second marriage, Davis volunteered for the Mexican War and served under his former father-in-law, Zachary Taylor, as a colonel of the First Mississippi Regiment. Davis distinguished himself in the battles of Monterey and Buena Vista, where he was wounded. Returning home as a war hero, he resumed his political career. Davis had been elected to Congress in 1845, resigning his seat to fight in Mexico, and was rewarded upon his return when the Mississippi legislature elected him to the United States Senate in 1847.

After his 1851 gubernatorial loss to Foote, Davis retired to his Warren County plantation until 1853, when President Franklin Pierce appointed him secretary of war. In 1857, at the end of the Pierce administration, the Mississippi legislature once again elected Davis to the United States Senate. Davis, who modeled his Senate career after that of John C. Calhoun, became one of the staunchest and most articulate supporters of state rights on the floor of the Senate.

During the 1850s national politics had dramatic effects on Mississippi. Most Mississippians viewed the 1854 Kansas-Nebraska Act which allowed these territories to vote whether to become slave or free states as the dawning of a new era for the expansion of the cotton kingdom. Few had the foresight of state rights Congressman Wiley P. Harris of Monticello, who opposed the measure because he saw it leading to a stalemate on the issue of slavery in the territories.

In 1856 the Democratic candidate, James Buchanan, won the presidency. His chief qualification, from his party's perspective, was that he had been out of the country as an ambassador during the confrontations between pro- and anti-slavery forces in Kansas, highlighted by the activities of John Brown. Therefore, he could not be called to account for any role in the affair. However, as soon as Buchanan walked into office, he had to deal with the question of "Bleeding Kansas." He appointed

Robert Walker of Mississippi as territorial governor of Kansas, hoping that would satisfy Southerners who wanted to make sure that their side had an opportunity to make Kansas a slave state. Many Democrats felt that the Lecompton Constitution, which was submitted by pro-slavery forces from Kansas as their document for statehood, would solve the issue; however, the constitution raised an uproar in Washington. Stephen Douglas, the chief architect of the Kansas-Nebraska Act, was shocked at the illegal means used to adopt the constitution. When the principled Robert Walker spoke against the Lecompton Constitution, its demise was assured, and Congress postponed the admission of Kansas as a state.

The rift between the Northern and Southern sections of the nation widened in the late 1850s. The Supreme Court decision of 1857 in the Dred Scott case, which upheld slaveholders' rights, offended free soilers, who were also outraged as William Walker led efforts to make Nicaragua an American colony. Walker was very popular among Mississippians; both Democratic and Whig newspapers supported his scheme.

At the Southern Commercial Convention of 1859, which met in Vicksburg, pro-slavery advocates went so far as to propose the reopening of the African slave trade. Two Mississippi delegates, former governor Henry Foote, who had returned from California to attend the convention, and Isaac Patridge, editor of the *Vicksburg Whig*, resigned their seats and walked out in protest.

John Brown's 1859 raid on the federal arsenal at Harper's Ferry, Virginia, served as the backdrop for Mississippi politics that year. The legislature

Above: *On February 18, 1861, in front of the state capitol at Montgomery, Alabama, Mississippi's Jefferson Davis took the oath of office as provisional president of the Confederacy. On the rostrum with Davis were Alexander H. Stephens, vice-president; William L. Yancey, leader of the Secession Party; and Howell L. Cobb, president of the Confederate Senate. Courtesy, Mississippi Department of Archives and History*

Above, left: *The Civil War halted construction on Longwood in Natchez. Imported interior woodwork and furnishings, then at sea, never reached Natchez. Begun by wealthy plantation owner Haller Nutt in 1860, the house today is a reminder of the impact the Civil War had on the state's economy. Preserved in its incomplete state, the house is maintained by the Pilgrimage Garden Club. Courtesy, The Pilgrimage Garden Club, Natchez*

The Battle of Shiloh brought the war to the northern border of Mississippi. It was one of the bloodiest battles of the Civil War, claiming more battle casualties, North and South, than the American forces suffered in all of the battles of the Revolutionary War. At Shiloh, the Union had 12,163 casualties; the Confederacy, 10,699. Courtesy, Library of Congress

The Ninth Mississippi Infantry around a campfire in Pensacola, Florida, are dressed, as were many Confederate soldiers, in non-regulation clothes made by their families. These Mississippians inspired a British journalist to describe them as "great long-bearded fellows in flannel shirts and slouched hats, uniformless in all save brightly burnished arms and resolute purpose." Courtesy, Library of Congress

passed resolutions requesting neighboring states to cooperate in case a similar incident occurred in the Deep South. The legislature also appropriated $150,000 for additional armaments for the militia of the state. Although there was no evidence of slave revolts in Mississippi, the reaction of white Mississippians to the Brown raid indicated how anxious Southerners had become about threats to the system of slavery.

Somehow, both Northerners and Southerners lost sight of their common objectives during the late 1850s. For example, except for slavery, John J.

Pettus could have run for governor in 1859 in almost any state on the same issues as he favored in Mississippi. He wished to support the state university, build a levee system, and provide the state with a comprehensive railroad system.

As a result of their inability to establish common ground for North and South, neither the Democrats nor the Republicans offered a true national candidate in the 1860 presidential contest. Lincoln was not even on the ballot in Mississippi. The election results in Mississippi were predictable: John Breckenridge (Southern Democrat), 40,464; John

Earl Van Dorn of Port Gibson, one of Mississippi's best-known generals, led a highly successful raid against Union troops at Holly Springs on December 20, 1862, burning Grant's store of supplies. The action temporarily diverted Grant from Vicksburg. Courtesy, Mississippi Department of Archives and History

In his report on the Battle of Shiloh, General Braxton Bragg wrote that he never considered a military success complete "until every enemy is killed, wounded or captured." Bragg was given command of the Army of the Mississippi to replace P.G.T. Beauregard in late 1862. Courtesy, Mississippi Department of Archives and History

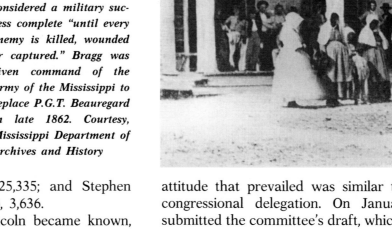

Bell (Constitutional Union), 25,335; and Stephen Douglas (Northern Democrat), 3,636.

When the election of Lincoln became known, Mississippians prepared for separation from the Union. The evidence seems overwhelming that they initially felt that Lincoln would let the South leave the Union peacefully.

Governor Pettus summoned the legislature into special session to consider Mississippi's options. Meanwhile, members of the state's congressional delegation met with Pettus. Albert G. Brown, Jefferson Davis, and L.Q.C. Lamar—three of Mississippi's most prominent state righters—were in favor of cooperative action with other Southern states. Most members of the delegation, however, wished to see Mississippi pursue the more radical course of immediate secession. On November 26, 1860, Pettus delivered to the legislature a rousing address on the need to escape "Black Republican" rule. The legislature issued a call for a special state convention, with the election of delegates to take place on December 20.

The only real decision before the convention in Jackson on January 7, 1861, was whether to secede immediately or cooperate with the other Southern states. Although cooperationist Lamar was chosen to head the ordinance drafting committee, the attitude that prevailed was similar to that of the congressional delegation. On January 9 Lamar submitted the committee's draft, which called for an immediate severing of the tie between Mississippi and the United States. The cooperationists lost on a vote to delay secession and then lost by a 70-29 vote on an amendment that would have required the convention's decision to be submitted to the people in a referendum. With those skirmishes behind them, the delegates then voted 84-15 in favor of immediate secession.

Opposition to secession came primarily from three areas of the state. Two of these had few slaves, the sparsely-settled piney woods and the northeastern hill region, a Jacksonian Democratic stronghold that simply wished to be left alone. The other was the Old Natchez District, which did not wish to have the stability of its world upset by secession and possible war. Leadership for secession came primarily from ambitious young politicians seeking new opportunities for the expansion of their power and wealth.

Once the decision had been made, most Mississippians rallied to the cause of the Republic of Mississippi. The new republic retained the existing state constitution with only slight modifications, primarily in military matters. The convention sent a delegation representing the Republic of Mississippi

to Montgomery for the organization of the Southern confederacy. On January 26, the convention adjourned. It reconvened on March 29 to ratify the constitution of the Confederate States of America. Meanwhile, one of Mississippi's moderate secessionists, Jefferson Davis, was inaugurated as the provisional president of the new government on February 18, 1861, in Montgomery, the "Cradle of the Confederacy." All these events had taken place before Lincoln was inaugurated president of the United States.

Despite the general feeling that Mississippi would be allowed to leave the Union in peace,

Governor Pettus and the legislature took some precautionary measures. In November 1860, at Pettus' request, the legislature created eighty-one companies of troops. The first shot in the Mississippi theater of the war was fired on January 11, 1861, from the bluffs overlooking Vicksburg, when artillery forces sent a warning shot in the direction of a United States Navy steamer, the *O.A. Tyler.*

More serious confrontations were in store at Fort Pickens in the Pensacola harbor, and at Fort Sumter in the Charleston harbor. Of all Union military installations in the seceding states, only these island forts had resisted Confederate occupation. Mississippi volunteers rushed to Pensacola, but Fort Sumter produced the engagement that began the Civil War. Immediately after that April 12-13 incident, President Davis called upon Mississippi to furnish the Confederacy with 8,000 men for a twelve-month service commitment. Mississippi regiments were organized and sent to Virginia and Tennessee.

In 1861 the only major military action in Mississippi was along the Gulf Coast. During the summer Confederate forces on Ship Island were forced to withdraw to the mainland when the Union naval pressure became overwhelming. Union forces then used the island as a base of operations for their attack on New Orleans, which fell in April 1862. Mississippians' attention then shifted to the activities of Union General Ulysses S. Grant in Tennessee. After victories on the Tennessee and Cumberland rivers in April 1862, Grant moved to Shiloh.

Located in Tennessee, Shiloh is important to Mississippi history because the battle there set the stage for the northern Mississippi campaigns. This was the first major engagement of the war for many Mississippians. The first day of battle, April 6, General Albert Sidney Johnston and his Confed-

Top, left: *After Corinth was occupied by Federal troops, slaves flocked in from outlying areas for Union assistance or to join the Union forces. The provost marshal was the man responsible for the government of an occupied city. He was head constable, police-court judge, health department, and distributor of financial aid. Courtesy, Mississippi Department of Archives and History*

Left: *Construction on the CSS Arkansas, rebel ironclad, was begun in Memphis early in 1862. When the Union fleet attacked, the Arkansas was towed down the Mississippi and up the Yazoo River to Liverpool near Yazoo City, where it was completed and launched on July 14, 1862. Courtesy, Mississippi Department of Archives and History*

Above: *Illinois troops, camped outside the courthouse in Oxford, guarded some of the 1,200 Confederate prisoners taken during Grant's march south in late 1862. Grant reached Oxford on December 5, but Van Dorn's raid on his supplies at Holly Springs delayed his advance toward Vicksburg. Courtesy, Mississippi Department of Archives and History*

Top: *Cotton bales stacked on barges were used as protection by Admiral Farragut's Union naval force as they attempted to go upriver past the Confederate guns at Vicksburg in pursuit of the CSS Arkansas. Courtesy, Mississippi Department of Archives and History*

erates almost pushed the Union army into the Tennessee River. Johnston's forces, however, were undisciplined and failed to take full advantage of their superior position. The Confederates suffered a crushing blow when Johnston was mortally wounded on the afternoon of the first day of battle. Late that afternoon and during the night Union reinforcements arrived.

On April 7, in spite of the arrival of Confederate reinforcements led by Mississippian Earl Van Dorn, the Union forces gained the advantage. General P.G.T. Beauregard, the new Confederate commander, skillfully disengaged his far-outnumbered forces and retired to Corinth, Mississippi. The Union forces, now under Grant's superior, General Henry Halleck, failed to make the victory a rout when they did not pursue Beauregard. High casualties on both sides, more than the total fighting at the First Bull Run (the war's first battle), left neither army in any condition to carry on the fight. Not until the end of May did Union forces occupy Corinth after the Confederates withdrew to the South. General Earl Van Dorn attempted to retake Corinth in October 1862, but he failed at a high cost in casualties.

The ultimate Union goal in the western theater of the war was the capture of Vicksburg. After the fall of New Orleans in April 1862, victories over Confederate forces had followed at Baton Rouge and Natchez. By May 18, six of Farragut's gunboats were anchored just below Vicksburg.

Vicksburg was also of major importance to the Confederates. Even if the Union controlled the rest of the river by holding Vicksburg, the Confederates could keep a vital link between the eastern

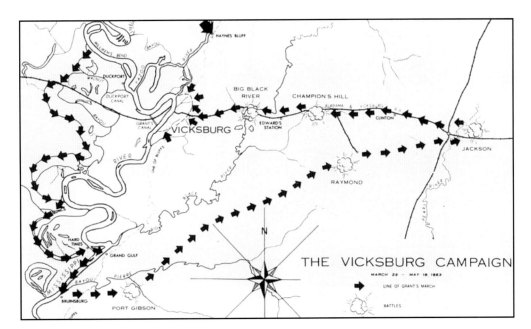

THE VICKSBURG CAMPAIGN
MARCH 29 - MAY 18, 1863

This map of the Vicksburg campaign shows Grant's route from the starting point of his campaign at Milliken's Bend, Louisiana, to a point on the Mississippi River south of Vicksburg. Grant's armies moved through Port Gibson, Raymond, Jackson, Champion Hill, and over the Big Black River to Vicksburg. Courtesy, National Park Service

Confederacy and soldiers and vital foodstuffs from as far away as Texas. Should Vicksburg fall, however, the Union could easily isolate the western section, concentrate on the eastern Confederacy, and utilize the river for commerce and communications.

From the bluffs, Confederate guns controlled the Mississippi at the hairpin turn of Desoto Point. In spite of his own doubts—already having withdrawn to New Orleans once—Farragut bombarded the city from the river in mid-June 1862, without success. By the end of the month, with the support of Union rams coming downriver from Memphis, Farragut's forces controlled the entire Mississippi—except for the four miles in front of Vicksburg.

Farragut's first plan was simply to go around the "Gibraltar of the West," as Confederates had begun to call Vicksburg. A group of soldiers went ashore to cut a canal across Desoto Point and divert the river through it. If successful, the river would bypass the city. The river, however, would not cooperate. Having already reached its early summer crest, the Mississippi fell rapidly, and the Union construction crews could not dig deep enough to make the bypass practical.

Meanwhile, the Confederates prepared a direct challenge for Farragut: the ironclad C.S.S. *Arkansas*. On July 14, the *Arkansas* left its Yazoo City berth for the Mississippi River. Along the way it forced three Union gunboat challengers out of the Yazoo. Lieutenant Isaac Brown, captain of the *Arkansas*, then ran the gauntlet of Union gunboats above Vicksburg and tied up at the city's wharf.

Nathan Bedford Forrest from Hernando enlisted in the Confederate Army as a private but ended the war as a lieutenant general, one of the Confederacy's most brilliant cavalry leaders. Operating in north Mississippi and west Tennessee, the task of defending Mississippi after the fall of Vicksburg was Forrest's. After winning the Battle of Brice's Crossroads, he was asked his secret for victory. He is said to have replied, "Git thar fust with the most men." Courtesy, Mississippi Department of Archives and History

Admiral David Porter's fleet ran the Confederate blockade of the Mississippi River at Vicksburg on April 16, 1863, with eight gunboats and two transports. The operation was vital, for it gave Grant the means to cross the river from Arkansas. Courtesy, Mississippi Department of Archives and History

Farragut now had a Confederate ironclad ram between himself and his supply base at New Orleans. He prepared to steam past Vicksburg and shell the *Arkansas* in hopes of sinking or disabling it. Setting out on the night of July 15, Farragut's men were unable to see the *Arkansas* on their run past the Vicksburg batteries. Once again, the ironclad seemed destined to foil Farragut. Farragut attempted to launch attacks against the ironclad for several more days. Finally, he and his forces retreated to the New Orleans and Baton Rouge area.

The *Arkansas'* end came ironically. With a land force marching alongside, the *Arkansas* descended the mighty Mississippi, only to have a mechanical failure. What the Union had been unable to do the Confederates were forced to do. With the *Arkansas*

Field photography was in its infancy when this photograph was made of an encampment at Vicksburg, circa 1864. The process used by the photographer was the wet-collodion glass negative plate that had started to replace daguerreotypes, ambrotypes, and tintypes in the 1850s. Courtesy, Old Courthouse Museum, Vicksburg

out of commission, the Confederates had to sink it rather than let it fall into Union hands.

Late in 1862, the defenders at Vicksburg braced for another Union assault. The Confederate general in charge of the defense of Vicksburg was John C. Pemberton, a native of Pennsylvania and an 1837 West Point graduate. Although a Northerner, he chose at the time of secession to cast his lot with the Southern cause. He commanded the Confederacy's Department of South Carolina, but was unable to get along with South Carolina's governor; therefore, President Davis transferred him to Mississippi.

Union General William T. Sherman began an amphibious operation against Vicksburg in December 1862, planning to enter the Yazoo upriver and then approach Vicksburg through its back door. Three of his divisions landed from their transports in an unsuccessful effort to cross the bottoms to Walnut Hills a few miles north of Vicksburg. After several days of intense fighting on the Chickasaw Bayou, Sherman retreated.

By that time, Grant himself had come into the area to assume overall command of the important Vicksburg operations. He headquartered at Milliken's Bend, Louisiana, on the Mississippi about twenty miles above Vicksburg. On the one hand, Grant knew that somehow he needed to get to the

high ground north or south of Vicksburg in order to avoid the bluffs. On the other hand, he could not afford the type of disaster that had befallen Sherman at Chickasaw Bayou.

With several operations having failed, Grant carefully masked his next moves against Vicksburg. First Union General McClernand began to build a road on the Louisiana side of the Mississippi south of Milliken's Bend; Pemberton interpreted that as a continuation of the earlier activities of Sherman. Therefore, Pemberton sent Confederate reinforcements to the Yazoo River area. Then, on April 16, Union Admiral David D. Porter led eight gunboats and two transports past the Vicksburg batteries, and Pemberton knew that he had misinterpreted Grant's activities. Grant's scheme had been successful so far.

Grant's operation now began to rapidly unfold. To keep the Confederates off balance, Union Colonel Benjamin H. Grierson launched a three-regiment cavalry raid that began in La Grange, Tennessee, and ended at Baton Rouge. Pemberton's strategic reserve was used in a futile effort to halt Grierson's destruction of railroads along his path, especially the link between Jackson and Meridian.

Union forces were now in position for their trans-Mississippi march. A Union attack against Snyder's Bluff, northeast of Vicksburg, tied up

Union troops set up dugouts in the hillside of Vicksburg during the siege of 1863 to serve as living quarters. The Shirley House, in the background, was taken over by General John Logan. The house and campsite are now in the Vicksburg National Park. Courtesy, Old Courthouse Museum, Vicksburg

On May 14, 1863, Grant's army walked into the evacuated city of Jackson. One of General William T. Sherman's young sons was given the honor of raising the American flag over the state capitol, now called the Old Capitol. Courtesy, Mississippi Department of Archives and History

In pursuit of Pemberton's army, the Union forces reached the Big Black River after the Battle of Champion Hill. General Sherman's forces, equipped with a pontoon transport, were able to build a bridge across the Big Black River in less than twenty-four hours, allowing his armies to move on toward Vicksburg in May of 1863. Courtesy, Library of Congress

additional Confederate forces and added to Pemberton's confusion. Meanwhile, the bulk of Grant's force had marched down the Louisiana side of the Mississippi to a point across the river from Bruinsburg. On April 30, 1863, Grant launched a massive amphibious assault, the largest in American history until the attack on North Africa in World War II. Unopposed, Grant placed 24,000 men and 60 cannon on the Mississippi side of the river in a matter of hours. Confederate General John S. Bowen and his men arrived and attempted to destroy Grant's beachhead. Holding the Union forces at bay with his vastly outnumbered Confederates, Bowen finally broke off the engagement after eighteen hours of fighting.

Grant then marched his men through Port Gibson to Raymond, where there was a brief skirmish. Grant's troops divided, with a major

contingent under Sherman going on to Jackson. Meanwhile, Pemberton was receiving conflicting orders. Earlier, President Jefferson Davis had ordered him to defend Vicksburg at all costs; now, General Joseph E. Johnston, who had arrived in the area from Tennessee and raised another Confederate army, ordered him out of Vicksburg to help stop the Union advance.

Pemberton refused to leave Vicksburg. As a result, Johnston had to withdraw his army from Jackson to Canton. Sherman moved into Jackson with little difficulty. Finally, Pemberton decided that in order to defend Vicksburg it would be best to stop Grant's forces before they got there. He therefore pulled a large force out of the city and moved toward Raymond, hoping to cut off Grant's supply lines. Johnston sent new orders to Pemberton, stating the need for Pemberton to have his army north of the Southern Railroad.

As Pemberton moved toward that destination, he stumbled into the most critical battle of the Vicksburg campaign. On May 16 he met Union General McPherson's force at Champion Hill, near Edwards. During the course of that one-day battle the crest of the hill changed hands three times. But at day's end, Union forces were on that commanding position. Late that afternoon the Confederates were in full retreat, leaving behind a number of cannon.

Grant and his men felt victory close at hand. They relentlessly pushed the Confederates to the Big Black River. The Confederates were so shocked by this time that they failed, once across the river, to burn the bridge. They quickly raced to Vicksburg to the protection of the city's guns. Grant was now at Vicksburg's back door. In just twenty days, he had marched more than 200 miles, won five battles, and inflicted over 8,000 casualties on the Confederates. If Johnston and Pemberton had ever joined their forces in one place, they would have outnumbered Grant. But in this particular series of confrontations, Grant proved to be a superior general. He kept the two Confederate armies guessing—and separated.

Once at Vicksburg, Grant attempted two assaults. In both cases, however, Union casualties were too great. By May 25, Grant ordered his generals to prepare for siege operations against the city. For over a month the people of Vicksburg suffered. Confederate morale sank when it became obvious that Johnston was not going to risk his army in a rescue attempt. Meanwhile, Grant

The relentless bombardment of Vicksburg forced many of the citizens to live in caves during the forty-seven-day siege. One of the most famous accounts of the hardships that civilians endured is My Cave Life in Vicksburg *by Mary Loughborough, published in 1864. Courtesy, Mississippi Department of Archives and History*

received reinforcements and patiently awaited the city's surrender. On July 3, 1863, Pemberton met with Grant in the middle of the battlefield to discuss terms of surrender. The following day the Confederates laid down their arms and marched out of the besieged city. They signed paroles promising not to fight again. Officers were allowed to keep their side arms and horses.

After the fall of Vicksburg, the remainder of the Mississippi phase of the war was of little strategic consequence, but that did not mean that the fighting in the state stopped. Because Johnston had retaken Jackson while Grant had laid siege to Vicksburg, it was necessary for Sherman to once again march on Jackson. Encountering stiffer resistance than had been offered in May during the initial capture of the capital, Sherman lay siege to the city, which he bombarded for several days. To avoid being trapped, on the night of July 16 Johnston evacuated his army to the east across the Pearl River.

The only major military activity in the state after the summer of 1863 occurred in northeast Mississippi, which Nathan Bedford Forrest held in

The Warren County Courthouse was built by slave labor in 1858. During the siege of Vicksburg it dominated the skyline. It is now in use as the Old Courthouse Museum.

Confederate hands for another year. He achieved a victory over Union forces at the Battle of Brice's Crossroads on June 10, 1864. Later, Forrest left half his cavalry force in Mississippi while he led the remainder of his men on a daring raid on Memphis. That was the last significant action to occur in the Mississippi area, for Forrest and others had to turn east and attempt to halt Sherman's forces moving through Georgia. The war officially ended for Mississippi when General Richard Taylor surrendered the Department of Alabama and Mississippi on May 6, 1865, less than a month after Lee's surrender to Grant at the Appomattox Courthouse.

During the war, Mississippians focused much of their attention on the military phase of the conflict, but that did not mean that important activity was not happening on the home front. With most of the military action outside the state in 1861, Mississippi concentrated on the problems of wartime government. Pettus ran for reelection in 1861; his only major opponent, Madison McAfee, was persuaded to withdraw from the race. Even with the continuity of Pettus as governor, the chaos of the war was evident in the civilian administration in Mississippi. Since Pettus had not really thought war would

come, the state found itself unprepared in April 1861. However, Pettus seized the initiative and served the state well, especially in his ability to keep militiamen from desertion.

In the 1863 elections Charles Clark, a former Whig from the Delta who had converted to Democracy in the late 1850s, won the governorship. His victory may have been due in part to his being a wounded Confederate veteran, but more than likely it instead marked a conservative trend away from the fire-eating Democrats. Clark's most important task as governor was to reorganize the militia in the state, but he had little success. He and the legislature also tried to establish controls on the economy, but contraband trade continued without interruption.

Another major concern for white Mississippians was the changes the war had caused in their relationship with slaves. Even before the arrival of Union forces in an area, local whites were very concerned about slave uprisings. Slaves were not allowed to go to the nearby towns without a white escort. As Union troops came closer, the news of the impending fall of the area to Union occupation spread throughout slave quarters.

With the occupation of Natchez and Vicksburg by Union troops, those Mississippi River towns became havens for both black refugees from behind Union lines and runaways from nearby plantations. Toward the end of the war, plantations simply did not have an available work force. For example, in late 1863, only 10 percent of the plantations between LaGrange, Tennessee, and Holly Springs were even occupied. Plantation owners who attempted to keep their operations running were caught between the necessity to provide for both whites and blacks on the plantation and to cope with periodic Union raids. Many planters were forced to sell their cotton to factors in Union-occupied Memphis; therefore, they were technically trading with the enemy.

By mid-1863, white nonslaveholder support for the war began to diminish in parts of the state. Some nonslaveholders began to conclude that the conflict was "a rich man's war and a poor man's fight." In the piney woods county of Jones, a former Confederate sergeant, Newton (Newt) Knight, organized a group of deserters and draft-dodgers into an organization to resist conscription and impressment of agricultural products. Supported by a significant part of the local population, including slaves and women, Newt Knight's band fought a guerilla campaign against pro-Confederates in Jones, Covington, and Jasper counties during late 1863 and throughout 1864. Although Confederate General Leonidas L. Polk sent two expeditions into south Mississippi in

1864, which captured and hung some of the Knight company, guerilla warfare in the "Free State of Jones" continued until the war's end. Though not as extensive, similar expressions of non-slaveholder discontent with the war were erupting in parts of northeast Mississippi by mid-1863.

As the war progressed, Mississippians had to learn to do without goods they had secured from abroad before the war. Under wartime conditions, "coffee" consisted of a concoction made from corn, okra, or dried sweet potatoes; "tea" came from dried raspberry leaves; and horse collars were made from cornshucks.

Sometimes the daily routines of wartime would be broken by the military presence. Citizens found their lives in disarray when Union troops came into a community, often on raids. Following Sherman's sentiments that a war needed to be brought to the civilian population, Union raiders would break up pianos and furniture, slaughter livestock, scatter books, and burn homes and businesses.

The economic devastation of the war went far beyond the destruction of real estate. During the war Mississippians found it necessary to use cotton as a medium of exchange. However, with the general difficulty in getting the cotton to the European market and more specific problems of Union raiders burning thousands of bales of cotton, the crop proved to be an undependable medium of exchange. The governments of the Confederacy and Mississippi were in equally difficult straits as those faced by individuals. Bonds and paper currency were issued with no backing except the faith the people had in the government. The final economic blow, of course, occurred with the freeing of the slaves. Not only did slaveowners lose a sizable investment in slaves but they had to come up with alternative labor arrangements after the war.

The war took a heavy toll on Mississippi. Although accurate records were not kept, it is estimated that 78,000 Mississippians were active in the conflict. Three-fourths were lost to the Southern cause for various reasons: killed in battle, medically discharged, discharged for being either too old or young, or dying in service in incidents unrelated to battle, usually because of disease. Of those still on the service rolls at the end of the conflict, about 30 percent were unaccounted for. Many of those who did return home at the end of the conflict brought with them physical and emotional scars, which helped shape the Reconstruction years.

Jackson was twice occupied by Union troops in 1863. Ulysses S. Grant captured it on May 14, and William T. Sherman attacked it on July 12, burning factories, and destroying railroads. Courtesy, Mississippi Department of Archives and History

Above: *The Battle of Corinth occurred between October 3 and 4, 1862. Courtesy, Mississippi Department of Archives and History*

Left: *Shadowlawn, a white-columned antebellum home in Columbus, has fourteen-foot-high ceilings and period furnishings. Courtesy, Mississippi Development Authority/ Division of Tourism*

This page: Along the Natchez Trace Parkway visitors can relive a part of Mississippi's colorful past. Photo by Harold Young, courtesy, University Press of Mississippi

Right, top: This statue of Brigadier General Lloyd Tilghman is located at Vicksburg National Military Park. Photo by Matt Bradley

Right, bottom: This row of cannons looms quietly in the Vicksburg National Military Park. Photo by Matt Bradley

BRIGADIER·GENERAL·LLOYD·TILGHMAN·C·S·A
COMMANDING FIRST BRIGADE OF LORING'S DIVISION
KILLED·MAY·16·1863
NEAR·THE·CLOSE·OF·THE·BATTLE·OF·CHAMPION'S·HILL·MISS·

Above: *This Faience pitcher from France was excavated from the Father-land Site. Courtesy, Mississippi of Archives and History*

Right: *This handpainted emblem is from the flag of the 14th Mississippi Infantry Regiment, C.S.A. Courtesy, Mississippi Department of Archives and History*

Right: *The offical seal of the State of Mississippi has remained unchanged since 1817, when it was adopted. Courtesy, Mississippi Department of Archives and History*

Longwood, one of numerous antebellum homes preserved today in Natchez. Unfinished at the time of the Civil War, the five-story house has an octagonal design. Courtesy, Mississippi Development Authority/Division of Tourism

Sailing in Mississippi's coastal waters. In 1849, vacationers from New Orleans established the nation's second-oldest sailing organization in the Gulf Coast community of Pass Christian. Courtesy, Mississippi Development Authority/Division of Tourism

Facing page left: *Friendship Cemetery in Columbus was the site of the first Decoration Day, a precursor of the modern Memorial Day. On April 25, 1866, the women of Columbus decorated the graves of both the Union and Confederate dead with flowers. The graveyard contains a number of impressive headstones, such as the weeping angel pictured here. Courtesy, Mississippi Development Authority/Division of Tourism*

Facing page right: *Gluckstad Cemetery at St. Joseph Catholic Church in Gluckstadt. This Madison County community was originally settled in the late nineteenth century by German immigrants. Courtesy, Mississippi Development Authority/Division of Tourism*

Civil war veterans, bonded together by their common experience, often held reunions. This group gathered in Oktibbeha County in the 1890s. As the veterans grew older, national organizations were founded to commemorate the Confederacy: the United Confederate Veterans in 1889; the United Daughters of the Confederacy, 1890; and the Sons of Confederate Veterans, 1896. Courtesy, Mississippi Department of Archives and History

CHAPTER VI

THE POST-CIVIL WAR ERA

It is generally accepted that the Reconstruction era began in 1865 and ended in 1876. Mississippi's Reconstruction, however, began with the fall of Vicksburg in 1863 and ended with the Democratic overthrow of Republican rule in 1875. The military phase of the process ended even sooner. In the last quarter of the nineteenth century, while the nation entered the Gilded Age of millionaires and general economic progress, Mississippi and the rest of the South were adjusting to new relationships between the races and between the region and the nation at large.

At the end of the war, Mississippi was in need of economic reconstruction. Emancipation caused an immediate loss of 60 percent of the slaveowners' wealth. Mississippians had also lost more than 60 percent of their livestock during the war. The neglected land was in poor condition. Former slaves fled the plantations for nearby towns and cities to enjoy their new freedoms and escape the badge of slavery. The massive flood of migrants into these areas put pressures on agencies for food, clothing, and shelter that not even the Freedmen's Bureau, an agency chartered by Congress to help the ex-slaves, could alleviate. Members of Congress considered the idea of giving each freedman "forty acres and a mule" from confiscated plantations. Various methods of economic reconstruction were discussed, but it was soon apparent that Reconstruction would be basically political in nature.

White Mississippians had about a two-year period during the administration of President Andrew Johnson to conduct what might be called "self-reconstruction." Although there was a federal military presence in the state, Congress had not yet imposed its plan on the South. Johnson announced toward the end of May 1865 that, excluding high-ranking Confederates and large property holders, Southerners who were willing to take an oath of allegiance to the United States would immediately be given amnesty and have their rights as citizens restored. In keeping with the Lincoln-Johnson idea of a lenient Reconstruction, Johnson appointed William L. Sharkey, a widely respected lawyer and judge, as the provisional governor of Mississippi.

Sharkey, a Mississippian who had been a pre-war Whig and Unionist, called for the state's citizens to begin drafting a new constitution. The only requirement imposed on the constitution was an admission that secession and slavery were illegal. Johnson also suggested that property-holding blacks be permitted to vote, but the constitution-makers were in no mood to go beyond what was required of them.

Former Whigs dominated the proceedings at the convention, assembled in the state capitol in August 1865. Secessionists, even moderates such as Albert

Newt Knight led a deserter band in south Mississippi during the Civil War. Convined that the Civil War was for the rich man's gain and fueled by class and religious divisions that had existed in the piney woods from the earliest days of white settlement, the Knight company fought an inner civil war with Confederate supporters in the area around Jones County. Courtesy, Mississippi Department of Archives and History

Above: *Wartime conditions created choices for slaves. Many left the plantations and congregated in towns under federal control. After the Emancipation Proclamation in June 1863, freedmen tried to find family members separated during slavery. Mass marriages took place as former slaves were now able to cement family bonds. In Vicksburg, between April and November 1866, more than 1,500 marriages between freed people took place. Courtesy, The Historic New Orleans Collection*

Above, right: *At the end of the Civil War more than 435,000 slaves in Mississippi were suddenly free and faced with the necessity of finding food, clothing and shelter. Jobs for wages, formal education, and the rights of citizenship were new challenges for Mississippi's black population. Courtesy, Mississippi Department of Archives and History*

Gallatin Brown and L.Q.C. Lamar, were blamed for the war and thus were unpopular figures on the Mississippi political scene. Out of the eighty-eight delegates elected to the convention, seventy-one had been Whigs before the war. In one form or another, ex-Whigs and Unionist Democrats dominated white Mississippians' politics during Reconstruction and remained strong throughout the remainder of the nineteenth century.

The 1832 constitution was adopted with the required additions; by the end of August the convention had done its work, called for fall elections, and adjourned. However, in spite of the wishes of many white Mississippians, there would be no return to an antebellum status quo. A constant reminder of that fact was the presence of largely black federal troops—mainly ex-slaves.

The fall elections proceeded with racial problems looming as a backdrop. Most candidates for office agreed that legislation was needed to control the freedmen. The issue that divided candidates was

More than 17,000 black Mississippians served with Union armies, and many were among the Federal troops stationed in Mississippi after the war. The men pictured were among the black units used in combat. Courtesy, The Old Courthouse Museum, Vicksburg

whom to blame for secession and a failed war. The Whigs split. Ultra-Unionists nominated Ephraim S. Fisher for governor, while moderates countered with former Confederate General Benjamin G. Humphreys. Although Humphreys had been a Unionist in 1860, he had been a full participant in the rebellion. Democrats offered William S. Patton, also a Unionist. The results of the election could not have been clearer: the voters selected the moderate Whig over both the moderate Democrat and the ultra-Unionist Whig. In keeping with the course of moderation, the legislature elected William L. Sharkey and James L. Alcorn as Mississippi's United States senators.

What passed for moderation in Mississippi was not interpreted as such in Washington. Radicals in Congress saw the election of Humphreys and Alcorn, both Confederate military veterans, as Mississippi's way of defying the Reconstruction process.

The Mississippi legislature passed a law entitled "An Act to Confer Civil Rights on Freedmen, and for other purposes," ostensibly designed to protect the rights of freedmen. It allowed blacks to own property and to testify in a court of law, but only against other freedmen. Most sections of the law, however, concentrated on the "for other purposes" part of the title. This legislation marked the beginning of the infamous "black codes" movement in the Southern states, designed to control the former slaves. A labor section of the law called for blacks to submit a signed labor contract by January of each year or face imprisonment for vagrancy. Another section allowed black orphans or abandoned children under the age of eighteen to be "apprenticed" to white guardians. In practice, that usually meant an apprenticeship to one's former

master. Northerners were angered by such legislation, and the Freedmen's Bureau courts in the Southern states voided many of the labor contracts, arguing that they were enforceable only if applied equally to both races.

In 1867 Mississippi's legislature repealed most of the provisions of the Black Code, primarily because of the poor image it had given the state but also because many areas of the state were not enforcing portions of the law. However, the provisions concerning vagrancy, which helped guarantee an annual supply of labor for the cotton fields of the state, were retained.

Although the cotton market had held during 1865 and 1866, the following year it plummeted, due both to overproduction and declining demand. By the late 1860s good cotton land was selling for only twenty-five to thirty-three cents an acre. Cotton prices did not even cover debts, and farmers were being forced to sell land at "fire-sale" rates in order to satisfy creditors. Conditions improved during 1869 when Mississippi farmers began to protect themselves against low cotton prices by raising less cotton and more foodstuffs.

Although the general economy suffered, railroad development offered a new area of growth. Immediately after the war, considerable mileage of the state's railroads fell into the hands of creditors from the Northeast and Europe, primarily British investors. Rail development was renewed in 1867 and continued until the national depression of 1873.

The Civil War was especially devastating to the Delta economy. Due to Grant's armies and a lack of maintenance during the war, many of the Mississippi River levees were in disrepair. The situation was complicated by the fact that the old levee boards had failed to pay back prewar bond

President Andrew Johnson quickly sent a pardon for Benjamin Grubb Humphreys (above) when he was elected governor of Mississippi in 1865. A Delta planter, Humphreys had served as a brigadier-general in the Confederate army. Humphreys' administration overlapped with the administration of the first military governor of Mississippi, General Edward O.C. Ord. Both men had to deal with the confusion of a military-civil government.

The pressing need for labor in the cotton fields precipitated a series of political actions. The Mississippi Legislature enacted the "Black Code" in November 1865, in an attempt to force freedmen into yearly contracts with planters. This act in turn led the United States Congress to place the state under martial law, and eventually led to the passage of the Fourteenth and Fifteenth amendments to the Constitution. Courtesy, The Old Courthouse Museum, Vicksburg

issues. In 1867, the legislature created a Liquidating Levee Board that not only took care of old debts but also allowed for new funding. It was several years before the levees were back in place.

Concurrent to "economic reconstruction" was the changing political establishment of the late 1860s. In March 1867 the Radical Republicans in Congress forced upon President Johnson their plan of Reconstruction. As a result, Mississippi was placed in a military district with Arkansas. In order to be readmitted to the Union, Mississippi was required, first, to allow blacks to vote, and, second, to remove from voting rolls ex-Confederates who were disqualified by the pending Fourteenth Amendment. Excluded from government were all persons who had made an oath of allegiance to the Union and then had broken it by participating in the Confederate government or armed forces. The approximately 2,500 Mississippians affected by the provision included many of the state's established leaders.

Major General Edward O.C. Ord, commander of the Arkansas-Mississippi military district, was initially in charge of the Radical Republican phase of Reconstruction. During the summer of 1867, he sent registrars throughout the state to enroll voters

The Freedman's Bureau was created by the federal government to supervise the readjustment of freed slaves. It provided food and supplies to the needy, schools and medical care, served as an economic and legal watchdog, and even attempted land reform. Courtesy, Mississippi Department of Archives and History

according to the provisions of the Congressional Reconstruction Act. When the rolls were closed that fall, Mississippi had 79,176 blacks and 58,385 whites registered.

The stage was set for a battle between politicians of various stripes for control of Mississippi. Anticipating an opportunity to win control of the state, especially with an electorate with a large black majority, Republicans were busy organizing blacks throughout the state into Union Leagues and Republican Clubs.

Not all Mississippi Republicans of the Reconstruction era fit the negative stereotype. For example, Charles W. Clarke was a carpetbagger but also an idealist who became dedicated to the Republican cause in the state because of the great suffering he had seen as an employee of the Freedmen's Bureau. Clarke sought to improve the quality of life of all Mississippians. For the most part, the scalawag element of the Republican party was made up of former Whigs who simply aligned themselves with the party closest to their economic philosophy. In fact, as Mississippi's Reconstruction experiment became more radical in nature, many of them moved to the Democratic party, giving it a more conservative flavor.

During the early stages of Reconstruction, both parties attempted to gain control of the black vote. Democratic leaders such as Albert Gallatin Brown gave up after several attempts proved unsuccessful. Republicans had more success, and blacks performed important and necessary grassroots work for their party. Mississippi was not, however, under "Black Republican" rule. Only a few blacks occupied important offices in the state. Except in counties such as Yazoo and Warren, which had large black populations, political leadership was still seen, even by most white Republicans, as a "for whites only" enterprise.

As the fall of 1867 approached, the leadership of the Constitutional Union party, representing the traditional white voters of the state, called for a white boycott of the elections for delegates to the 1868 constitutional convention. Since the Congressional Reconstruction Act required a majority of the registered voters to participate in the election, they hoped to scuttle the proposed convention. The ploy backfired when blacks turned out in high numbers for the Republican ticket. More than 90 percent of the 76,016 persons voting supported the Republican's delegate slate.

With seventeen blacks among the ninety-seven delegates present at the 1868 constitutional convention in Jackson, the conservative white press declared it to be a "black and tan" convention. Of course, the "tans" (white Radical Republicans) controlled the meeting.

Out of the proceedings came a document that was in many ways progressive. For example,

the new constitution outlawed dueling, prohibited lotteries, and established a board of public works; in addition the term for governor was extended from two to four years. Future apportionment of the legislature was to be based on qualified voters; this action was designed to encourage voting in the state. Also, a comprehensive system of public education was provided—although the document did not indicate whether schools would be segregated or integrated. Black delegates agreed to the provision, pleased that blacks would gain access to an education. In some respects, the constitution was conservative, reversing many Jacksonian Democratic provisions of 1832, making many offices appointive, and placing no limitation on gubernatorial secession.

The new constitution contained more stringent requirements against ex-Confederates voting and participating in government than those of the Fourteenth Amendment. Anyone who had supported secession or assisted the Confederacy in any way was prohibited from holding office. Faced with a document designed to ensure the dominance of Republicans, Democrats came up with new tactics after the convention adjourned on May 18. Their strategy was to reject the document at the polling place. The Constitution of 1868 was the only Mississippi constitution ever submitted to the voters for ratification.

White Democrats used every weapon in their arsenal to discourage blacks from voting. The Ku Klux Klan, which appeared in the state earlier in the year, used threats and outright violence. The federal military counteracted this intimidation but was unable to thwart more indirect means such as the rumors of poll watchers recording the names of blacks who had voted Republican. Such lists, according to rumors, would be distributed or even published in local papers.

By such efforts Mississippi accomplished what no other Southern state was able to do: it defeated a Radical Republican state constitution. With more than 120,000 votes cast, the constitution failed by fewer than 8,000 votes—a close vote that indicated a rough future for Reconstruction in the state. After the provision regarding ex-Confederate voting and officeholding was separated from the rest of the constitution, the main document passed in another vote in November 1869; the provision was defeated.

On the same 1869 ballot, the citizens of Mississippi elected James L. Alcorn governor of the state. Alcorn was the head of a group of Republicans including Adelbert Ames, the military governor of the state, and John R. Lynch, a prominent black politician. Ironically, Alcorn, a Mississippian, defeated a conservative carpetbagger, Louis Dent, the brother-in-law of President Grant.

As Radical rule unfolded in the state, Mississippi's legislators quickly showed their willingness to go along with their Radical friends in Congress. The legislature quickly ratified the Fourteenth and Fifteenth amendments. It also selected Ames for one of the United States Senate seats and Hiram R. Revels, a black politician, for the other. Mississippi thereby became the only Southern state to elect blacks to the United States Senate—Revels and, later, Blanche K. Bruce.

As is often the case with successful political movements, the Republicans, having defeated their common opponents, began bickering among themselves. Alcorn attempted to build political alliances between Mississippi whites and the

Above: *The Ku Klux Klan was organized in Pulaski, Tennessee, in December 1865 to promote white supremacy and preserve "the Southern way of life." It operated actively in northern Mississippi until 1871 when federal laws made it illegal to wear masks for purposes of intimidation. This photograph of a Klan member in the custody of the United States district attorney was taken in 1871 in Tishomingo County. Courtesy, Herb Peck*

Facing page: *The 1850s were years of extensive levee building, when 310 miles of levees were constructed in the Delta along the Mississippi River. These levees were heavily damaged by the war and the flood of 1867. The levees were repaired and reconstructed in the 1880s with convict labor. Courtesy, The Historic New Orleans Collection*

James L. Alcorn, a wealthy planter from Coahoma County, was a Whig who served briefly in the Confederate Army as a brigadier general. After the war he joined the newly created Republican party and became Mississippi's first Republican governor. Courtesy, Mississippi Department of Archives and History

General Adelbert Ames, a Union war hero from Maine, was sent to Mississippi by President Ulysses S. Grant as military commander and provisional governor. After civilian control was restored, Ames was elected to the Senate from Mississippi. In 1873 he was elected governor, choosing to stay in Mississippi because he "had a mission . . . to help the colored men of the State." With the takeover of the legislature in 1875 by Democrats who brought impeachment charges, Ames left the state and never returned. Courtesy, Mississippi Department of Archives and History

Republican party, but Ames and others felt he was selling out the principles of equality in doing so. Alcorn was especially criticized for not appointing any blacks to judicial positions. On the other hand, the court system was the only aspect of Reconstruction that conservative whites would later recall with anything less than displeasure.

Finally, in the election of 1873, Ames directly challenged Alcorn for the governorship. Alcorn had been appointed as the state's other United States senator in 1871; therefore, the state's two senators were now opposing one another. One of the issues in the campaign was Alcorn's lukewarm support of Grant in the 1872 presidential campaign and the suspicion that he allowed his supporters to assist Grant's opponent Horace Greeley. Alcorn, in quite a turnabout from 1869, received the support of many Mississippi Democrats, including L.Q.C. Lamar. Still, Ames won the contest overwhelmingly, with a vote of 69,870 to 50,490.

The decisive result convinced conservative whites that there was no way to defeat the Radical Republicans at the polls. Sporadic, but possibly orchestrated, violence occurred throughout the state over the next two years. In 1874, after riots in Vicksburg, the Democrats gained the upper hand in Warren County.

The final battles in the war to overthrow the Republicans occurred in the elections of 1875. In January a "taxpayers' convention" was held in Jackson. The purpose of this meeting was to present a united front of conservative whites against Governor Ames, who had weakened his position in the state by calling for higher taxes to provide needed services. The fact that Mississippi's property tax rate was still well below the national average had no effect on the delegates to the convention; they saw a good "non-racial" issue to use against Ames.

Though in the guise of a taxpayers' movement, the anti-Ames forces returned to old tactics. The legislative seats were up for grabs, and the Democrats were determined to use any means necessary to achieve victory. As the by-then traditional violence of the election season began, Ames and James Z. George, along with L.Q.C. Lamar, a leader of the so-called "white liners," agreed to a truce. However, George was unable to enforce the agreement. Riots occurred at Clinton and Yazoo City, and sporadic violence increased throughout the state. Black militiamen attempted to quell the disturbances. Governor Ames telegraphed

Hiram Revels was sworn into the United States Senate on February 25, 1870. Elected by the Mississippi legislature, he became the nation's first black senator. Born free in North Carolina, he came to Mississippi in 1868 to teach freedmen. Revels later became the first president of Alcorn University, serving until 1882. Courtesy, Mississippi Department of Archives and History

President Grant for assistance, only to be told that Mississippi had to take care of its own affairs.

Violence and intimidation produced results, and the 1875 elections in Mississippi were a resounding victory for the Democrats. The new legislature was overwhelmingly Democratic; sixty-two of the seventy-four county governments went into the Democratic column. The new legislature wasted little time in getting to the main business at hand. In the early days of 1876, the legislature impeached and convicted the Republican lieutenant governor. Governor Ames agreed to resign rather than face similar embarrassment. Within months the executive branch was completely in the hands of Democrats.

Black Mississippians were not suddenly removed from politics with the end of Reconstruction. Although blacks were not allowed within the inner circles of decision making, they continued to hold some offices in the state of Mississippi until the turn of the century. For example, twenty-one black legislators survived the Democratic flood tide of 1875. In 1890 six blacks still served in the legislature. Blacks continued to vote in large numbers throughout the 1870s and 1880s.

Whatever gains were made during Reconstruction were not long lasting for black Mississippians for whom sharecropping replaced slavery. The sharecropper worked a small plot of land that belonged to a landowner, and, in return, received a share of the proceeds. The crop lien law made it

John R. Lynch of Natchez, son of an Irish plantation manager father and a slave mother, was a self-educated photographer when he was elected to the Mississippi legislature in 1869. He was elected Speaker of the House in 1872 at the age of twenty-four and was the first black from Mississippi elected to the U.S. House of Representatives, where he served three terms. He later moved to Chicago and became a successful lawyer. Courtesy, Mississippi Department of Archives and History

Left: *L.Q.C. Lamar of Oxford, who had been the chief author of the Ordinance of Secession, became the most powerful man in Mississippi politics after Reconstruction. He served in the United States Congress, played a major role in the 1875 Democratic takeover, and was elected to the United States Senate. President Grover Cleveland appointed him associate justice of the U.S Supreme Court. Courtesy, Mississippi Department of Archives and History*

Above: *Sharecroppers accumulated large debts at country stores, where they were furnished a line of credit for such necessities as food, clothing, seed, fertilizer, and tools. Under the 1867 crop lien law the sharecropper had to remain on the land working until the debt was paid. They were rarely ever able to free themselves from debt. Courtesy, The Historic New Orleans Collection*

Above: For twenty years after Reconstruction, Robert Lowry, an attorney from Brandon, shared the governor's office with John M. Stone of Iuka. Lowry placed strong emphasis on railroad construction. More track was laid during his eight years in office (1882-1890) than in all the preceding years. Most of these new tracks crossed the Piney Woods and the interior Delta lands. Courtesy, Mississippi Department of Archives and History

Above, right: Henry McComb came to Mississippi from Delaware after the Civil War. He transformed a pre-war trunk line into the Mississippi Central Railroad, and then expanded that railroad into the New Orleans, St. Louis, and Chicago line before turning it all over to Illinois Central Railroad. Courtesy, McComb Public Library

legal for a creditor to satisfy a debt by attaching future earnings; the law virtually guaranteed that a sharecropper would stay on a particular plantation until his debt was paid.

In spite of the weak position of blacks in Mississippi, the new political powers in the state used the fear of "black domination" to keep the majority of whites in line. This era of Mississippi politics is variously known as the Bourbon Era, the Redeemer Era, or the Rule of the Brigadiers. The terms are both useful and misleading. The term *Bourbon* indicated that the same politicians who were in power in pre-Civil War Mississippi had reassumed their places (as with the House of Bourbon in post-revolutionary France). The term *Redeemer* similarly indicated that politicians were "redeeming" the state from the rule of Republican carpetbaggers and scalawags. The term *Brigadier* designated a Confederate military leader who was now in the civilian government of the state.

Five politicians dominated the government of the state of Mississippi during the Redeemer period: John M. Stone, Robert Lowry, L.Q.C. Lamar, James Z. George, and Edward C. Walthall. Stone and Lowry monopolized the governorship from 1876 until 1896. Lamar, George, and Walthall, known as the Mississippi Triumvirate, ran the political scene from their positions as United States senators. They were not, however, identical in their political views. George was the most progressive of the three, earning the name the "Great Commoner." When Lamar was appointed by President Cleveland as secretary of the interior in 1885, Walthall replaced him in the Senate. Walthall was the most conservative of the three; his previous position as a railroad lawyer was reflected in his voting record in the Senate.

In keeping with the attitudes of the triumvirate, many Mississippi businessmen began to devote time and money to industrial development. Railroading, the most prosperous industrial sector of the Mississippi economy, grew tremendously with the help of inducements such as tax exemptions and subsidies. The most outstanding career in railroad building was that of Henry McComb, who in 1874 began the Chicago, St. Louis and New Orleans

Although Mississippi's major crop was cotton, the state had only nine of the 905 textile mills in the United States in 1890. The Mississippi Mills, which had been established at Wesson just after the Civil War, was the state's largest manufacturer. Courtesy, Mississippi Department of Archives and History

This photograph shows a timber crew in the Piney Woods with a crosscut saw. In the late 1880s, the crosscut saw replaced the axe as the basic tool for felling trees. Its arrival in a lumber camp was a major event, and people came from miles around to watch the new tool in use. Courtesy, University of Mississippi Library

Railroad. Three years later, this line became a part of the Illinois Central system. The other major industry in Mississippi following Reconstruction was textiles. The leading entrepreneur in that area was Colonel J.M. Wesson, who founded Mississippi Cotton and Woolen Mills in 1866. By 1890 there were nine textile mills in Mississippi, employing 1,184 workers.

Industrial enterprises that emerged tended to be closely tied to agriculture. Lumber mills and cottonseed-oil factories sprang up throughout the state. By 1890 there were 338 lumber mills dotting the countryside and eight cottonseed-oil factories producing fertilizer and cattle feed.

In spite of the obvious needs of the state, both industrial and agricultural, Redeemer politicians continued to dominate the political scene and call for low taxes and barebones services. They were not without opposition. Both within and without the Democratic party, alternatives were offered. During the 1870s, the Grange, an organization of farmers

Above: *Black men in Mississippi were able to register to vote for the first time in 1867 under Reconstruction guidelines established by Congress. Many white Democrats boycotted politics, including voter registration, creating a sizable black majority among registered voters. The first election of delegates to the Constitutional Convention of 1868 resulted in election of seventy-eight whites and sixteen blacks, mostly Republican. Courtesy, Mississippi Department of Archives and History*

Left: *Legal separation of the races did not exist immediately after Reconstruction. Separate schools were provided in 1878; intermarriage was forbidden in 1880; and segregation legislation, known as "Jim Crow" laws, began in 1888 with a law requiring separate facilities for blacks in railroad accommodations. By 1890 social segregation was the pattern throughout the state. Courtesy, Mississippi Department of Archives and History*

Above, left: *The ideas and personality of James Z. George of Carroll County dominated the 1890 constitutional convention. He had played a leading role in toppling the Republican party in 1875, and his role in restoring white supremacy had won him great popularity with white voters. He served as United States senator from 1881 to 1887. Courtesy, Mississippi Department of Archives and History*

Above, right: *Because of the poor agricultural conditions in Mississippi during the 1890s, small farmers tried to wrest political control from the Democratic leaders. Many farmers joined the Populist party, whose leader was Frank Burkitt of Chickasaw County. Courtesy, Mississippi Department of Archives and History*

Facing page: *Established by the Mississippi legislature in 1884, the "Mississippi Industrial Institute and College for the Education of White Girls of the State of Mississippi in the Arts and Sciences" was the first state-supported college for women in the nation. Uniforms were adopted to achieve a type of democracy among the students who came from widely varying backgrounds. Today it is called Mississippi University for Women. Pictured here is the first graduating class. Courtesy, Mississippi University for Women*

more concerned with technical agricultural matters than politics, spoke out against the crop lien system. They were successful in establishing a state railroad commission and state college of agriculture. In the 1880s the Farmers' Alliance replaced the Grange as the major outlet for the farmers' protest.

The Farmers' Alliance became more active in politics than the Grange had been, railing against the abuses of the sharecropping system and the convict-lease system. The convict-lease system had arisen as a means of taking care of convicts when the state did not have sufficient prisons. The practice of leasing convicts to plantation owners led to corruption and brutality. An important part of the scheme was the infamous "pig law," whereby a person could be sentenced to three years in prison for stealing swine, cattle, or property of more than $10 in value. Blacks, primarily, were imprisoned under this law and immediately sent to work on plantations.

Although the Farmers' Alliance had little success in electing its candidates to office, the legislature did adopt some of its programs. A campaign under the leadership of Frank Burkitt, editor of the Okolona *Chickasaw Messenger,* got the crop lien and pig laws repealed. Finally, in 1889, the Farmers' Alliance persuaded the state's politicians to consider a critical part of its platform, a new constitution.

The resulting Constitution of 1890 crystallized the changes that had occurred in Mississippi since Reconstruction. The primary purpose of the constitutional gathering was to disfranchise black Mississippians, a step many whites thought necessary in order to protect their own positions. Toward this end, the laws of segregation, or "Jim Crow," were enacted. In 1888 the state had passed a law requiring separation of blacks in railroad accommodations and facilities, opening the floodgates to all kinds of segregation laws. By the end of the century, all facilities in Mississippi were segregated, ranging from restaurants to cemeteries. The Constitution of 1890 formalized the same principle in the political arena.

The delegates to the constitutional convention wished to disfranchise black voters without openly violating the Fourteenth Amendment. White reformers felt black participation in voting had cheapened the process by allowing vote buying, vote stealing, and other fraudulent activities. Also, with blacks removed from the process, white political infighting could occur without the fear of black voting tipping the balance. A series of requirements

were drawn up that did not mention blacks specifically but were targeted against them nevertheless. Voters were required to pay a poll tax each year, and it had to have been paid for two years prior to an election in order for the voter to be eligible to vote. There was a clause requiring voters to be residents of the state for two years and the precinct for one year and to have been registered at least four months before the election. Then, there was the "understanding" test, which required the potential voter to understand a clause of the Mississippi constitution. The registrar was the judge of whether or not the potential voter had understood the passage correctly.

The Constitution of 1890 was not submitted to the people for approval. But delegate votes indicated an unusual and ironic alliance against the measures among the Delta and hill counties. Indeed, the poll tax would disfranchise hill-county whites as well as Delta blacks. In 1892 the new voting rolls showed 56,587 whites and only 6,648 blacks registered to vote in Mississippi.

By the end of the century, many whites had convinced themselves that the only way for them to guarantee white control was to have laws that kept blacks at the bottom of society. In addition, the legislature cut funding for all elementary and secondary education, and black schools suffered the most.

Behind all the "racial decisions" was a grim economic reality. During the 1880s and 1890s, Mississippi farmers were hard pressed financially. The Populist party was unsuccessful in the state because the Constitution of 1890 had ensured that there would be no biracial voting coalition to challenge the Democrats. Small white farmers were losing their farms, and they struck out politically against blacks. The end of the century would not bring an end to Mississippi's political and racial troubles.

Federal programs, initiated by FDR's New Deal, became a part of the daily lives of Mississippians. The largest was the Works Progess Administration, or WPA. Others were the CCC (Civilian Conservation Corps), FSA (Farm Security Administration), REA (Rural Electrification) and NYA (National Youth Administration). Courtesy, Mississippi Department of Archives and History

FROM PROGRESSIVISM TO THE NEW DEAL

Two legislative actions symbolically marked the beginning of the new century. First, in 1900 the legislature appropriated one million dollars for the building of a new capitol on the site of the old state penitentiary, signaling a new and more prominent role for state government. Then, in 1902, the legislature passed the direct Primary Law, creating an all-white primary election system for nominating candidates of the Democratic party. This system increased grassroots participation in the nomination of candidates for the various offices and replaced the old convention system, which tended to be controlled by political insiders. However, the system included white males only. Since winning the Democratic nomination meant for all practical purposes that the candidate would win the general election, the primary law guaranteed that the white community would dominate the election process. At the same time, blacks had been effectively eliminated from the electoral process. This period, 1903-1923, became known in Mississippi as the "Redneck Era." It was marked by considerable political participation by common white folks, derisively termed by their upper-class political opponents as "rednecks."

James K. Vardaman, known as the White Chief, was the first governor elected after the enactment of the primary law. Twice he had unsuccessfully sought the nomination for the governorship under the convention system. Once able to appeal directly to the voters, this spellbinding speaker was elected governor in 1903, making him the first Progressive to be elected governor of Mississippi. Progressives wished to open government to democratic processes and squelch corruption, especially in the voting process. But Vardaman's campaign and administration exemplified the contradictions in Southern Progressivism. Vardaman used race-baiting tactics in his campaign, stating that black schools should receive tax monies only in proportion to the amount of taxes blacks had contributed. On the other hand, he persuaded the legislature to increase funding of all public schools, established a textbook commission to select uniform textbooks, and abolished the convict-lease system. Despite his racial demagoguery, Vardaman, on at least one occasion, called out a militia unit to prevent the lynching of a black man.

Edmund Noel, who had been the author of the primary law, was elected governor in 1907. He

COTTON.
AMERICA'S KING.
GREETS
AMERICA'S PRESIDENT

Above: *When President Theodore Roosevelt visited Vicksburg in 1907, he was greeted with a parade through an arch made of bales of cotton. Courtesy, The Old Courthouse Museum, Vicksburg*

Facing page: *Jackson was a small town of 8,000 when construction began on the New Capitol in 1901. The grand design by Theodore Link was in the classical Beaux Arts style that dominated American architectural design at that time. The building was completed in July of 1903. Courtesy, Mississippi Department of Archives and History*

continued to call for Progressive legislation and programs as Vardaman had done. The work of the state and county health boards was enlarged. In 1910 a pure food and drug law, patterned after the national legislation, was enacted. Mississippi also passed a child labor law in 1908 that set minimum wages and maximum hours while prohibiting night work for children under twelve.

In 1907, Mississippi had an unwelcome visitor, the boll weevil. By the fall of 1909 the pest had covered the southwestern third of Mississippi. As the boll weevil's territory expanded, the experts of the newly created agricultural experiment stations encouraged farmers to plant crops other than cotton, but only a few enlightened farmers followed the advice.

It was in the realm of education that Mississippi made its greatest strides in the years before World War I. Building upon the work of the Vardaman administration, subsequent governors and legislatures created a system of agricultural high schools, with at least two high schools for each county (one for whites and one for blacks). Access to education

was thereby guaranteed to rural children. In another development, the consolidated school law of 1910 marked the beginning of the end for the one-room school.

In higher education, there was both expansion of the system and improvement of its administration. In 1910 a state normal school was created at Hattiesburg for the training of teachers. The same year colleges of the state were placed under the control of a single board of trustees. Mississippi continued throughout the Progressive era to earmark a high percentage of the state budget for education.

With improvements in education came a change in the status of women in the state. Nellie Nugent Somerville of Greenville spoke throughout Mississippi and other states on behalf of women's suffrage. Although the state of Mississippi did not pass such a suffrage law, the Nineteenth Amendment to the United States Constitution, ratified in 1920, cleared the way for Mississippi women to vote. In 1923, Nellie Somerville became the first woman elected to the Mississippi legislature.

Somerville's daughter Lucy followed her mother's example. Graduating Phi Beta Kappa from an all-girls college in Virginia, she attended the University of Mississippi Law School, where she graduated at the top of her class. She married fellow classmate Joseph Howorth and they practiced law, first in Greenville and then later in Jackson. Lucy Somerville Howorth was elected to the state House

of Representatives in 1931 and later served in New Deal agencies in Washington during the 1930s. She stayed on in Washington after the New Deal years as a judicial officer for the Veterans Appeals Board and the War Claims Commission. In 1984 she was inducted into Radcliffe College's Women's Hall of Fame.

The political scene in Mississippi during the early twentieth century was dominated by Vardaman's attempts to gain a United States Senate seat. When Senator Hernando Money retired in 1907, Vardaman and John Sharp Williams challenged one another for the vacant seat. Although the state legislature elected the senators, a popular "straw vote" was considered binding. Williams, a congressman from Yazoo City, declared himself the choice of "the good people" of Mississippi. Vardaman, of course, was running as "the people's candidate." Using his race-baiting tactics again, he called for the modification of the Fourteenth Amendment and the outright repeal of the Fifteenth Amendment, which guaranteed civil rights to blacks. The election was extremely close. The Democratic state committee finally declared Williams the winner by a 648-vote margin.

Vardaman had another chance to gain a Senate seat when Senator Anselm McLaurin died in late 1909. Many Progressives felt that the governor should simply appoint Vardaman, since he had come so close to winning in 1907. Governor Noel, however, appointed Colonel James Gordon of

James K. Vardaman ushered in a new era of politics, sometimes called the "rise of the rednecks," an era that championed the white working class. His inaugural address set the tone of his administration: "It is rather the honest laborer, who in the sweat of his face, in time of peace, maintains the commerce of the nations, and in time of war fight its battles . . . We need more help from that class of people." Vardaman worked for progressive reform in every area except race relations. Courtesy, Mississippi Department of Archives and History

Pontotoc County to serve as an interim senator. The legislature then constituted itself as a caucus for the purpose of electing a candidate who would hold the senate seat until the 1911 election. The leading contenders in the legislative caucus were Vardaman and LeRoy Percy, a Delta planter from Greenville. Vardaman sought, but did not receive, an open vote. Three other candidates eventually withdrew in favor of Percy, who defeated Vardaman in the caucus vote.

That did not end the fight, however. Theodore G. Bilbo, a legislator from Pearl River County and a Vardaman supporter, came forward to say that he had accepted a Percy supporter's bribe in order to expose the tactics of the opposition. Both the legislature and a Hinds County grand jury investigated Bilbo's allegations and declared them groundless. Bilbo, although severely censored by his colleagues, survived expulsion from the state senate by a single vote. Ironically, this incident launched Bilbo's career as a statewide politician. As he would later say, he did not care what people said about him, "just so long as they were talking about him."

The year 1911 was characterized by one of the most heated political campaigns in the state's history. Earl Brewer was chosen governor and Theodore Bilbo was elected lieutenant governor. Their races paled beside the United States Senate race, as Vardaman, who once again challenged Percy for the seat, made the secret vote of the caucus and the Bilbo bribe the major issues. This time Vardaman won the Democratic primary without a runoff, with Percy a distant third in the race. The Vardaman victory, coupled with Bilbo's election, marked the beginnings of a "redneck machine" in the state. With Bilbo's victory, Vardaman had proven that he could transfer his vote-getting ability to others.

Earl Brewer had no opposition during the Democratic primary, but once in office, he found Lieutenant Governor Bilbo was his greatest opponent. Brewer and the anti-Vardaman faction counterattacked. Brewer attempted to have the Burns Detective Agency check on Bilbo, but the legislature would not appropriate the funds to cover the investigation. In 1913 a grand jury brought an indictment against Bilbo for accepting a bribe, but he was acquitted of the charges.

In spite of this infighting, Brewer continued the Progressive reforms initiated by Vardaman and Noel. The state's judiciary was modernized. The

The abusive convict lease system that had supplied labor for public and private contractors for thirty-five years was abolished by Governor James K. Vardaman's administration. Courtesy, Mississippi Department of Archives and History

legislature increased appropriations for education during each session from 1912 through 1917. The licensing of teachers was improved, and stronger state regulation of banking was adopted.

Brewer's successor in the governor's chair was Theodore G. Bilbo. Bilbo had done such a good job of keeping his name before the public that he was able to win the Democratic nomination in 1915 without a runoff. He immediately moved to consolidate his position. His handpicked candidate, the twenty-six-year-old first-term legislator Martin "Mike" Conner, was selected as Speaker of the state House of Representatives. Lee Russell, another Bilbo supporter, headed the state senate as lieutenant governor.

With this kind of support, it is not surprising that Bilbo's administration achieved much success. Progressive legislation breezed through the two houses. New agencies were created: a highway department, board of law examiners, board of pharmacy, board of pardons, and department of game and fish. Needed facilities were built: a state tuberculosis sanitarium and a training school for delinquents. The fee system, which so often had led to corruption, was abolished for many county offices. Also, Mississippi ratified the national prohibition amendment during Bilbo's term in office.

Bilbo's record of accomplishment might have been even greater if it had not been for the coming

Above: *Children working in the seafood industry on the coast and in the cotton and woolen mills of southern Mississippi prompted several years of agitation for a child-labor law. A 1908 law set the minimum work age at twelve and established a ten-hour work day. These shrimp pickers were photographed in Biloxi by Lewis Hine in 1911. Courtesy, Mississippi Department of Archives and History*

of World War I, when local and state concerns tended to be pushed aside. Even before the war, Mississippians were being called for military service. During 1916, as General John Pershing's expeditionary force was chasing Pancho Villa into Mexico, Mississippi volunteers created three independent infantry battalions. Several companies of the National Guard were called into service as the 1st Mississippi Infantry Regiment, which was posted briefly at Fort Sam Houston in Texas but never made it to Mexico. During World War I this unit was reactivated as the 155th Infantry Regiment.

In addition, 56,740 young men from Mississippi were either inducted or enlisted during World War I. Over one third of a million Mississippians were registered for military service, approximately half of them black and half white. Another "draftee" was the 1917 Mississippi Centennial: the state had been planning a major exposition in Gulfport to celebrate its one hundredth year, but with the war effort taking precedence, the military converted the buildings into a naval station. After the war one of the buildings was used as a veterans' hospital.

A political casualty of the war was James K. Vardaman. He had opposed American entry into the war because he felt that British imperialism was as much to blame for the conflict as anything else. Vardaman was one of a handful of senators and congressmen to vote against American entry into the war. The patriotism of those who questioned American involvement was suspect, and, as a result, Pat Harrison defeated Vardaman for the Senate seat in 1918 amid cries of "Herr von Vardaman" and "Kaiser Vardaman." In running for the Senate,

Above: Pictured here is the administration building for the University of Southern Mississippi. Courtesy, Mississippi Department of Archives and History

Top: The State Teachers Association argued that the state needed more and better-educated teachers for the public schools. Their efforts led to the establishment in 1910 of the Mississippi Normal College "to train teachers for the rural schools of Mississippi." It is now the University of Southern Mississippi at Hattiesburg. Courtesy, Mississippi Department of Archives and History

Facing page, bottom: Arguments for school consolidation began as early as 1903. After consolidation was authorized in 1910, one-room schools began to be eliminated, but it took almost half a century to do it. A one-room school can still be seen in Lucedale, where it has been restored as a historic site. Courtesy, Mississippi Department of Archives and History

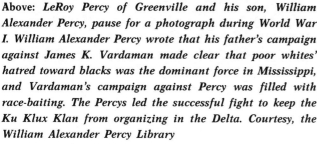

Above: *LeRoy Percy of Greenville and his son, William Alexander Percy, pause for a photograph during World War I. William Alexander Percy wrote that his father's campaign against James K. Vardaman made clear that poor whites' hatred toward blacks was the dominant force in Mississippi, and Vardaman's campaign against Percy was filled with race-baiting. The Percys led the successful fight to keep the Ku Klux Klan from organizing in the Delta. Courtesy, the William Alexander Percy Library*

Above, right: *Theodore G. Bilbo's political career, which spanned thirty-eight years, began and ended in controversy. He appeared on the political scene in a vote-buying scandal, and his career ended in 1947 when the United States Senate considered charges that he had accepted bribes during World War II. Courtesy, Mississippi Department of Archives and History*

Facing page, bottom: *Senator Pat Harrison of Gulfport, pictured here with Eleanor Roosevelt, was an early supporter of Franklin Delano Roosevelt and backed most of the early New Deal legislation. He broke with the administration over the Supreme Court packing scheme, the anti-lynch law, and the wage and hour law. Harrison was one of Mississippi's most popular politicians and served in the Senate from 1918 to 1941. Courtesy, Mississippi Department of Archives and History*

Harrison had given up his United States House of Representatives seat. Bilbo ran for that position but was defeated by Paul B. Johnson, Sr. Bilbo's defeat was primarily due to his campaigning for Congress when many voters felt he should have spent his time performing his duties as governor. Also, many voters blamed Bilbo for the unpopular dipping-vat law, designed to eradicate the cattle tick by a required dipping procedure. Some were so upset by this "invasion of their individual rights" that they dynamited some of the vats.

Although Bilbo was defeated in 1918, the "redneck machine" was still ready for the state races in 1919. There was a great deal of infighting in the organization for the gubernatorial nomination. Bilbo endorsed Lee Russell, causing a split with Attorney General Ross Collins, who refused to step aside in Russell's favor. Russell led the contestants in the first primary and defeated the Delta candidate, Oscar Johnston, in the runoff.

As was the case with most American farmers, the years after World War I marked the beginning of an agricultural depression for the Mississippi farmer. Cotton prices, which had been very high due to wartime demand, suddenly collapsed. In 1920 Mississippi farmers were further hurt by a short crop year, the first in years that had not gone above

Hundreds of pieces of liquor legislation and decades of agitation against selling liquor resulted in statewide prohibition in 1908. The statute remained in effect until 1966 when Mississippi, the last state in the nation to do so, repealed prohibition and enacted a county option liquor law. Courtesy, Mississippi Department of Archives and History

a million bales. A small independent farmer in 1923 could have made, at most, $300 for a full year's labor. Further complicating the farmer's plight was the fact that the number of Mississippi sharecropping farms had doubled from 1890 to 1930, with the average farming unit decreasing in size from 122 acres to 55 acres.

During this time, many blacks left Mississippi for better opportunities elsewhere. What had been a sporadic exodus became a stream during the early 1900s and increased steadily through World War II and the postwar years. Blacks were leaving sharecropping farms behind as they went to the towns and cities of Mississippi and surrounding states. Many blacks left the South altogether, having either bought a passenger ticket or hopped a freight car of the Illinois Central bound for Chicago.

The Russell administration was the last of the "Redneck Era" in Mississippi. The Bilbo machine, racked by factionalism, saw its political power diminish. While Mike Conner was still Speaker of the state House of Representatives, he had split with Bilbo over the Russell candidacy. The first legislative session during the Russell administration accomplished nothing, whereas the second session was dominated by a fight over control of the Yazoo-Mississippi Delta Levee Board. Walter Sillers, a young Bolivar County legislator, and other representatives from the Delta, won that battle by limiting the board to elected members from the district itself.

In some respects, the Russell years saw a continuation of the policies of earlier adminis-

Above: *The attitude of this group of men in Vicksburg, ridiculing the idea of women voting, won the day. The Mississippi legislature refused to allow women to vote or sit on juries. Mississippi women were able to vote only after other states ratified the Nineteenth Amendment to the Constitution in 1920. The 1984 Mississippi legislature finally ratifed the amendment. Courtesy, The Old Courthouse Museum, Vicksburg*

Right: *The four million acres in the interior of the Mississippi Delta were sparsely settled until the turn of the century, primarily because of flooding. Levee construction enabled the railroads to come in and help settle the land. This land office was set up in Yazoo City in the late nineteenth century.*

The timber boom changed the way of life for people in the Piney Woods. Dozens of sawmill towns sprang up, offering educational, social, and economic opportunities not previously available. The move from isolated homesteads to sawmill towns altered attitudes, habits, and customs that had been characteristic of Piney Woods' pioneer society. Hattiesburg and Laurel both started as sawmill towns in the 1880s and went on to become two of the largest cities in the state. The group pictured here is at the Eastman-Gardiner mill near Laurel. Courtesy, Lauren Rogers Library, Laurel

Women voters probably gave Henry L. Whitfield his victory over Theodore G. Bilbo. In the 1923 race for governor, women were allowed to vote for the first time, and Whitfield, who was president of Mississippi State College for Women, had the faithful following of large numbers of students, faculty, and alumnae. Courtesy, Mississippi Department of Archives and History

trations. The state legislature passed a record $18-million budget in its first session during his term of office. During the second legislative session of his term, most of the budget was earmarked for education and welfare needs. Teachers' pay continued to be increased, and bond issues were allowed for new buildings at the state colleges. A $20-million bond issue was also approved for highway improvements. The way was cleared for this highway program when the legislature finally limited county boards of supervisors to control of county roads only. Also passed during Russell's administration was a constitutional amendment that guaranteed a four-month term for all Mississippi schools and a provision to help poor counties meet that goal.

The official end of the "redneck era" of Mississippi politics was marked by the defeat of its leaders in 1922-1923. Vardaman was defeated by Congressman Hubert D. Stephens for John Sharp Williams' United States Senate seat in 1922. The following year Henry L. Whitfield, who had been dismissed in 1920 as president of Mississippi State College for Women because of his failure to support Lee Russell, defeated Bilbo for the governorship. The two met in the runoff, with

Vardaman giving his support to Whitfield, perhaps the decisive element of the contest. Also contributing to Whitfield's success were the votes of newly enfranchised females, for he had been a very popular president of the Industrial Institute and College (now the Mississippi University for Women).

During his administration Whitfield took steps to confront the powerful timber industry. Throughout the early twentieth century, timber companies from outside the state had purchased huge tracts of land in Mississippi. Because of heavy debt and property taxation, these operators cut timber as rapidly as possible. The agricultural census of 1908 indicated that Mississippi was the third largest timber producer in the nation. The timber industry created a subculture of lumber mill towns throughout the piney woods. In some instances, companies provided railroad cars for schools that traveled along with the crew as it moved from one stand of pines to the next.

Reformers felt that the state needed more control over this giant industry. During the Vardaman administration, the legislature had passed a law aimed at the timber companies: it limited land ownership by a single corporation to 1 million dollars (this was later increased to 2 million dollars). Whitfield's administration, however, afforded relief to the industry. First, the legislature repealed the law limiting the land holdings of a corporation. Second, a severance tax replaced the property tax on forest lands, taking some of the financial pressure off timber growers and allowing them more latitude in decisions regarding the cutting of timber. It would remain to the Civilian Conservation Corps of the New Deal to replace forests felled during the period from 1880 to 1930.

Whitfield had a good record overall in getting his agenda through the legislature. He advocated

Facing page: The one-room cabin was the common house style among both black and white sharecroppers and small hill farmers in east Mississippi. The per capita income of the people of Mississippi in 1932 was $125. Courtesy, Mississippi Department of Archives and History

Below: The flood of 1927, one of the state's greatest disasters, inundated the low, flat Delta, which is part of the Mississippi River flood plain. Just as the 1890 flood led to improved levees, the 1927 flood spurred new federal efforts at flood control. A series of reservoirs at Arkabutla, Sardis, Enid, and Grenada were built in the hills along the eastern rim of the Delta to trap floodwater during the rainy season and release it during dry months.

taxation of "visible property" through privilege, luxury, income, and profits taxes; although the legislature elected not to enact a comprehensive tax reform package it did approve an ad valorem tax. A former college president, Whitfield took a special interest in education. Delta State Teachers College was established during his term as governor, and the Mississippi Normal College in Hattiesburg had its name changed to Mississippi State Teacher's College.

In 1927 Mississippians faced a major and prolonged natural disaster. On April 21, 1927, a little over a month after Governor Whitfield's death on March 18, the Mississippi River broke through the levee at Mound Landing, eighteen miles north of Greenville. Remembered as the Flood of '27, its devastation was enormous: two million acres went underwater and over 185,000 people were affected. The American Red Cross, in its major project of that year, coordinated the relief efforts. When the final tally was in, 40,000 homes had been destroyed, along with 21,000 other buildings, and an unknown number of livestock and poultry were lost. The 1927

Delta crops were decimated.

The 1927 flood also caused heightened racial tension in the Delta. Whites, operating the eighteen Red Cross refugee camps set up on the levees and near the Delta, demanded hard labor of destitute blacks who were seeking relief from the Red Cross. LeRoy Percy, a Delta planter from Greenville, saw the aid as the only means of keeping blacks in the area: "If we depopulate the Delta of its labor, we should be doing it a grave disservice." Finally, the Red Cross, in response to black complaints, created a Colored Advisory Commission, which helped assure fairness in the distribution of relief.

In the governor's race of 1927, Theodore Bilbo once again announced his availability for office. Dennis Murphree, who had assumed the governorship upon Whitfield's death, was Bilbo's strongest opponent. Bilbo defeated Murphree in the runoff by a margin of 10,000 votes, with over 284,000 cast.

Unlike his first administration, Bilbo's second term in office was spent fighting the legislature. Bilbo set the tone when he attempted—and failed—to replace Thomas L. Bailey as Speaker of the House. Bailey, in turn, appointed members of the anti-Bilbo faction to all important committee chairmanships. Since the legislature accomplished nothing during the regular session, Bilbo called it into extraordinary session in 1928, but again nothing constructive was accomplished.

Bilbo was determined to get his program through the legislature. In the summer of 1929, he called a second extraordinary session. Federal matching funds were available for highway improvements, and Bilbo wanted to take advantage of the opportunity. But when the legislature did pass an insignificant highway bill—after two-and-a-half months in session—Bilbo vetoed the measure.

The greatest controversy of Bilbo's second term concerned the governor's relationship with the colleges of the state. In the summer of 1930, Bilbo replaced the presidents of the University of Mississippi, the Mississippi State College for Women, and Mississippi A&M. The Southern Association of Colleges and Schools withdrew accreditation from these colleges until 1932, when Mississippi created a constitutional board of trustees somewhat removed from political interference.

There were bigger problems with which the Bilbo administration had to contend. In 1930 Mississippi felt the brunt of the Great Depression. The state's revenues for the year had been only half of its expenditures. Bilbo called the legislature into session in January 1931, and it passed legislation allowing the state to paper over the problem with bond issues: $5 million for highway construction; $1 million to the agricultural board for relief; and $6 million to cover operating deficits. Although these measures gave temporary relief, the problem grew.

As Mississippi stepped deeper and deeper into the Depression, candidates lined up to guide the state out of the economic mess. In 1931, with almost one-fourth of its farms in default, the state was looking for new political leadership. Only 19 of the state's 140 legislators returned for the 1932 session. As of January 1, 1932, the state had issued $13 million in warrants (glorified IOUs).

Mike Conner, Paul B. Johnson, Sr., and Hugh White, a lumber millionaire from Columbia, were the leading candidates for governor in 1931. Conner defeated White in the second primary by a vote of 170,690 to 144,918. By the time Conner assumed office, the state debt stood at over $50 million, and its credit rating was so low that businesses demanded cash from state agencies for any

Above: *Highway construction has always been a major political issue in Mississippi. During Hugh White's first administration (1936-1940), major emphasis was put on building highways. Successive administrations have expanded the state highway system to 10,651 miles. Courtesy, Mississippi Department of Archives and History*

Facing page: *Funds for the War Memorial Buidling were appropriated by the state legislature in 1938 for a "war veterans memorial." The sculpture, designed by Albert Ricker, depicts soldiers in World War I. Completed in 1940, it was the home of the Mississippi Department of Archives and History and the Mississippi Historical Society for over 30 years.*

purchases. The property tax rate had already been increased as much as practicable. Conner came up with a sales tax as the means of getting the state out of its financial straits. He proposed a 3-percent tax on all retail sales.

Leading the forces against the sales tax was Dr. James Rice of Natchez. His efforts culminated in a convention of 5,000 in Jackson to protest the proposed tax. On the other side of the issue, Willard F. Bond, the state superintendent of education, organized mass meetings throughout the state in support of the tax. Passed by a two-vote margin in the legislature, the law provided for a 2-percent tax on the sales of all retail items. Mississippi was the first state in the nation to pass a comprehensive sales tax.

Taxation was not enough to solve all the state's financial problems. Conner tried innovative approaches to state expenditures as well. He took direct control of the state's prison at Parchman and operated it at a profit. He also created "mercy courts," advisory groups that considered reducing the sentences of long-term prisoners.

Mississippi was suffering from the twin ills of unemployment and low income. Many Mississippians simply could not find work, and most of those who had jobs were poorly paid. New Deal programs of the Roosevelt administration, beginning in 1933, helped greatly. By 1934 there were 57,728 Mississippians employed on some type of Civil Works Administration project. All together, during Conner's four years in office, $50 million in federal funds came to Mississippi.

Probably at no time during Mississippi's history did the state's representatives in Washington play such a critical role as they did during the Great Depression. At the beginning of the New Deal, the state's United States senators were Byron "Pat" Harrison and Hubert Stephens. Harrison, as chairman of the Senate Finance Committee, was in a key position to help the New Deal, and he made sure Mississippi got its share of New Deal money.

Although New Deal programs were a great help, they sometimes inadvertently caused problems. During the 1930s, in the depths of the Great Depression, the federal government paid farmers to reduce the acreage they had in production. Some landowners took advantage of the situation by pushing tenant families off the plantation and pocketing all of the federal incentive money for themselves. The owners also found that, especially with growing centralization and mechanization, it was cheaper to pay wage laborers when needed rather than share the proceeds of the crop with sharecroppers. Sharecropping seemed doomed; the 1930 census was the last in which blacks made up a majority of the Mississippi population. New Deal programs were simply unable to reach those most in need of assistance.

The New Deal did provide Theodore Bilbo with a position at the United States Department of Agriculture. His political opponents stated that all he was doing was clipping newspaper articles about the agency; they dubbed him the "pastemaster general." In 1934 Bilbo challenged Stephens for the latter's Senate seat. Although Stephens had gone along with Roosevelt, it was apparent that he was not a New Dealer. Bilbo campaigned as 100 percent in favor of Roosevelt's programs. In the election, Bilbo led Stephens by fewer than 8,000 votes out of almost 200,000 cast. Once in the Senate, Bilbo fulfilled his promise to the voters of Mississippi that he would support Roosevelt fully. He even went so far as to support Roosevelt's candidate for the majority leader of the Senate, Alben Barkley of Kentucky, over his fellow senator from Mississippi, Pat Harrison. Barkley won the office by a margin of a single vote. During his Senate career, Bilbo established the most consistent New Deal voting

record of any member of the Senate.

In 1935 Mississippians elected a businessman as governor over a proven politician. Paul B. Johnson, Sr., had been a congressman and the runner-up in the 1931 governor's race. But his opponent, Hugh White of Columbia, was offering an alternative to "politics as usual." The son of a wealthy lumberman, White had entered his father's business and at the age of twenty-six had even been elected as mayor of Columbia. He used his office as a means to attract industry to Columbia. In 1931, building on that reputation and his record of public service, he had run for governor on a Balance Agriculture with Industry (BAWI) platform. Running on a similar platform in 1935, White defeated Johnson by a margin of approximately 12,000 votes out of over 250,000 cast.

As governor, "the father of Mississippi industrialization" had a large task before him. He was leading a state that had only 922 miles of paved roads in a system of over 6,000 miles. The imbalance between agriculture and industry was great. The annual agricultural payroll was $186 million as compared with $14 million for industry.

White first gave attention to the dire needs of the highway system. The legislature responded with a $42.5 million program without a dissenting vote, and by 1940 Mississippi had over 4,000 miles of paved roads. The change had been accomplished with revenue from a gasoline tax of six cents per gallon, in addition to $40 million that, since 1937, came from federal funds.

With the highway program in place, White called the legislature into special session in 1936 to consider his BAWI program. The program was passed, and it did boost industry for Mississippi. White indicated that in its first six months in operation, the BAWI program had been responsible for 2,500 new jobs with an annual payroll of $1.5 million. However, BAWI did not fully implement White's dreams of a promised land, partly because certain businessmen, especially state bankers, never embraced the idea, and had in fact opposed it from the beginning.

In 1939 Paul B. Johnson, Sr., again a candidate for governor, called for a halt to programs like

Paul B. Johnson, Sr., like populist governors before him, disliked industrialization, believing it to be against the interests of the average man. Nevertheless, industry continued to develop during his administration, and when he left office the state had the largest treasury surplus in its history. Johnson is pictured on horseback on the lawn of the Governor's Mansion, along with Lieutenant Governor Dennis Murphree, who succeeded Johnson at his death in 1943. Courtesy, Mississippi Department of Archives and History

White's BAWI. Johnson felt that politicians should be concerned with the "little man," or as he more graphically described the situation, "the runt of the litter." An old ally of Huey Long, Johnson campaigned for higher homestead exemptions, free textbooks in schools, and a three-dollar car tag (all similar to programs in Long's Louisiana). In the Democratic primary, Johnson defeated Mike Conner in the runoff by a wide margin, almost 30,000 votes.

Once in office, Johnson accomplished much of what he had proposed during the campaign. He dismantled BAWI, replacing it with the more modest program within the newly created Mississippi Board of Development. The board had only advisory powers, and its primary function was planning future development. It proved to be ineffective and was abolished soon after the end of Johnson's term.

Johnson's other programs were more popular and long-lasting. The homestead exemption was increased from $3,500 to $5,000. Appropriations for welfare were increased by 75 percent. The greatest achievement of the Johnson administration was a 1940 law that provided free textbooks for the first eight grades. The law was expanded in 1942 to cover all grades. A few weeks before the end of his term, Johnson died of a heart attack. But he had established a record as an excellent governor.

On the eve of World War II, Mississippi remained a rural state. Jackson was rapidly growing, emerging in 1930, with a population of 48,242, as the state's largest city. However, most Mississippians lived in rural areas. In 1940 over 80 percent of Mississippians lived outside towns and cities. World War II would have a tremendous social and economic impact on the state of Mississippi.

Keesler Air Force Base was opened on Biloxi's Back Bay in June 1941 as a major training center for pilots. After the war Keesler Field remained as the permanent electronics training center for the United States Air Force. Today it is a major part of Gulf Coast life. Courtesy, Mississippi Department of Archives and History

WORLD WAR II AND CIVIL RIGHTS

World War II marked a major turning point for the state of Mississippi. If one looks merely at the statistics, the story of Mississippi during World War II has a familiar refrain: last in war contracts, last in war production facilities, and tied for last in privately financed facilities. But economic statistics do not tell this particular story well, for they do not reflect the transformation of Mississippi in the years following World War II. As a result of the war, the state's citizens had a greater exposure to outside society and culture than at any time since the Civil War. More than 141,000 mechanics and 336,000 basic trainees went through Keesler Field during the course of the war. In addition, countless others went to Camp Shelby or found employment at the shipyards on the coast. At the same time, Mississippians were enlisting in the armed forces in record numbers.

The United States was preparing for the possibility of war long before officially entering it in 1941. In 1940, as a result of the first peacetime draft in American history, 160,000 Mississippians had registered with the Selective Service. In November 1940, a total of 3,681 Mississippi National Guardsmen were activated. Camp Shelby, located near Hattiesburg, was reopened and enlarged that summer. Because of the mild climate and large amounts of land available, Mississippi became a prime location for training facilities and military bases. Keesler Field was established at Biloxi in 1940. Other posts used in the war effort included Camp McCain near Grenada and Camp Van Dorn near Centreville. Air installations included bases at Greenville, Columbus, Jackson, Laurel, Greenwood, and Meridian. There were several smaller air facilities scattered throughout the state.

The state's largest private employer during the war years was the Ingalls shipyard in Pascagoula. In 1938, as the first major initiative under the BAWI program, the state built a shipyard and then leased it to Ingalls. Even before the American entry into the war, Ingalls employed 3,000 workers. The new facility, featuring the latest in shipbuilding technology, in 1940 launched the world's first all-welded ship, the *Exchequer.*

The Mississippi Gulf Coast enjoyed a rapid recovery from the Depression. Workers, men and women, flocked to the coast for jobs in war-related industries. Towns in the region boomed, but there were problems associated with this sudden influx of population, especially in housing, transportation, and public health. Black and white troops were trained separately, but in close proximity to one another, and outbursts of racial unrest occurred sporadically. Serious riots occurred in 1943 at Camp Van Dorn and Camp McCain.

The wartime situation called for various adjustments by the civilian society. The legislature

In June of 1940, Ingalls Shipyard launched its first ship, which was also the world's first all-welded oceangoing cargo carrier, the Exchequer. *Before many more cargo liners could be made, Ingalls retooled for the war effort, and a nonstop production schedule built 100 vessels. Courtesy, Ingalls Shipyard, Pascagoula*

passed laws on special matters ranging from citizen cooperation with blackouts to restricted trade in goods such as tires. Goods needed in the war effort, gasoline, for example, were rationed at home. Mississippi's law against sedition led to an important United States Supreme Court decision. Mississippi law had stated that refusal to salute, honor, or respect the Mississippi or United States flag could result in imprisonment for up to ten years. In a 1942 case, *Taylor* v. *Mississippi*, the United States Supreme Court ruled in favor of R.E. Taylor, a Jehovah's Witness, that Mississippi had infringed on Taylor's religious rights as protected under the First Amendment.

World War II was a watershed for Mississippi in many ways. The mechanization of Mississippi agriculture, begun after World War I, accelerated during World War II. The mechanical cotton picker had first been introduced in 1938 and was being used in some large operations by the end of the war. With the introduction of large-scale, capital-intensive agriculture, profitable farming on a small scale became almost an impossibility.

Mississippi's economy began to show signs of diversification. Although cotton remained king, other agricultural products, such as livestock, soybeans, and poultry, began to make up a significant part of the Mississippi farm economy. Manufacturing, too, was making inroads: there was

an increase of 700 factories and 25,000 jobs in the manufacturing sector between 1939 and 1947.

In 1943 Thomas Bailey defeated former governor Mike Conner in the Democratic runoff election. A 1909 Millsaps College graduate, Bailey had studied law and begun his law practice in Meridian. He was first elected to the legislature in 1915. He served as Speaker of the House during twelve of his twenty-four years in that body. As governor, Bailey was able to accomplish his major goals, the authorization of a four-year medical school in Jackson and increased aid to education. A major accomplishment in education was the creation of the state's first teacher retirement program. In September 1946 Governor Bailey was diagnosed as having cancer; he died two months later.

Lieutenant Governor Fielding Wright succeeded to Bailey's office. Wright, who had been in the legislature and served a term as Speaker beginning in 1936, was the first politician from the Delta to be governor since Earl Brewer. As governor he called for a special session of the legislature in 1947 that approved a teachers' pay raise and state matching funds for a federal school lunch program.

Wright ran for a full term as governor in 1947 and became the first candidate since Bilbo in 1915 to win the governorship without a runoff. He received 200,000 votes. His closest opponent was

Beginning his political career with a temporary appointment by Paul B. Johnson, Sr., when Pat Harrison died, James O. Eastland (above) of Doddsville endeared himself to farmers and states righters. In 1943 he started a permanent political career in the United States Senate where he became chairman of the powerful Judiciary Committee in 1956 and president pro tempore in 1972. He retired from the Senate in 1979, after thirty-seven years of service. Eastland died in 1986. Courtesy, Mississippi Department of Archives and History

Paul B. Johnson, Jr., with only 112,000 votes.

During the legislative session of 1948, the legislators kept their attention on the needs of the state. More than one half of the senators and representatives were first-term members. They were also young, fifty-seven of them under the age of forty. They adopted a series of progressive laws, including a workmen's compensation law.

During the 1940s, both Senate seats were vacated. In 1941, when Pat Harrison died, Governor Paul B. Johnson, Sr., appointed James O. Eastland to the position until an election could be held. Eastland chose not to run for the remainder of Harrison's term, which expired in January 1943. However, in his brief first term as a senator, Eastland endeared himself to the sharecroppers and

tenant farmers of Mississippi: he sponsored legislation that protected their rights to share with landlords in the sale of cottonseed, which during the war was worth more than ever before. The voters remembered the favor, and in 1942 when Eastland decided to run for a full term, he defeated the incumbent Wall Doxey of Holly Springs in the second primary by almost 20,000 votes. Eastland remained in the Senate from 1943 until 1979.

The other Senate seat was held by Theodore Bilbo, who was reelected to office in 1946. During the campaign, Bilbo urged voters to use any means necessary to keep blacks from voting. His tactics led to a call in the Senate for an investigation of possible intimidation of voters. These charges were whitewashed by fellow Democrats. There were, however, more substantiated charges that Bilbo had taken bribes from war contractors. The investigation was postponed after Bilbo, diagnosed as having oral cancer, requested that he be given an opportunity to answer the charges. Bilbo died in 1947, without ever having returned to the Senate.

In the special election to fill Bilbo's seat, a unique situation occurred. Since there was no time for a primary before the fall general election, the legislature decided that the person with the greatest number of votes, not necessarily a majority, was to be the victor. With only 27 percent of the vote, a forty-six-year-old state circuit judge from Kemper County named John Stennis was elected to the seat.

During World War II President Franklin Roosevelt's policies caused a rift between the national and state Democrats. In the 1944 presidential contest, Mississippi had sent an anti-FDR delegation to the Democratic convention. Although Roosevelt won the nomination, three of the Mississippi electors pledged to vote for Senator Harry Byrd of Virginia in the general election. Bilbo had not helped the situation: among his last acts in office was an attack on the Fair Employment Practices Commission.

Behind the scenes, rumblings within the Democratic party could be heard in Jackson as President Truman led the national party to take a strong stand for civil rights. In February 1948, Governor Wright called a state Democratic meeting in Jackson, where Mississippi Democrats debated their position in relation to the national party. Debate continued, and a meeting of Southern Democrats was scheduled to convene in Birmingham immediately after the national convention.

At the convention, Hubert Humphrey, mayor of

John C. Stennis, a young judge from DeKalb, began his political career when he was elected to complete Bilbo's unexpired term in 1947. He became a powerful and respected figure in the United States Senate through his work on the Armed Forces Committee and as chairman of the Senate Ethics Committee. He served for seven terms, until 1988. Courtesy, Mississippi Department of Archives and History

Frank Smith, a former president of the Mississippi Historical Society, is the author of five books. He represented the Delta in the United States Congress for twelve years before his defeat by Jamie Whitten in 1962. He was appointed by President John F. Kennedy to be a director of the Tennessee Valley Authority, an office he held for ten years.

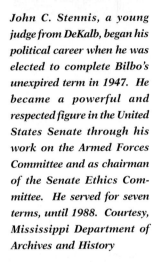

Minneapolis, Minnesota, presented the majority report on the civil rights plank. Walter Sillers of Mississippi presented the minority report, basically taking a state rights position on the issue. When the convention adopted a strong civil rights plank for the platform, the Mississippi delegation walked out.

As agreed, disaffected Southern Democrats gathered at the States' Rights Party convention in Birmingham. Strom Thurmond of South Carolina was nominated for president and Fielding Wright was nominated for the vice presidency. In the general election that fall, Mississippi voted 87 percent for the States' Rights (commonly called Dixiecrat) ticket.

Not all Mississippi Democrats, however, had left the national fold. In fact, the divided mind of the state party was apparent throughout the 1950s. In 1950 the hottest political contest in the state was the fight for the seat of the retiring Will Whittington in the Delta district. Frank Smith, a racial moderate, campaigned for the "little man" against the "Delta aristocrats." Smith won the seat and remained in

office for twelve years. He later served as one of the directors of the Tennessee Valley Authority, a reward for his steadfast loyalty to the national Democratic party.

In 1951 Hugh White won his second term in office as governor, defeating Paul B. Johnson, Jr., in the runoff by fewer than 10,000 votes. With White's previous record as governor, this election had not been a traditional hill-county versus Delta contest but a vote on White's policy of economic development through industrialization.

White's administration had to deal with the 1954 *Brown* v. *Board of Education* Supreme Court decision that overturned the fifty-eight-year-old "separate but equal" education system. Anticipating the decision, White called upon the state legislature in its 1953 session to build modern facilities for black children, stating that it was the "legal and moral obligation" of the state to equalize the schools. The legislators responded with plans for massive school consolidation and extensive building programs.

When the *Brown* decision was handed down, Mississippi whites reacted in a variety of ways. The legislature limited the usual biennial appropriations to schools to one year. In Indianola, a group organized the Citizens' Council in the summer of 1954 to resist the decision. Circuit Judge Tom P. Brady of Brookhaven wrote *Black Monday* condemning the *Brown* decision and became one of the leaders of the Citizens' Council. He would later serve as associate justice of the Mississippi Supreme Court. The council grew rapidly, claiming 80,000 members by 1956. By then, to be a self-avowed moderate on the issue of race was to become an outcast in the white community. Politicians had to go along or face sure retribution at the polls. Some ministers who criticized the Citizens' Council were forced from their pulpits. A chaplain at the University of Mississippi was asked to resign because he invited a black speaker during Spiritual Emphasis Week. During the next ten years, from 1954 to 1964, the civil rights movement and white resistance to it dominated the state.

During the 1950s racial incidents brought unwanted publicity to Mississippi. In the summer of 1955, a fourteen-year-old youth from Chicago, Emmett Till, was visiting relatives in Tallahatchie County. On a teen-age dare, he "talked fresh" to the attractive wife of the owner of a local crossroads store. That night her husband and brother-in-law killed Emmett. Several days later his body, chained to a gin fan, was dragged from the Tallahatchie

All white male juries such as the one pictured above at the 1955 trial for Emmett Till's murder were mandated by Mississippi's 1890 constitution. It was not until 1968 that Mississippi women were allowed to serve on juries. Courtesy, Mississippi Department of Archives and History

River. Although it was known throughout the community who had killed the young man, and although a trial was held, no one was ever convicted of the crime. Others, such as the Reverend George Lee of Belzoni, an NAACP (National Association for the Advancement of Colored People) activist, were killed for their political activities.

Much of the nation regarded the 1950s as a period of calm. In Mississippi, however, it was a decade of political realignment and social turmoil. The voters ratified an amendment to the Mississippi constitution in 1954 that authorized the legislature to abolish public schools if it felt it necessary in order to preserve segregation. Over the next ten years, the state legislature passed forty laws, resolutions, and amendments to thwart the implications of the *Brown* decision. During this period, the "doctrine of interposition" was resurrected. This state-rights philosophy claimed the state had the constitutional right to interpose itself between the people of Mississippi and the power of the national government by refusing to follow orders from Washington.

In the 1955 governor's race, James P. Coleman, whose platform advocated the use of legal action to forestall integration, defeated Paul B. Johnson, Jr., in the runoff. As governor, Coleman pursued a moderate course. He would not, as Alabama had done, ban the NAACP. He vetoed a legislative bill designed to hinder efforts of civil rights investi-

The plaque adopted by the Citizens' Council was often seen on the outskirts of towns and cities among the welter of signs announcing the local civic organizations. By 1958 there were approximately 80,000 paid members of the Citizens' Council. In 1960, the state began funding the group at $5,000 per month. Courtesy, Mississippi Department of Archives and History

gators.

Racial unrest continued in the state during the Coleman years. Mack Charles Parker, accused of assaulting a white woman, was murdered by a lynch mob in Poplarville. When Clennon King attempted to enroll at the University of Mississippi, he was committed to a state mental hospital on the theory that any black who tried to integrate Ole Miss had to be crazy.

In 1959 Ross Barnett, the Citizens' Council candidate, was elected governor of the state. The Citizens' Council dominated his administration. The state's Sovereignty Commission, during Coleman's term, had functioned as an arm of the legislature, spreading the word that Mississippi had the constitutional right to be left alone by the national government. Under Barnett, it became an agency that subsidized the Citizens' Council and spied on civil rights advocates and supporters of racial integration.

The earliest civil rights activity in Mississippi centered in McComb. Bob Moses, Harlem-born and Harvard-educated, came to McComb in 1961 to lead a voter registration project for the Student Nonviolent Coordinating Committee (SNCC). After a great deal of harassment, the project was discontinued. SNCC then turned most of its voter registration efforts in 1962 to the Delta, especially Leflore County and its county seat, Greenwood. Meanwhile, the NAACP was active in quiet ways throughout the state.

Mississippi was featured on national news in 1962 as the integration crisis unfolded at the University of Mississippi. James Meredith, an air force veteran, carefully planned his attempted enrollment at the university, including notification of the Department of Justice concerning his plans. President Kennedy sent United States marshals to Oxford to protect Meredith. On September 30, rioting began on campus, with a newsman and bystander killed and many others injured during the night of violence. National Guard troops were quickly committed, and President Kennedy ordered 20,000 federal troops to the scene.

More violence was in store. The state field director of the NAACP, Medgar Evers, who had given the organization vital new direction and a higher profile in the early 1960s, was assassinated in the driveway of his home in Jackson in 1963. Evers' murderer was Byron de La Beckwith, a member of the Greenwood Citizens' Council. Beckwith was charged with the crime but released after two mistrials in 1964. Evers' martyrdom, however, helped galvanize the Mississippi phase of the civil rights movement, and Beckwith was finally brought to justice in 1994 when a Hinds County jury convicted him of Evers' murder.

Civil rights leaders in the state, feeling that the right to vote was the critical link to other citizenship rights, planned a mock-election alongside the regular election for state offices in 1963. Aaron

Above: *The restoration of the Old Capitol, 1959-1961, required the rebuilding of interior space, but much of the original material was preserved, including the outer brick walls, splendid Ionic columns, and the lintels over the windows. Initiated by Governor James P. Coleman, the restoration cost over $1,500,000 and preserved one of the finest Greek Revival buildings in the nation. Courtesy, Mississippi Department of Archives and History*

Above: *James P. Coleman of Ackerman led a movement for thirty years advocating a constitutional convention to replace the 1890 constitution. Elected governor in 1955 just after the Supreme Court decision declaring separate schools for the races unconstitutional, Coleman faced increasing racial tensions. Courtesy, Mississippi Department of Archives and History*

After his election as governor in 1959, Ross Barnett, Jackson attorney, became the leader of Mississippi's resistance to school integration. During the Barnett administration, the White Citizen's Council exercised enormous influence within state government. Photo by Ed Williams

Henry, president of the state's NAACP, was the candidate for governor, and Ed King, a white native of Vicksburg and chaplain at Tougaloo College, completed the ticket as the candidate for lieutenant governor. They received 80,000 votes in their unofficial November 1963 balloting. Although this election had no legal standing, it did emphasize the dramatic impact that black voting could have on Mississippi politics.

The following year, a major change took place in the Mississippi civil rights movement. All the civil rights organizations, which had already banded together in 1963 under the umbrella organization COFO (Council of Federated Organizations), now prepared for a massive voter registration and education drive. The results of that effort came to be known as the Freedom Summer of 1964.

Feeling that the national media had paid little or no attention to the suffering and even deaths of blacks in the South as they had asserted their rights, COFO called upon Northern university students, many of them white, to volunteer a summer for organizing and teaching efforts in Mississippi. They "invaded" the state that summer, living in Freedom Houses and teaching in Freedom Schools. The schools had two purposes: supplementing the underfunded black schools of Mississippi with innovative curriculum and instruction and building a future generation of local civil rights activists.

Other Freedom Summer volunteers canvassed

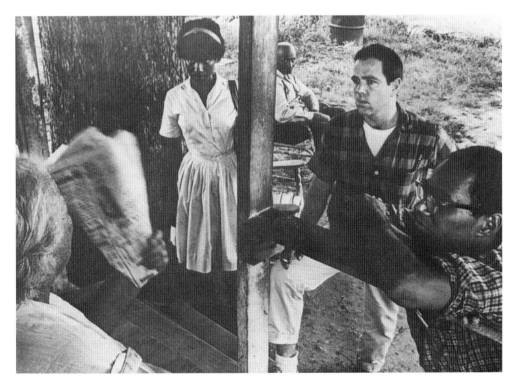

Bob Moses (right), one of the most effective civil rights organizers in Mississippi, came from New York City's Harlem to conduct voter registration and "Freedom Schools." He was one of the founders of the Mississippi Freedom Democratic Party. Photo by Danny Lyon

Civil rights activists worked together under the Council of Federated Organizations (COFO) to register black voters, organize Freedom Schools, and conduct the Mississippi Summer Project of 1964 which brought hundreds of young people into the state to help with voter registration. This "freedom house" was a COFO headquarters in Moss Point. Photo by Tamio Wakayama

Medgar Evers' death is commemorated each spring in Mississippi with the Medgar Evers Homecoming Celebration. Evers, Mississippi field secretary of the NAACP, was killed by a sniper's bullet in 1963, two weeks after direct-action protests, led by Evers, began in downtown Jackson. Courtesy, Mississippi Department of Archives and History

neighborhoods and communities to find and instruct persons willing to register to vote. Although there were some incidents of violence during the first couple of months of the summer, especially at Canton, the COFO staffers and volunteers attempted to foster trust and hope within the black community. But the "long, hot summer of 1964" had its costs: 1,000 arrests, 35 shootings, 35 churches burned, and 31 homes and buildings bombed, including the Jewish synagogue in Jackson.

In June, three civil rights workers disappeared in the area near Philadelphia, Mississippi. Initially, whites argued that the disappearance was a publicity stunt to gain sympathy and national media attention for the civil rights movement. The FBI and other federal agencies became involved in the search for the three: Andrew Goodman, James Chaney, and Michael Schwerner. Their bodies were found buried in an earthen dam in Neshoba County forty days after their disappearance. Florence Mars, a businesswoman, Clay Lee, a Methodist pastor, and others in the Philadelphia community called upon their fellow white citizens to help bring the murderers to justice. As it turned out, rather than coming to trial in state courts for murder, Cecil Price, a Neshoba County deputy sheriff, and six other defendants were tried and convicted in

Aaron Henry, a Clarksdale pharmacist, held the longest and most sustained leadership of the black community in Mississippi. He served as president of the Mississippi chapter of the NAACP from 1960 to 1993. He participated in the Freedom Rider movement and served as chairman of COFO in the 1960s. He was a founder of the Mississippi Freedom Democratic Party and a leader the the 1970s' merger of the Loyalist and Regular Democrats. Courtesy, Mississippi Department of Archives and History

Fannie Lou Hamer, a sharecropper from Sunflower County, became a political activist when she was denied the right to register to vote in 1962. She became a worker in the Student Nonviolent Coordinating Committee, was a founder of the Mississippi Freedom Democratic Party and the Freedom Farmers' Cooperative, and ran for the United States Congress as a Loyalist Democrat. Courtesy, Mississippi Department of Archives and History

federal court for violating the civil rights of Goodman, Chaney, and Schwerner.

Civil rights activists also launched a major challenge to the all-white delegation headed to the Democratic national convention that summer in Atlantic City. The challengers, known as the Freedom Democratic Party (FDP), were a biracial group.

Although there was no doubt that President Lyndon Johnson would be nominated by the Democrats, he wanted to avoid any alienation of Southern whites or any show of discord at the convention. Efforts to compromise with the FDP proved futile. Delta sharecropper Fannie Lou Hamer, who emerged as a strong leader of the FDP, observed, "We didn't come all this way for no two seats when all of us is tired." Although the FDP delegates were not seated, they won the war, for in 1968 the Mississippi delegation was biracial.

Freedom Summer was the high-water mark of

the civil rights movement in Mississippi. The next year, thanks in large part to the Selma-to-Montgomery march, the Voting Rights Act of 1965 was passed by the United States Congress. This act revolutionized Mississippi politics—along with the Civil Rights Act of 1964 and the Twenty-fourth Amendment (1964) outlawing the poll tax. Blacks capitalized on the opportunity to participate in the political process and gain access to restaurants, motels, and other public facilities.

In order to draw attention to the "all-pervasive and overriding fear that dominates . . . in Mississippi," James Meredith planned to walk from Memphis to Jackson in 1966. Just across the Mississippi state line, he was peppered with birdshot and slightly injured. Other civil rights workers came to Mississippi to complete the march. At that time Stokely Carmichael introduced the slogan "black power," and the freedom movement in the United States turned in radical new directions. Many civil rights activists left the South and moved out of mainstream American politics. Other dedicated workers, however, remained in Mississippi.

In the late 1960s Mississippi politics began to follow a more moderate course. Although Paul B. Johnson, Jr., defeated J.P. Coleman for the governorship in 1963 because Coleman was perceived by the voters as too moderate, Johnson proved to be a calming force in the state. Rather than offering defiance, as Governor Barnett and Mayor Allen Thompson of Jackson had done when confronted with integration, Johnson, in his inaugural address, called for reconcilation and remained behind the scenes as white restaurants and hotels were integrated. Court-ordered desegregation of the public schools in many Mississippi cities proceeded uneventfully as segregationists labeled Johnson "ambivalent Paul." The public schools were integrated without major incident, although in areas of heavy black population, many whites deserted public schools for white academies. The Citizens' Council established its own system of schools and 35 percent of Jackson's white students left the public schools in 1971-1972. Prior to the end of the decade the trend reversed as the Citizens' Council ceased its operation of schools. Many other private schools were closed during the 1980s.

By the beginning of Governor Johnson's administration, however, Mississippi's future had already been determined. In 1964 the "battle for the ballot" reached the United States Supreme court in the case United States v. Mississippi, which

In 1910 Biloxi was the leading exporter of raw oysters in the world. Although the industry has been damaged by hurricanes, pollution, and occasionally fresh waters from the Bonnet Carre spillway, Biloxi is still a major shipping center for oysters and shrimp. Courtesy, Mississippi Department of Archives and History

toppled the voting provisions of the Mississippi Constitution of 1890. Only 6.6 percent (28,000) of the black voting-age population had been registered to vote in Mississippi in 1964. Two years later, as Governor Johnson quietly encouraged county election officials to register black voters, there were 176,000 blacks registered to vote in the state.

Nevertheless, accommodation was not complete. In the 1967 governor's race, the voters of Mississippi had a clear choice. John Bell Williams, one of the state's congressmen and a champion of states' rights and segregation, opposed State Treasurer William Winter, a moderate, in the runoff for the governorship. In spite of Winter's defeat, other election results indicated a change in Mississippi politics. Twenty-one blacks were elected to local offices that year, and Robert Clark, the grandson of a slave, was elected to the state House of Representatives from Holmes County.

Johnson's attempts to heal the racial tensions in the state were influenced by his efforts to industrialize Mississippi. During his term in office, 549 industrial plants were built or expanded, and 38,631 jobs were created. In spite of these efforts, Mississippi's struggle to climb the economic ladder was frustrating. Although there were yearly increases in per capita income throughout the 1960s, the state was still ranked at the bottom, and the dollar gap between Mississippi and her sister states actually increased. World War II, however, had clearly sparked a transformation of the Mississippi economy. In 1965 Governor Johnson invited Hugh White to a celebration of the news that industry had just surpassed agriculture as the state's prime employer. Even old economic mainstays, such as commerce on the Mississippi River, had taken on new economic vitality. By the 1940s the towboat had replaced the steamboat of an earlier era as the means of moving bulk cargoes along the river, and by the 1970s, Greenville, both a port and a barge-building center, had earned the title of "Towing Capital of the World." New industries also developed in the World War II era and after, such as the oil industry, which began to flourish after oil was discovered in Yazoo County in 1939.

Beginning with World War II, the Mississippi economy also benefitted from the infusion of federal money associated with the military-industrial complex developed during both the war and the Cold War that followed. Camp Shelby near Hattiesburg and the National Aeronautics and Space Administration testing facility in Hancock County had major impacts on local economies by the late 1960s.

During World War II and the years that followed, the agricultural revolution begun by the New Deal accelerated in Mississippi. The drain of labor from rural areas during the war coincided with the beginnings of mechanization. After the war, mechanical cotton pickers, together with the use of newly-developed herbicides to control weeds, allowed plantation owners to grow more with fewer workers. As a result, the sharecropping system in Mississippi began to disappear. Whereas in the 1920s and even 1930s blacks had exercised the option of going to the North to escape the poverty and second-class citizenship of Mississippi's Jim Crow system, in the 1950s and 1960s they were literally displaced from the plantations and farms of the South by machines and chemicals. In 1940 more than one of every two jobs in Mississippi had been in farming; twenty years later, fewer than one in five people earned their living by working the land.

The mechanization of the post-World War II years also led to diversification of the agricultural economy. During the 1960s, soybeans surpassed "King Cotton" in acreage, although for many years cotton still remained the state's leading cash crop. By the 1960s, however, land formerly devoted ex-clusively to the production of cotton was used increasingly for a variety of purposes. Many former cotton fields were transformed into woodland or pasture; others were planted with a variety of crops: corn, peanuts, pecans, rice, sugar cane, and sweet potatoes. In the Delta, beginning in the early 1960s, a number of planters turned from cotton cultivation to catfish farming. Large ponds were created, where the fish were fed on grain, forwarded to a number of processing plants that grew up in the area, then shipped around the world. A sizeable part of this operation was centered around Belzoni, which became known as the "Catfish Capital of the World." By the late 1980s, Mississippi operations supplied almost 70 percent of the country's catfish production.

Together, World War II and the civil rights movement ushered in profound changes for Mississippi. Indeed, these two events transformed the state more than the Civil War and Reconstruction ever had. Much of the state's distinctive political, economic, and social systems began to crumble under the pressure of war and the black freedom movement. In the final three decades of the twentieth century, the process of change begun in the World War II and civil rights era continued to unfold.

With the development of diesel boats during World War II that could haul larger loads and required smaller crews, an independent towing boom began on the Mississippi River, based at the river ports of Greenville, Vicksburg, and Natchez. In the 1950s and 1960s traffic on the river nearly doubled. Boats towed petroleum products, chemicals, coal, grain, asphalt, and gravel. The industry peaked in 1981 with nearly 450 million tons of cargo on the river. Courtesy, Gil Ford Studio

Hugh White (left) and Mike Conner (second from left) meet at White's inauguration in 1936. During the Great Depression, these two governors supported bold measures to bolster the state's economy, such as the establishment of a state income tax and the BAWI program. Courtesy, Mississippi Department of Archives and History

Clarksdale plantation owner and his tenants in front of the plantation store, 1930s. From the end of the Civil War until after World War II, the sharecropping/tenant system dominated Mississippi agriculture. Plantation owners also frequently owned general stores, which provided the "furnish" for tenants and sharecroppers. Courtesy, Mississippi Department of Archives and History.

Right: *Cliff Finch, a Batesville lawyer and former segregationist ally of Governor Ross Barnett, emerged from the gubernatorial election of 1975 as the surprise winner against two formidable challengers, Democrat William Winter and Republican Gil Carmichael. After his term as governor, Finch ran unsuccessfully for U.S. President in 1980. Courtesy, Mississippi Department of Archives and History*

Below: *In 1959 and 1960, civil rights protesters held wade-ins on the beaches of the Mississippi Gulf Coast to protest the fact that blacks were excluded from all but a few segregated slivers of the twenty-six mile beach. Courtesy, McCain Library and Archives, University of Southern Mississippi Libraries*

The Grand Opera House opened in Meridian in 1890 and attracted major shows to this east Mississippi community. Although closed in the 1920s, it remained undisturbed and was reopened in 1988. The building is currently being restored to its late-nineteenth century splendor. Courtesy, Mississippi Development Authority/Division of Tourism

Above: *The engines for the Space Shuttle are tested at the John C. Stennis Space Center in Hancock County, NASA's facility for rocket propulsion testing.   Courtesy, Mississippi Development Authority/Division of Tourism*

Left: *The Lauren Rogers Art Museum, located in Laurel, was founded in 1923 as a memorial to the deceased child of one the area's prominent timber families. The museum houses major collections of Native American baskets, Japanese woodblock prints, and nineteenth and twentieth century European and American paintings, including works by Jean-Baptiste Camille Corot, Winslow Homer, Albert Bierstadt, and Mary Cassatt. Courtesy, Mississippi Development Authority/Division of Tourism*

Left: *Part of the Catherine Marshall Gardiner Native American Basket Collection at the Lauren Rogers Art Museum in Laurel. The collection includes 800 Native American baskets from around the world. Courtesy, Mississippi Development Authority/Division of Tourism*

Below: *Visitors to the Mississippi Craft Center, located on the Natchez Trace Parkway, can find examples of a wide array of Mississippi crafts, from native American to folk to contemporary creations. The Center is operated by the Craftsmen's Guild of Mississippi. Courtesy, Mississippi Development Authority/Division of Tourism*

Right: *Walter Place is a grand antebellum home located in the north Mississippi town of Holly Springs. It was spared destruction during the Civil War primarily because it served as the temporary residence of Julia Grant, wife of Union general Ulysses S. Grant, during the Union occupation of north Mississippi. Courtesy, Mississippi Development Authority/Division of Tourism*

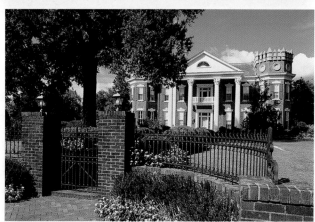

Bottom right: *Many Mississippi communities hold festivals during the summer and early fall, celebrating everything from the state's musical traditions to its ethnic heritage to its foodways. The Mize Watermelon Festival, held each July, features watermelon-eating and seed-spitting contests. Courtesy, Mississippi Development Authority/Division of Tourism*

Above: *The Grand Casino is the largest casino in Tunica County and one of the biggest in the world, with almost 150,000 square feet of gaming space. Despite its size, the Grand Casino, like most in the state, is actually located on a floating barge. Courtesy, Mississippi Development Authority/Division of Tourism*

Middle far left: *In Bentonia, located between Yazoo City and Jackson, one can still hear local blues men perform from the front porch of the Blue Front Café. Courtesy, Mississippi Development Authority/Division of Tourism*

Left: *The blues originated in the Mississippi Delta, and although many blues singers have died or left the state, the music can still be heard at various juke joints in the area and at the numerous annual blues festivals held in Delta communities. Courtesy, Mississippi Development Authority/Division of Tourism*

Middle left: *Square Books, along with many other thriving stores and restaurants, is located on the courthouse square in Oxford. The square is a focal point of life in this small university community; a number of other Mississippi towns have similar downtown squares, which encircle the local courthouse. Courtesy, Mississippi Development Authority/Division of Tourism*

Right: *Downtown Jackson, the largest city in Mississippi and its state capital. Located on Le Fleur's Bluff on the Pearl River, the city was named for Andrew Jackson. Courtesy, Mississippi Development Authority/Division of Tourism*

The Canton Flea Market, held on one day in May and one day in June in downtown Canton, is one of the South's oldest and largest events of its kind. Over 1,000 market vendors sell everything from used goods to collectibles to handcrafted arts and crafts amidst a carnival-like atmosphere. Courtesy, Mississippi Development Authority/Division of Tourism

MODERN MISSISSIPPI

In the 1960s outsiders often thought of Mississippi as almost another country, with its one-party state, seemingly backward economy, and racial segregation and disenfranchisement. In the last three decades of the twentieth century, however, Mississippi largely shed these distinctive political, economic, and social characteristics that defined the state for much of its history. Indeed, over the last thirty years, Mississippi has changed dramatically.

Political transformation in Mississippi began to occur once restrictions on black voting were lifted in 1965 and thousands of black Mississippians were added to the voter rolls. By the 1970s and 1980s, the winning candidates for governor, all Democrats, appealed to white and black voters alike. William Waller, after his victory in 1971, became the first governor since Reconstruction to appoint blacks to positions within his administration. In 1975 Cliff Finch, in his working man's "lunch box" campaign, sought its base unabashedly in a black/poor white coalition. William Winter, a "self-avowed moderate" during the 1960s, was elected governor in 1979. In 1983 Bill Allain also won the governor's chair by attracting a coalition of blacks and poor whites. Running on a platform of economic development, education improvement, and "basic, drastic change," Ray Mabus, a Harvard-educated lawyer, won the governor's race in 1987 by polling eight of nine black votes (about 30 percent of all registered voters by 1987) and half of the white votes.

While black voters by the 1970s proved crucial to the success of moderately-progressive Democratic candidates, the ability of black candidates to win elective office themselves came somewhat slower. For many years after the passage of the Voting Rights Act of 1965, the Mississippi legislature passed a number of laws designed to dilute black voting strength. This continuation of the 1950s strategy of massive resistance to civil rights persisted, in some cases, into the early 1980s. Ultimately, black voters had to sue the state to force it to obey the federal voting rights legislation. As a result, although Robert Clark of Holmes County became in 1967 the first black elected to the state legislature in the twentieth century, he remained the sole black member for twelve years. In 1979, after the state finally settled a fourteen-year-old reapportionment dispute, sixteen additional black members were elected as lawmakers.

The political power of black Mississippians in the legislature and beyond has continued to grow since 1980. Today, forty-five of Mississippi's 174 legislators are African American. In addition, by the late 1990s, Mississippi had hundreds of additional black elected politicians, more than any other state, including over 500 city and county officials, almost 100 law enforcement officers, and nearly 150 education administrators. By the mid-1980s black candidates had also gained control of the black-majority Delta Congressional district. In 1982 and 1984, Robert Clark lost close elections in

The administration of William Waller (1972-1976) signaled the beginning of a new era of Mississippi politics ushered in by passage of the federal Voting Rights Act. In the early 1960s Waller had served as Hinds County District Attorney; his office tried twice, unsuccessfully, to prosecute Byron De La Beckwith for the murder of Medgar Evers. Courtesy, McCain Library and Archives, University of Southern Mississippi Libraries

this district to Webb Franklin, a white Republican. In 1986, however, Mike Espy, a young black man from Yazoo City, in his first political race, defeated Franklin. Espy continued to hold the seat until 1992 when President Bill Clinton chose him to be Secretary of Agriculture, the only Mississippian to serve in a presidential cabinet in the twentieth century. His successor, Bennie Thompson, a life-long civil rights-activist and politician from Hinds County, continues to hold the Delta Congressional seat today.

While black candidates have been helped by the requirement of the Voting Rights Act to create black-majority voting districts, black office seekers by the 1990s also had some success winning elections in white-majority areas. For instance, in the 1990s, the people of Corinth, with a black population of less than 15 percent, elected E. S. Bishop, a former black school administrator, to two terms as their mayor. Several other white-majority towns have also selected black candidates as their chief executives in recent years, including Hattiesburg, the state's third-largest city, which chose Johnny DuPree over a white incumbent in the 2001 election. In 1996, Fred Banks, Jr. of Jackson, who worked as a civil-rights lawyer in Mississippi during the late 1960s, won a seat on the Mississippi Supreme Court from central Mississippi's white-majority district.

As black politicians have increasingly assumed positions of power and influence in the state, they have formed alliances with white Democrats to pro-

mote programs important to black Mississippians. A countervailing weight to this black/white Democratic alliance, however, has been the re-emergence of the Republican party in Mississippi. As the Democratic party became increasingly associated with the civil rights movement in the 1950s and 1960s, many white Mississippians—conservatives who had stayed in an increasingly liberal Democratic party primarily because it had long supported white supremacy—transferred their political allegiance to the Republican party. By the 1960s, the state's white voters regularly preferred the Republican presidential candidate, and the state Republican party moved to offer its first serious candidates for statewide office. In 1963 and 1967, Rubel Phillips, the first viable Republican candidate for governor since Reconstruction, made a respectable showing. In 1978, Thad Cochran, a Republican, won election to the U.S. Senate primarily because the independent candidacy of Charles Evers, brother of civil-rights martyr Medgar Evers, split the state's Democratic vote with Maurice Dantin. Despite the circumstances of this election, Cochran, currently completing his fourth term, has proved to be a popular senator, appealing to a wide spectrum of Mississippi voters with his moderate agenda. In 1988 another Republican, Trent Lott, who had served as U.S. Representative from south Mississippi's district since 1972, won the other U.S. Senate seat, after the aging John C. Stennis declined to run for an eighth term. By 1994, when the Republican party gained control of the U.S.

Congress for the first time in forty years, Mississippi Republicans had established themselves as major players in the Republican resurgence. Longtime Mississippi Republican leader Haley Barber was elected chairman of the Republican National Committee in 1993 and played a key role in engineering the Republican landslide of 1994. When Bob Dole resigned as Senate majority leader in 1996 to run for vice-president, the top two leadership positions in the Senate were held by Cochran and Lott. Senate Republicans chose Lott over Cochran as their leader, a post the junior Mississippi senator held until the Republicans lost control of the Senate in 2001.

Mississippi Republicans also had success in the state political arena during the 1990s. In the 1991 election, a little-known Vicksburg businessman, Kirk Fordice, tapped into a rising sentiment against "professional politicians" to defeat incumbent governor Ray Mabus. Fordice thus became the first Republican governor in Mississippi since the Democrats forced Adelbert Ames to resign in 1876. Fordice also became the first governor since the nineteenth century to succeed himself when he won reelection over Democratic challenger Dick Molpus in 1995, a second term made possible due to a change in the state constitution advocated by a string of Fordice's Democratic predecessors.

In his eight years in office, Fordice garnered headlines but accomplished little. The headlines detailed often outrageous statements made in national forums by the governor, regular safaris to Africa, and an ongoing marital dispute. The governor's self-styled posture as a political outsider, however, was perhaps the greatest factor in limiting his effectiveness. The Mississippi political system had long placed most power in the legislative branch, and Fordice's disdain for the political process weakened what little power a Mississippi governor actually had. In addition, much of the Fordice agenda was ignored by a state legislature that remained firmly in the hands of a sizeable Democratic majority. Unlike other southern states, the Republican resurgence in Mississippi has not yet been extended to either the legislature or most statewide positions below the governor's chair.

While the Republican party in Mississippi will likely continue to develop on the local level, by the end of the twentieth century the state's two political parties were already extremely competitive in the most prominent statewide elections. Indeed, no gubernatorial election had ever been closer in

Mississippi than the 1999 contest. Democrat Ronnie Musgrove, a former lieutenant governor, received only 8,300 more votes than Republican Mike Parker, a former U.S. congressman. Because two independent candidates garnered a smattering of ballots, neither man received at least 50 percent of the votes or a majority of electoral votes (based on state House districts), both requirements for election as outlined in the state constitution. After Parker refused to concede the race, the selection of the state's governor was thrown into the state House of Representatives for the first time in the state's history. With an almost three-to-one Democratic majority, the legislative body selected Musgrove in a largely party-line vote.

Beyond politics, the economic changes that began in the state during the 1930s and 1940s accelerated in the final decades of the twentieth century. By the dawn of the twenty-first century, Mississippi was still a state with few large urban areas where agriculture remained important. But the state had also experienced significant population changes and

Robert G. Clark has been a member of the Mississippi House of Representatives since his historic election to that body in 1967. He currently serves as Speaker Pro Tempore for the House. A teacher by training, Clark has been a persistent advocate for the improvement of Mississippi's educational system. Courtesy, McCain Library and Archives, University of Southern Mississippi Libraries

Rubel Phillips ran for governor of Mississippi in 1963 as a Republican, only the second Republican gubernatorial candidate since 1881. Phillips tried to capitalize on the state's white animosity toward the national Democrats, which increased after the Kennedy administration's efforts to force the enrollment of James Meredith at Ole Miss in 1962. Phillips' campaign slogan was "K.O. the Kennedys." Courtesy, McCain Library and Archives, University of Southern Mississippi Libraries

suburban growth, a further diversification of its agricultural economy, and a significant expansion of its non-agricultural sector. In the half century after World War II, most states in the so-called Sun Belt experienced significant population growth. Mississippi's population growth, however, has been much slower than that of many other southern states, although between 1970 and 2000, the state grew by over half a million residents. While Mississippi continued to add new residents in the 1990s, after the 2000 census, the state learned that its number of U.S. Congressional districts would be reduced from five to four.

Even so, in the last three decades of the twentieth century, for the first time in over half a century, the state reversed a long trend of population outmigration. In fact, part of the recent population growth has included a number of blacks and whites (or their children) who returned to Mississippi after having left the state in the Great Migrations from the state between 1920 and 1970. In addition, Mississippi's recent new residents have also included hundreds of northern retirees who settled in the state in the 1990s, attracted to Mississippi as an alternative to traditional retiree destinations like south Florida and by the state's income tax exemption, beginning in 1995, of most forms of retirement income.

Other segments of Mississippi's growing population have added a dose of diversity to the state's demographic profile. In the 1990s, the fastest-growing segment of Mississippi's population, as in many other parts of the country, was the Hispanic population. While the number of residents in the state claiming Hispanic ancestry remains relatively small compared to other locales, their numbers grew by more than 100 percent between 1990 and 2000. In the late 1970s and 1980s thousands of Vietnamese immigrants settled on the Mississippi Gulf Coast. The earliest arrivals secured jobs in the area's struggling seafood industry and were attracted by the similarities between Vietnam's coastal region and the Mississippi coast. Other Vietnamese immigrants soon followed, and by the beginning of the twenty-first century, the Vietnamese helped revitalize the Gulf Coast seafood industry and established a vibrant culture centered around the Point Cadet area of Biloxi. Beginning in the late 1960s, hundreds of people of Indian ancestry began to arrive in Mississippi. Most came not from the Indian subcontinent but from British colonies in Africa as those areas experienced

Governor Ronnie Musgrove in the Dixie National Rodeo Parade. Musgrove, whose hometown is Batesville, became Mississippi's sixty-second governor in 2000. During his first two years in office, Governor Musgrove focused on economic growth, highlighted by the deal that brought Nissan to the state, and education improvement, most notably the passage of his plan to raise the pay of Mississippi public school teachers to the Southeastern average within six years. Courtesy, Donald C. Simmons, Jr.

decolonization. This population has continued to grow within the state, with many of the new immigrants working as small businessmen in the Delta or professionals in the larger cities, such as the Jackson area. Although Mississippi continues to be an ethnically homogenous state, with well over 95 percent of residents of either Anglo-American (primarily Scots-Irish) or African-American heritage, projections of the population trends of the late twentieth century suggest that the state in the coming decades will become more ethnically diverse than at any point in its history.

Significant population shifts also occurred within Mississippi during the late twentieth century. While most cities in the state grew little or even lost population, the suburban areas around Jackson, in Desoto County, and along the Gulf Coast experienced significant growth. For example, during the 1990s the population of the north Delta county of DeSoto grew by 57 percent, as the area became a popular suburb of nearby Memphis, Tennessee. At the same time, people continued to leave many other parts of the Mississippi Delta. Most dramatic, in the last two decades of the twentieth century, Quitman County lost about a quarter of its population, but all but five of the region's eighteen counties saw their population decline during the same period. The recent depopulation of much of the Mississippi Delta coincided with the decline of the cotton farming that defined the region's economy for over a century. The area has struggled to reshape its economy in the wake of these changes, and today, the Delta is a region characterized by a few pockets of prosperity within large areas of what historian James Cobb has described as "rural ghettos."

Beyond the Delta, however, the decline of King Cotton has generally meant economic improvement, through a diversification of agricultural production and the development of a significant non-agricultural economy. While per capita income in Mississippi was only one-third of the national average in 1940, by the mid-1990s, that figured had climbed to almost 75 percent. The declining importance of cotton to the state's agricultural economy can be

Unlike most of Mississippi, the Gulf Coast area is one of wide ethnic diversity. This church, St. Rose de Lima Catholic Church, in Bay St. Louis, was dedicated in 1926 and serves a community that includes people from a variety of backgrounds: African, Creole, Italian, and Slavic. Courtesy, Diana C. Young

When the Vietnamese first began to arrive on the Mississippi Gulf Coast in the late 1970s, they initially worked primarily in the seafood processing plants. Within a few short years, however, many Vietnamese immigrants had built their own boats and established their own seafood businesses, and today, they play a dominant role in the Gulf Coast seafood industry. Courtesy, Mississippi Development Authority

seen by the fact that in 2001, the value of both Mississippi's forest products and its poultry and eggs were each worth more than the value of the state's cotton crop. During the 1980s and 1990s a number of technological innovations increased the productivity and output of Mississippi's lumber industry. By 1993 the value of the state's timber harvest regularly exceeded $1 billion, and by 1998, 10 percent of all Mississippi jobs were in the state's forest products industry. With over 60 percent of the state's land blanketed by forest, the timber business will undoubtedly remain central to Mississippi's economy for decades to come. Over the last thirty years, the poultry and egg products industry has emerged as the largest agricultural interest in the state. Much of the $1.5 billion industry (the fourth-largest in the nation) is located in a series of poultry-growing centers scattered around south-central Mississippi.

Beyond agriculture, Mississippi has continued the diversification of its economy begun during World War II in a variety of directions. The furniture industry, centered in northeast Mississippi, has emerged as one of the fastest-growing industries in the state over the last forty years. From modest beginnings in the early 1960s, the furniture industry today provides jobs for more than 25,000 people working in over 200 factories. Other

industries created because of World War II, or because of Cold War investments by the federal government, continued to be major economic engines for the state's economy into the twenty-first century. The state's largest private employer today is Litton Industries at the Ingalls Shipyard in Pascagoula, which opened in 1939 and first prospered as a major Navy shipyard during World War II. Today, Ingalls not only continues to build ships for the Navy but also builds a variety of vessels for nations around the world. The Mississippi Test Facility in Hancock County was created in the 1960s by NASA to test rockets for the Apollo moon missions. Now the facility known as the John C. Stennis Space Center has evolved into a multi-agency "city" that is home to not only most of NASA's rocket-testing programs but also thirty additional federal and

Workers at a Tyson Foods poultry processing center in Mississippi. In 1998 Mississippi's poultry industry provided jobs for more than 19,000 people. Courtesy, Mississippi Development Authority

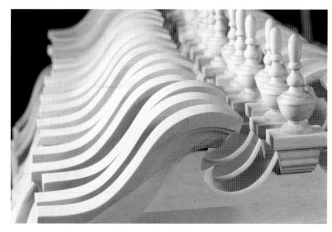

Above: *Headboards produced by Hood Furniture await delivery to furniture outlets around the country. Mississippi's furniture manufacturing industry is the second-largest in the United States, second only to North Carolina. Courtesy, Mississippi Development Authority*

Left: *Though the timber industry has been important to Mississippi's economy for over 100 years, the industry today is less labor-intensive, depending on machines to do much of the work once performed by humans, oxen, and mules. Courtesy, Mississippi Development Authority*

state agencies, including much of the U.S. Navy's oceanographic operation.

In the last decade or so, a number of new, multinational industries have invigorated the Mississippi economy. In south Mississippi a small long distance reseller eventually grew into a global communications giant during the 1980s and 1990s. In 1985, Bernie Ebbers headed Long Distance Discount Calling, headquartered in Brookhaven. By the late 1990s, through a series of acquisitions and mergers, Ebbers' company had morphed into WorldCom, Inc., with corporate headquarters in Clinton, just outside of Jackson. In 2001, the company had an international workforce of 90,000, but much of its growth was unfortunately built on a shaky foundation of apparently dishonest accounting. In 2002, WorldCom announced that it had overstated its 2001 earnings by almost $4 billion. Within months, the company became the largest ever to file for bankruptcy. Although the prosperity brought by WorldCom was relatively short-lived, state leaders continued their efforts to attract multinational

corporations to Mississippi. In early 2001, Nissan Motor Company decided to build a manufacturing plant near Canton after the state offered an attractive incentive plan worth almost $300 million. Set for completion in 2003, the $1.4 billion Nissan factory will employ over 5,000 people, as well as create related jobs for thousands of other Mississippians. Like WorldCom before its collapse, Nissan is bringing the kind of high-wage jobs to Mississippi that the state has long needed to further improve the personal incomes of its citizens.

No industry has had a greater impact on Mississippi's recent economy than the gaming industry. The creation of a casino gambling industry in the state, that is today only outstripped by Las Vegas and Atlantic City, was started almost unnoticed in 1990. Governor Ray Mabus proposed the creation of a state lottery to fund his ambitious BEST (Better Education for Success Tomorrow) education program that year. Widespread opposition to the lottery, led by the Mississippi Baptist Convention, killed the funding proposal for Mabus's

Old South meets the New South. When the Mississippi Test Facility was constructed out of the swamps of Hancock County in the mid-1960s, NASA builders had to turn to some tried-and-true methods to help complete the job. Renamed the John C. Stennis Space Center in 1988, today the facility employs more than 4,000 people and has an economic impact on south Mississippi in excess of $400 million. Courtesy, NASA

education package, but during the same year a proposal by a Natchez legislator to help the struggling economy of the old Mississippi River town sparked a casino boom in the state. The new legislation allowed local citizens in counties along the Mississippi River and the Gulf Coast to vote on whether to allow riverboat casinos to operate on their waters. The gambling statute, however, never required that the riverboats actually go anywhere, and soon, casinos were sprouting up along the Mississippi River and the Gulf Coast that technically were on the water but that hardly resembled boats. The largest "riverboat" casino in the state today is the Grand Casino in Tunica, which has 140,000 square-feet of gaming space, making it the third largest casino in the world. In 2001, the state had 31 casinos in seven locales around the state, but the center of the casino industry is located in Tunica County, with ten casinos, and the Gulf Coast, with twelve gambling operations.

The casinos have had a major economic impact on both of these areas. The Mississippi Gulf Coast originally developed in the nineteenth century as a tourist destination for people from New Orleans, the Mississippi Delta, and other locales. By the late 1960s, however, the area's status as a resort destination began to decline due to competition from

the development of more attractive beach areas in nearby Alabama and Florida as well as the devastation wrought by the Category Five Hurricane Camille that hit the Gulf Coast in August 1969. The arrival of the casinos brought the tourists back to the Gulf Coast and invigorated the region's economy, while virtually eliminating unemployment in the area. The transformation in Tunica has been even more dramatic, primarily because the county was one of the poorest in not only Mississippi but also the entire country, before the arrival of the first casino in 1992. In the ten years since, the unemployment rate has dropped from more than 25 percent to just over 6 percent. Welfare rolls have been cut in half, and a sleepy backwater dominated by catfish farms and cotton plantations has been transformed into a major tourist destination—complete with more than 6,000 hotel rooms (the county had one, twenty-room motel in 1992).

One other locale where casinos have become important in recent years is in east-central Mississippi, on the land of the Mississippi Band of the Choctaw Indians. For almost a century and a half following the removal of most of the tribe from the state in the 1830s, the Mississippi Choctaws remained mired in economic poverty; in the 1960s, unemployment among tribal members hovered around 75 percent.

Beginning in the late 1970s, under the leadership of Chief Philip Martin and a sixteen-member Tribal Council, the Mississippi Band of Choctaw Indians reemerged as a major economic force in the state, in part helped by new federal laws adopted in the 1970s that gave native American groups more autonomy over activity on their reservations. In 1979, the tribe created an 80-acre industrial park, where numerous manufacturing facilities were established, everything from companies producing supplies for the automotive industry to a business molding plastic cutlery for McDonald's. In 1994, the Choctaws opened their first casino, which quickly became the state's highest-grossing gambling concern. In 2000, they began construction on the $750 million Pearl River Resort; when completed, it will include a new casino and hotel and a recreation development. Today, the various Choctaw enterprises provide almost 10,000 jobs (with more on the way with the development of the new resort), and unemployment among the tribe is virtually non-existent. Despite their rapidly developing economy, the Mississippi Band of Choctaw Indians have managed to maintain a good deal of their traditional culture. They have their own school system; many tribal members still speak the native language; and

Top: *Though most often associated with New Orleans, Mardi Gras is also celebrated on the Mississippi Gulf Coast. During the weeks leading up to Lent, more than 20 parades roll through Gulf Coast communities, with Krewe members on elaborate floats throwing trinkets to onlookers. Courtesy, Diana C. Young*

Bottom: *The largest commercial investment made in a Mississippi casino project in the 1990s was the $650 million needed to develop the Beau Rivage Resort in Biloxi, completed in 1999. The Beau Rivage has almost 72,000 square-feet of gaming space, nearly 1,800 hotel rooms, twelve restaurants, and a marina. Courtesy of the Beau Rivage*

many craft traditions, such as basket making, and traditional recreational activities, such as stickball, continue to thrive.

While Mississippi political and economic life underwent significant transformations in the late twentieth century, the changes in social life have been even more dramatic. Perhaps most striking, the end of legalized racial segregation transformed race relations in the state. Although white resistance to the Civil Rights Act of 1964, which banned racial discrimination in public accommodations, continued in some of the state's more isolated hamlets well into the late 1970s, the growing black political power in the state ultimately assured the death of Jim Crow. Since that time, Mississippians have wrestled with the transition to a post-Jim Crow society. Although the results have been mixed, there is no doubt that a visitor from the Mississippi of 1960 would find the change in the state's race relations to be nothing short of revolutionary. Today, race relations are certainly no worse and probably much better in Mississippi and other southern states than in other parts of the country.

Racial conflict, of course, has not been eliminated with the death of Jim Crow. For example, Mississippi struggled for over twenty-five years to resolve a higher education desegregation lawsuit, originally filed in 1975 by Jake Ayers of Glen Allan, who claimed the state had underfunded its three historically-black universities—Alcorn, Jackson State, and Mississippi Valley State—for decades. Although a U.S. District Court originally dismissed the lawsuit, the U.S. Supreme Court ruled in 1992 that Mississippi had not eliminated all vestiges of segregation from its university system. State leaders and the black plaintiffs wrangled over how to implement the Supreme Court decision for the next decade, finally agreeing to a settlement in early 2002 that would direct over $500 million during a seventeen-year period to improve facilities and programs at the three historically-black institutions.

Continuing racial divisions also reemerged in recent debates over displays of Mississippi's Confederate history. In 1993 the National Association for the Advancement of Colored People (NAACP) sued Mississippi, claiming the state's use of a Confederate battle symbol in its flag—adopted in 1894 in the midst of efforts to disfranchise black voters and tighten racial segregation—violated black citizens' civil rights. When the Mississippi Supreme Court ruled on the matter in 2000, it disagreed with the NAACP's contention but also noted that Missis-

Phillip Martin, a World War II veteran, has served as the elected Chief of the Mississippi Band of Choctaw Indians since 1979. In 1997 Chief Martin and Governor Kirk Fordice signed an agreement in which the state of Mississippi recognized the sovereignty of Choctaw tribal government. Courtesy, Mississippi Band of Choctaw Indians

sippi actually had no official state flag, since no mention had been made of the banner when the state updated its laws in 1906. Governor Ronnie Musgrove appointed a commission, chaired by former Governor William Winter, to investigate what the state should do regarding the adoption of a state flag. After a series of contentious public hearings around the state, the commission recommended the adoption of a newly-designed flag without the Confederate symbol. Most of the state's business and political leadership endorsed the new design, hoping that the change would benefit economic development efforts and avoid negative publicity for the state. In an April 2001 referendum to choose between the new flag and the old one, however, two-thirds of those who voted went for the traditional flag. The vote split largely along racial lines, with most whites claiming that their votes had been to preserve their Confederate heritage, not perpetuate racial animosity, and most blacks arguing for the establishment of a state symbol untainted by the legacy of slavery and racial violence.

While the 2000 flag vote seemed to confirm William Faulkner's oft-repeated quote that in Mississippi "the past is never dead; it's not even past," Mississippians in recent years have also made efforts to confront directly their racial history. In 1994, a biracial jury in Hinds County convicted Byron de la Beckwith of murdering NAACP leader Medgar Evers in 1963. Beckwith had been tried for the crime twice before soon after the murder, but in both instances, all-white jury trials ended in mistrials. Beckwith died in prison in 2001. In 1998 a multiracial Forrest County jury convicted another long-suspected murderer of a 1960s civil rights activist. In 1966, a group of Klansman, led by imperial wizard Sam Bowers, firebombed the home of Hattiesburg NAACP leader Vernon Dahmer. Although Dahmer fought off the attackers while his family escaped, he died from smoke inhalation shortly after the attack. At the time, Bowers and thirteen other Klansmen went on trial. An all-white jury actually convicted four of the men (itself a noteworthy event), but four separate attempts to convict Bowers all ended with a hung juries. When new evidence surfaced in the mid-1990s, however, Bowers was retried again, convicted and sentenced to life imprisonment. Since 1993, at least six other investigations have been reopened into civil-rights related killings that took place around the state in the 1960s.

Measuring how much individual racial attitudes have actually changed in Mississippi over the last thirty years remains an impressionistic task, but it is clear that the most visible and violent manifestations of racial animosity have all but disappeared from the state. The political empowerment of Mississippi's black population has certainly helped usher in a period of changed relations between white and black Mississippians, one in which racial harmony, or at least harmonious coexistence, prevails. At times, both black and white Mississippians are more cognizant of the changed racial landscape in their state than outsiders who still remember the dark days of racial segregation and civil rights strife. Such was the case in the 2002 battle to secure the nomination of Federal Judge Charles Pickering of Laurel to the Fifth Circuit Court of Appeals. While national civil rights organizations and liberals blasted Pickering for his past as a racial segregationist in the 1950s and early 1960s, almost all black leaders in Laurel supported the nomination, citing Pickering's efforts toward racial reconciliation, beginning in 1967 with his testimony against Sam Bowers in the first round of Vernon Dahmer mur-

Top: *In many Mississippi communities during mid-June, black residents celebrate Juneteenth, the day when slaves received the news of the Emancipation Proclamation. In 1991 in Hattiesburg, Johnnie Dupree, local businessman and political leader, was the King of Juneteenth. Ten years later, he was elected mayor of the city. Also pictured is Hattiesburg businesswoman and neighborhood mentor Lillie McLaurin. Courtesy, Diana C. Young*

Bottom: *Confederate reenactors gather at the Confederate monument in Hattiesburg on Confederate Memorial Day. It is a legal state holiday in Mississippi, observed on the last Monday of April. Courtesy, Diana C. Young*

der trials. Many local blacks, primarily Democrats, viewed Pickering as a fair, upstanding Christian, despite his Republican politics and racial history. As one local black leader told the *New York Times* during the controversy, "if the judge has moved beyond his past, I think we should all try to do the same." In assessing the current state of race relations in Mississippi, a paraphrase of Martin Luther King, Jr., might best capture the reality: we ain't where we want to be, and we ain't where we should be, but thank God we ain't where we were.

The story of Mississippi public education in the three decades since the 1960s illustrates both the dramatic changes and persistent continuities that have defined Mississippi society since the civil rights movement. In 1970, after one hundred years of almost complete school segregation, Mississippi and many other southern states were ordered by the U.S. Supreme Court to desegregate their schools immediately. Despite Mississippi's stubborn battle in the 1950s and 1960s to prevent such integration, the transition to a unitary school system in the early 1970s occurred without violence. Although white resistance to "forced integration" persisted in a variety of ways, most notably in the white flight from public schools in the Mississippi Delta and the state's larger urban areas, by the 1990s Mississippi, like most other southern states, had public schools that were significantly more integrated racially than schools in the Northeast or Midwest with significant black populations.

At the same time, the end of the dual system of public education created opportunities for educational reformers to push for long-overdue improvements in the state's educational system. During the battle over civil rights in the late 1950s and 1960s, state leaders had largely neglected the state's educational problems: low teacher pay, inadequate funding, the lack of a compulsory attendance law, high dropout rates, and an ineffective system for administering the public schools. In his campaign for governor in 1979, William Winter made education reform the centerpiece of his platform. After his election, the new governor rallied public opinion to convince the state legislature to pass the most significant education legislation in the state's history. The Education Reform Act, passed in a December 1982 special session of the legislature, created publically-funded kindergartens, established a compulsory education measure, gave teachers a much-needed salary boost, and funded a variety of other new programs to bolster public

The New York Society for the Preservation of Mississippi Heritage, a group of transplanted Mississippians, started the annual Mississippi picnic in New York City's Central Park. Over 1,000 people with Mississippi ties, as well as some curious locals, generally turn out for the event. Courtesy, Mississippi Development Authority/Division of Tourism

education. In addition, the State Board of Education, which had been composed of three statewide elected officials (the state superintendent of education, the attorney general, and the secretary of state) was replaced by a lay board, which better represented the various public education constituencies across the state. Other attempts to improve the state's public education system followed in subsequent administrations. When one of Governor's Winter's aides, Ray Mabus, became governor in 1987, he attempted an even more ambitious project of education reform. Although the legislature balked at funding Mabus's entire BEST program, some of the governor's suggestions, such as continuing pay increases for teachers, were enacted. In 1997, over a veto by Governor Kirk Fordice, legislators passed the Adequate Education Program, which provides additional state funds to the state's poorer school systems in an effort to equalize some of the disparities between richer public and private schools and the state's most impoverished school districts. Despite all these efforts to improve schools in the state, educational achievement, by most benchmarks, still lags behind national averages, and the state's long obsession with racially-separate schools continues to cast a shadow over its project of creating a first-rate educational system.

Beyond the effects wrought by the civil rights movement on Mississippi society, life in the state has also been profoundly affected by the wide-ranging mass culture that increasingly defines American society. In the 1950s and 1960s, Mississippi was often rightly described as a "closed society." Today, of course, Mississippians have cable TV, VCRs, cell phones, computers, and all the other trappings of the information age that link them to the wider world. Culturally, the current generation of Mississippians share more with other Americans than they do with their Mississippi ancestors of fifty years ago. This Americanization of Mississippi has certainly played a role in eroding much of the former distinctiveness of Mississippi life, including many of the negative attributes. Many have bemoaned at least some of the effects of this cultural change, such as the replacement of unique downtown shopping districts by the ubiquitous Super Wal-Mart. At the same time, not all of the state's distinct characteristics have crumbled in the face of this recent Americanization. A relaxed, hospitable pace of life still characterizes social relations in Mississippi. Also, Mississippians have retained their strong devotion to their religious traditions despite their acceptance of many of the secular trends that define modern American life.

While much about Mississippi has changed in the last quarter century, one other constant has been the abiding devotion of Mississippians to their state. Shortly before his death in 1999, author Willie Morris noted that Mississippians "have a long and well-known history of rebellion, divisiveness and oppression, yet Mississippians from all walks of life, political opinions, races and ethnic backgrounds have an unsurpassing love for and dedication to their native soil." That attitude is what sustains the annual Way Up North in Mississippi picnic, held every June since 1979 in New York City's Central Park, where Mississippi transplants gather for some home cooking and entertainment. Similar feelings led a black woman in Hattiesburg, Osceola McCarty, who had to quit school in the sixth grade to help her family make ends meet and who worked hard all her life washing and ironing white people's clothes, to donate her life's savings of $150,000 to the largely-white University of Southern Mississippi in 1995 so that other poor Mississippi children might acquire an education. In the midst of all the alterations in the state's political, economic, and social life, Mississippi remains a unique place, one with a complicated past, and if willing to continue to make changes while clinging to her better traditions, a state with a promising future.

After the Hattiesburg washerwoman, Oseola McCarty, gave her life savings of $150,000 to the University of Southern Mississippi, she received a host of awards and honors, including an honorary doctorate from Harvard University and a Presidential Citizens Medal, presented to her by President Bill Clinton. Her gift inspired countless Americans to donate their time and resources to help others, such as media titan Ted Turner, who gave a billion dollars to the United Nations after he heard about McCarty's story. Courtesy, McCain Library and Archives, University of Southern Mississippi Libraries

This photograph of a family outing at Rawls Springs, near Hattiesburg at the turn of the century, could be from any decade. Diaries, letters, books and newspapers throughout Mississippi history have chronicled the importance of the family in Mississippi culture. Courtesy, Forrest Cooper

MISSISSIPPI CULTURE

A remarkable number of musicians, writers, and other artists have emerged from Mississippi's rich cultural heritage. Its art and culture reflect a complex pattern of influences: a frontier past, an Indian population, a strong farming tradition, and the presence of large numbers of African people and their culture. Contemporary annual events reflect these and other influences: the Choctaw Indian Festival, the Blessing of the Fleet on the coast, the Delta Blues Festival, and the Neshoba County Fair.

The bases for Mississippians' everyday life and culture have traditionally been the family and the church. Family gatherings were headed by a family patriarch, "Granddaddy"; family reunions, centered on specially prepared dishes, were attended by a large family network, sometimes numbering several hundred people.

For both black and white Mississippians, the church was a primary social and cultural institution. Week-long revivals, generally with morning and evening services, were held each year, usually after the cotton crop had been "laid by." These events also featured arrays of food, which were points of pride to the women, who also organized much of the week's activities.

Many rural churches in Mississippi gave budding artists their first opportunities to sing or play an instrument. One tradition—sacred harp singing, or the singing from "shaped note hymnals" in a unique cadence—was passed along through annual week-long teaching sessions.

Although Baptists and Methodists dominate the religious scene in Mississippi, the state became more religiously diverse as the twentieth century progressed. Catholics have always had a strong presence on the coast; with the arrival of a substantial Vietnamese community, those numbers have increased. Even within Protestantism there have been changes, as more and more Mississippians, both black and white, join Pentecostal churches.

Traditions and customs from the frontier days continue to exert an influence on contemporary Mississippi. Men whose fathers and grandfathers hunted for deer and bear in the Mississippi Delta still enjoy hunting or fishing on a regular basis. Quilting and canning traditions also continue among rural communities.

Among other traditions preserved is that of the Neshoba County Fair, a political and social institution begun in the nineteenth century. For many years it was thought that a candidate for

statewide office was not serious unless he had spoken at the Neshoba fair and officially announced his candidacy there. The fairground, which includes a group of permanent cabins clustered around Founder's Square, has been entered in the National Register of Historic Places.

Both Indians and blacks have special annual events that highlight their cultures. The Choctaws of the Mississippi reservations near Philadelphia have a Choctaw Indian Festival during the summer. The fair not only preserves Indian traditions, but also allows Oklahoma Choctaws a chance to visit and celebrate those traditions. In the 1970s, the Delta Blues Festival began at Freedom Village near Greenville. As the current generation of blues artists fades from the scene, this event allows audiences to hear traditional Mississippi blues as well as contemporary rhythm and blues artists.

Annual pilgrimages to visit architecturally outstanding older homes are popular in areas of the state that have antebellum homes. This tradition began with the Natchez Garden Club in 1932. The pilgrimages have been a popular and profitable way of preserving old homes and promoting historic preservation. Along the coast such traditions as the Blessing of the Fleet and Mardi Gras give that area a different cultural flavor.

Two musical traditions—blues and country music—found in Mississippi a rich environment for development. The blues, which grew out of field hollers, work songs, and the concurrent gospel music, came out of the Delta in the early twentieth century. Bluesmen Big Bill Broonzy, Charley Patton, Mississippi John Hurt, and many others sang about their hard times, troubled relationships, and traveling—to escape to better fortune.

The career of Broonzy typifies the life of a Delta bluesman. Born in 1893 in Scott, Mississippi, Broonzy was a farmer until World War I, when he joined the service. After the war he could no longer tolerate the treatment of blacks in Mississippi, and he left for Chicago in 1920. He recorded "race records," as they were known then, for Paramount Records. After enjoying a measure of success during the 1930s, Broonzy's career seemed to be at an end with the coming of World War II. After the war, however, he was rediscovered and played to sold-out audiences on a world tour. The music of

Facing page: *When Mississippi was settled, the state teemed with wild game: turkey, bear, rabbit, panther, and deer. Hunting has always been an important activity, both for sustenance and sport. By 1900, the only area left in the state with large populations of deer and bear was the Mississippi Delta. This Delta hunting party was photographed in the first decade of the century by J. Mack Moore. Courtesy, Old Courthouse Museum, Vicksburg*

Right: *Ethel Wright Mohamed, needlework artist of Belzoni, has detailed some of the activities at a Sacred Harp Singing. The song leader directs the four-part harmony in the church while outside "dinner on the grounds" is being prepared. Sacred Harp or shaped note singing was an outgrowth of the singing schools in the East, and can still be heard in northeast Mississippi today. Courtesy, Ethel Wright Mohamed*

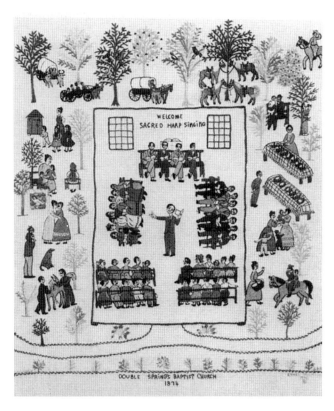

Below: *A widespread and popular outing in the first part of the century was the baptismal service. Rural churches often used creeks, lakes, and rivers to baptize new members. This well-attended service was photographed by J. Mack Moore near Vicksburg around the turn of the century. Many churches still have outdoor baptisms. Courtesy, Old Courthouse Museum, Vicksburg*

Broonzy, Robert Johnson, Willie Dixon, Howlin' Wolf, John Lee Hooker and others continues to be recorded and to influence both contemporary blues and other forms of American popular music.

Typical of the careers of the second generation of blues musicians is that of Muddy Waters (McKinley Morganfield). Born in Rolling Fork in 1915, Morganfield grew up in Clarksdale. There are several stories as to how he got the name Muddy Waters. He says that he got the name because he liked to play in a creek near his home as he was growing up. However, a good friend of his says Morganfield got the name Muddy Waters because "he used to `muddy' [gig fish] on Saturday and sell fish on Saturday nights." After playing the Delta juke joints during the 1930s, Waters went to St. Louis for a time. He did not leave Mississippi permanently, however, until after Alan Lomax had made a recording of his blues sound for the Library of Congress. Moving to Chicago in 1943, Waters got his big break in 1946 when Big Bill Broonzy introduced him to a record producer. Waters' first release, "Rolling Stone," became a big seller. He hit the peak of his record sales in the mid-1950s, and continued as one of the most influential of the bluesmen, with the popular British rock group, the Rolling Stones, taking their name from his *most* popular song.

Country music is another tradition whose development owes much to the state of Mississippi, and in particular to the "Father of Country Music," Jimmie Rodgers of Meridian. Born in 1897, Rodgers was a railroad worker at the age of fourteen. While riding the trains, black workers taught Rodgers work songs and the blues. In 1927, after he had developed tuberculosis, Rodgers cut his first record in Bristol, Tennessee. Five years later, soon after a recording session, the "Singing Brakeman" died. In that short span of time, Rodgers set the course of country music, combining the plaintive quality of the blues with the rhythms of mountain music and popularizing it through traveling shows and recordings.

Many other Mississippians have followed Rodgers into country music, including Conway Twitty and Tammy Wynette. An interesting contribution has been made by a black country music singer named Charley Pride. Growing up in Sledge, Pride listened to country music on the radio and later became a star performer in a field that once included only white entertainers. Two of country music's most popular stars of recent years hail from Mississippi—Faith Hill of Star and LeAnn Rimes of Pearl.

Music is only one art form to have folk expressions in Mississippi. The recording of folk tales as well

Above: *Quilting was still a daily part of Mississippi women's lives when this photograph was taken by Farm Security Administration staffer, Russell Lee, near Pace in 1939. The child is receiving what Pecolia Warner, a Vicksburg quilter, called "fireplace training." Courtesy, Library of Congress*

Facing page, top: *This Choctaw family group was photographed by M.R. Harrington in 1908 after a renewed attempt by the federal government to move more Choctaws to Oklahoma. The more traditional Indians resisted the removal efforts, but by 1910 only 1,000 Choctaw remained in Mississippi. They maintained and passed down many of their tribal customs and ceremonies that survive today. Courtesy, Museum of the American Indian, Heye Foundation*

as songs by John Lomax, who was born in Goodman, helped preserve Mississippi folk culture for future generations. Two "primitive" artists, Theora Hamblett of Oxford and Ethel Mohamed of Belzoni, have added to the body of Mississippi culture that has been admired in museums throughout the nation. Born a mile west of Paris, Mississippi, in 1895, Hamblett was primarily a painter, her work often visionary in content. Mohamed, born in 1906 in Fame, Mississippi, concentrated on stitchery. Her style, which features a flair for color, was greatly influenced by family and community traditions and her own memories.

Popular culture, unlike folk culture, tends to be "manufactured" for mass tastes. A prime example, however, of the interaction of folk and popular culture is the career of Elvis Presley. Born in Tupelo, Presley, who openly acknowledged his debt to the gospel and blues traditions, began his musical career

Left: *The first pilgrimage in the state was founded in 1932 in Natchez. Today Columbus, Holly Springs, Vicksburg, Woodville, Lawrence County, and other areas hold annual pilgrimages to open their historic homes and buildings to the public. Courtesy, Mississippi Department of Archives and History*

Above: *Tammy Wynette; born Virginia Wynette Pugh in Itawamba County, was one of America's leading country music singers and composers. She sold more than thirty million records and won two Grammy Awards. Courtesy, Public Broadcasting System*

Top, left: *Sam Chatmon of Hollandale was a favorite performer at the Delta Blues Festival. The son of a popular fiddler in Bolton, Chatmon joined his family's string band at the age of six. He was a member of the "Mississippi Sheiks" in the 1930s and toured with his brother as the guitarist and vocalist for the "Chatmon Brothers." Courtesy, Mississippi Educational Television*

Top, right: *B.B. King, born Riley B. King on a plantation near Itta Bena, has dominated the blues scene for more than forty years. He started his career at Radio WGRM in Greenwood in the late 1950s. Today he is the most successful blues performer in the world, having earned more awards and sold more blues and rhythm and blues recordings than any other performer. Photo by Kevin Westenberg. Courtesy, Lieberman Management LLC*

Above: *Leontyne Price was born in Laurel in 1927, the daughter of Kate and James Price, who gave her a musical start with piano lessons. A long-time member of her church choir, at age seventeen she decided to be a music teacher. She graduated from Ohio's Central State College and was awarded a scholarship to the Julliard School of Music. Price is pictured above in her role of Leonora in* Il Trovatore *at the Metropolitan Opera. Courtesy, Metropolitan Opera Association*

Elvis Presley was born in 1935 in this house in Tupelo. Successfully blending the country and black music that formed his background, he became the most important rock and roll singer of his time. By his death in 1977 he had produced more than one hundred single records that made the top of the charts in the music industry, and his influence is strongly evidenced in contemporary music. Courtesy, Mississippi Department of Economic Development

as a country music artist. In the late 1950s and in the 1960s Presley successfully integrated these Southern music traditions, popularized the sound, and became known as "the King of Rock and Roll."

Mississippians have also had a major impact on classical music. William Grant Still, born in 1895 on a plantation near Woodville, was one of the earliest black composers of classical music. He left home at the age of twenty to work with W.C. Handy in Memphis. Still's *Afro-American Symphony* (1931) was the first major piece by a black composer to be accepted by the American musical establishment. In 1938 he wrote an opera, *Troubled Island,* for which poet Langston Hughes wrote the libretto. This opera was so far ahead of prevalent social attitudes toward race that it was not performed until 1949. Other compositions by Still include *Song of a New Race, From the Delta* and another opera, *Lennox Avenue.*

Lehman Engel, born and reared in Jackson, became one of the great composers and writers of Broadway music. He composed the incidental music for Broadway productions of *Hamlet* and *Macbeth,* and wrote the score for the original Broadway production of *A Streetcar Named Desire.* In addition to these and other arrangements, Engel wrote several books on the technique of the musical theater.

Leontyne Price, who was born in Laurel in 1927 and grew up in the state, is Mississippi's great contribution to opera. She made her Metropolitan Opera debut in 1961 as Leonora in *Il Trovatore,* receiving a record forty-two-minute standing ovation. Since then Price has enjoyed fame as one of America's premier prima donnas, and has made major tours throughout Europe and around the world. Her performance in *Antony and Cleopatra* opened the Metropolitan Opera House when it moved to the Lincoln Center in 1966. She performed in *Aida* many times—always to a packed house—and returned to that role in 1985 to mark her retirement from opera. Since that time she has toured and devoted time to teaching the next generation of prima donnas.

Milton Babbitt, born in Philadelphia, Pennsylvania, in 1916, spent most of his childhood in Jackson, where he graduated from Central High School in 1931. He began composing at the age of five. Since his father was a mathematician, Babbitt tended to combine his interests in music and mathematics. He went to New York University, where he graduated in 1935. He was greatly influenced by Roger Sessions during the next few years. Babbitt joined the music faculty at Princeton in 1938 and in 1942 received one of its first master of fine arts degrees. Meanwhile, he had written *Music for the Mass* in 1941, for which he received the Bearns Prize. His pathfinding study *The Function of Set Structure in the Twelve-Tone System* was published in 1946. In 1958 he again became a pioneer when he began working with electronic music, publishing *Composition for Synthesizer.*

Mississippi has produced notable artists since the turn of the century. A tradition of excellence in art pottery was begun by George Ohr, who with his sons produced some of the finest pottery at the turn of the century from their Biloxi shop. That tradition was continued at the Shearwater Pottery in Ocean Springs, where in the 1920s Peter Anderson created everything from playful figures of coastal creatures to fine ceramic dinnerware. Peter Anderson, from time to time, employed his brother Walter in his pottery business. Walter Anderson, however, was destined to become famous for his watercolors. Trained at the Philadelphia Art Institute, Anderson returned to the Gulf Coast to pursue his life work of creating: paintings in both oil and watercolor, sculpture, ceramics, and furniture. Anderson painted a mural on the interior walls of the Ocean Springs Civic Center as a WPA project and completed another for the Ocean Springs High School. He refused in both cases to accept payment, arguing that it was the responsibility of an artist to give something back to his society. He is best remembered for his depictions of animal life on Horn Island, where he often stayed for weeks writing in his log book and sketching for his next watercolor project.

The Mississippi art scene was transformed after World War II. Art museums appeared throughout the state and associations offered marketing networks for artists. Karl and Mildred Wolfe began this cooperative concept with the art colony that was established at Allison's Wells, north of Canton in Madison County in 1948. Until it burned in the mid-1960s, Allison's Wells provided a place for

artists to come together and share their craft. Mississippi has continued to produce nationally known visual artists. Photographers William Eggleston and Dan Guravich are native Mississippians. Artists Bill Dunlap, Sam Gilliam, Wyatt Waters and Richard Barthe also hail from Mississippi.

Mississippi's contribution to American literature is great and diverse and rightly begins with a discussion of William Faulkner and Eudora Welty. William Faulkner is recognized as one of America's finest novelists—arguably the greatest. To many observers, Faulkner's accomplishment is especially noteworthy when one considers that he spent most of his life on his "little postage stamp" of Oxford and Lafayette County. Therein, however, lies Faulkner's greatness: the ability to universalize from the particular existence of the characters he created to inhabit his mythical Yoknapatawpha County and its county seat, Jefferson.

The most productive period of Faulkner's career was the late 1920s and 1930s. In rapid succession, the following appeared: *Sartoris* (1929); *The Sound and the Fury* (1929); *As I Lay Dying* (1930); *Light in August* (1932) and *Absalom, Absalom!* (1936). The Nobel Prize for Literature was awarded to William Faulkner in 1950; he received Pulitzer Prizes for his last two novels, *A Fable* (1954) and *The Reivers* (1962).

When Faulkner received the Nobel Prize in 1950, it was an honor long overdue. He had been ignored by many in the scholarly community until Malcolm Cowley edited *The Portable Faulkner* in 1946, allowing a wider public to see the range of this Southern genius. Faulkner's novels, long out of print, then went into new editions. He took the belated recognition with good grace. In his acceptance speech for the Nobel Prize, which has become a classic, he took the opportunity to tell his listeners his view of the human condition. Though some of his characters seemed to be beyond any redemption, Faulkner proved himself to be an optimist, telling his audience that he was confident that man has "a spirit capable of compassion and sacrifice and endurance."

Today an annual Yoknapatawpha Conference is held in his native town of Oxford, where scholars from all over the world gather to read papers and visit Rowan Oak, Faulkner's home, now designated a National Historic Landmark.

As Faulkner was writing in Oxford, other Mississippi authors were at work across the state. Eudora Welty was one of Mississippi's most enduring and endearing authors. Born in Jackson in 1909, she began her career in the 1930s and has remained in Mississippi—as did Faulkner—as a living symbol to her fellow citizens and a national literary figure. Welty attended Mississippi State College for Women before going to Wisconsin for her undergraduate degree. She then attended the Columbia University School of Business for a year. Returning to Mississippi in the midst of the Great Depression, she abandoned plans for a career in advertising and began writing articles on various communities for the WPA. Many of her observations appear in her fiction, and through the lens of her camera were preserved some of the best documentary images of Depression-era Mississippi.

In 1941, after having a number of her stories accepted for publication by magazines, Welty's first collection, *A Curtain of Green,* appeared. This work was followed by another collection, *The Wide Net,* in 1943. *The Golden Apples,* which appeared in 1949, solidified Welty's reputation as a short story writer. In honor of her accomplishments, Welty three times received O. Henry Memorial prizes. Meanwhile, she

Artist William Dunlap was born in Tupelo and educated at Mississippi College and the University of Mississippi. He won national acclaim with his monumental one-man show at the Corcoran Gallery in 1987. His work features the landscapes and people of Mississippi as well as his adopted Virginia and North Carolina. Courtesy, Jack Kotz

Shown in this self-portrait is Walter Anderson, Mississippi's most outstanding artist. Working primarily in Ocean Springs and on Horn Island, he produced watercolors, oils, pen-and-ink drawings, ceramic designs, large block prints, and murals, most depicting the natural world of Mississippi's Gulf Coast. Courtesy, Mrs. Walter Anderson

One of Mississippi's finest artists was Kate Freeman Clark of Holly Springs. A student of William Merritt Chase, she exhibited in New York City under the name Freeman Clark. When she moved back to Holly Springs in 1922, she abruptly quit painting, and at her death in 1957 she bequeathed to Holly Springs her home and several hundred canvases and sketches from her New York years. Courtesy, Marshall County Historical Society

Above: *Nobel Prize winner William Faulkner, born in 1897 in New Albany, lived most of his life in Oxford. He made the red clay land of north Mississippi, his fictional Yoknapatawpha County, familiar throughout the world. Since his death in 1962 his work has become increasingly valued. Courtesy, Jack Cofield Collection, Special Collections, University of Mississippi Libraries*

Above, right: *Eudora Welty was one of the major American writers of the twentieth century. Welty's use of comedy, her ear for realistic dialogue and dialect, and her sense of place complement her tragic vision, her lyrical descriptions, and her development of universal themes. Born in Jackson in 1909, she continued to live and work there until her death in 2001. Among her numerous honors and awards was the Pulitzer Prize in 1973 for* The Optimist's Daughter. *Courtesy, Random House, New York City*

Below, left to right: *Ellen Douglass, photo by Susie James; Stark Young, courtesy University Press of Mississippi; Elizabeth Spencer, photo by Chrissy Wilson; Ellen Gilchrist, photo by Thomas Victor; Richard Wright, courtesy, University Press of Mississippi; Margaret Walker, courtesy, Mississippi Department of Archives and History; Tennessee Williams, courtesy, International Creative Management; Barry Hannah, photo by Hunter Cole; Richard Ford, photo by Chrissy Wilson; Willie Morris, courtesy, Mississippi Educational Television*

wrote two novels, *The Robber Bridegroom* (1942) and *Delta Wedding* (1946). In 1954 she published the brief, lighthearted *The Ponder Heart*. In 1970 Welty published *Losing Battles*, set in the northeastern Mississippi hill country. She followed that fine effort with *The Optimist's Daughter* (1972), which won a Pulitzer Prize.

As Welty's career progressed, the accolades continued. She received two Guggenheim fellowships. In 1955 she was honored with the William Dean Howells Medal of the American Academy of Arts and Letters for "the most distinguished work of American fiction" produced in the past five years. In 1983 Harvard University invited her to deliver the William E. Massey, Sr. Lectures. These lectures became *One Writer's Beginnings*, an autobiographical account of growing up in a small state capital, which was a national best-seller.

A community of writers also emerged in Greenville, possibly under the influence of poet and writer William Alexander Percy, born there in 1885. He graduated from the University of the South (Sewanee) and the Harvard Law School. He made little use of his law degree, concentrating more on his plantation and his poetry. Percy wrote four volumes of poetry during his lifetime: *In April Once* (1920); *Sappho in Levkas and other Poems* (1924);

Enzio's Kingdom and Other Poems (1924); and *Selected Poems* (1930). Percy may have seen himself as a poet, but the literary world has most honored him for his autobiography, *Lanterns on the Levee*, and for creating a milieu in Greenville that encouraged young creative artists.

The writer most influenced by William A. Percy, at least on a personal level, was novelist Walker Percy. Although not a native Mississippian, Walker Percy spent his formative teenage years in Greenville in the home of his cousin, William A. Percy, who adopted him after the death of his parents. Walker Percy was born in 1916 in Birmingham, Alabama. He graduated from the University of North Carolina in 1937 and Columbia University Medical School in 1941. After contracting tuberculosis, he gave up his medical career and turned to writing. Percy's scientific interest and analytic mind, possibly sharpened by his medical training, are evident in his novels. On the other hand, his Catholic humanism makes him suspicious of the "accomplishments" of the scientific world. His first novel, *The Moviegoer* (1961), won the National Book Award. Other novels by Percy include *The Last Gentleman* (1966); *Love in the Ruins* (1971); *The Message in the Bottle* (1975); *Lancelot* (1977); *The Second Coming* (1980); and *The Thanatos Syndrome* (1987). One critic of his body of work stated, "Percy epitomizes the new Southern writer, both a descendant of the past and a man of the present."

Another member of the literary circle of Greenville is Charles Bell. Born in 1916, Bell, a youthful protege of William A. Percy, has been published in magazines ranging from *Ladies' Home Journal* to *Atlantic Monthly*. He has written several volumes of poetry, including *Songs for a New America* (1953) and *Delta Return* (1956).

A third member of the Greenville writers group born in 1916 was Shelby Foote, who is well-respected for both his fictional and historical work. During his early writing career, Foote concentrated on fiction, with no thought of writing history. His first novel was *Tournament* (1949). His novel *Shiloh*, which was published in 1952, led an editor to encourage him to write a one-volume treatment of the Civil War. Three volumes—and twenty years later—*The Civil War: A Narrative* was completed

(1958; 1963; 1974). During the 1950s, while writing *Civil War,* Foote received three Guggenheim fellowships. One critic said of *Civil War:* "It is a remarkable achievement, prodigiously researched, vigorous, detailed, absorbing . . . a monumental, even-handed account of this country's tragic, fratricidal conflict." Renewed interest in Foote's historical trilogy followed the writer's appearance as the primary commentator on Ken Burns' 1990 documentary, "The Civil War." In addition to his historical works, Foote also wrote a number of other novels, including September, September (1978).

Although not a native of Greenville, Ellen Douglas (Josephine Haxton) is closely associated with that river town, for it was there that she began her writing career. She was born in Natchez in 1921. A 1942 graduate of the University of Mississippi, she moved to Greenville when she married. Her first novel, *A Family's Affairs,* which was listed by the *New York Times* as one of the five best novels published in 1961, won for her a Houghton Mifflin Fellowship. Her productive career includes the following books: *Black Cloud, White Cloud* (1963), *Apostles of Light* (1973), and *A Lifetime Burning* (1982). *Apostles of Light* was nominated for the National Book Award in 1974. Douglas received National Endowment for the Arts grants in 1976 and 1986. Her son, Brooks Haxton, a rising young poet, also received an NEA fellowship in 1987. He has published six books of poetry, including *The Lay of Eleanor and Irene* (1985) and *Dead Reckoning* (1995).

Other small Mississippi towns have also produced writers. Stark Young, born in Como in 1881, attended the University of Mississippi and later went to Columbia for his master's degree. Young, a novelist, poet, translator, and editor, is best remembered for his work with the *New Republic,* where for twenty-six years he was the theater critic. His most widely recognized novel is *So Red the Rose* (1934). Young was also involved with a group of writers known as the Fugitives, who challenged the prevailing notion that all industrial progress was good. Along with historians and other intellectuals who felt similarly, they also became known as the Nashville Agrarians and published a book in the 1930s entitled *I'll Take My Stand.*

Elizabeth Spencer, born in Carrollton in 1921, has had a long and productive career as a novelist. She was educated at Belhaven College and Vanderbilt University. For a time, Spencer worked as a reporter for the *Nashville Tennessean.* She also taught English until she became a successful novelist. Her first novel, *Fire in the Morning* (1948), was rated by the *New York Times Book Review* as one of the three best novels published that year. The 1950s were a very productive period for her: a Guggenheim Fellowship financed a two-year stay in Italy, which she used for collecting material for *The Light in the Piazza* (1960). Among her other novels are *The Voice at the Back Door* (1956), *No Place for an Angel* (1967), *Marilee* (1981), and *The Salt Line* (1984).

Ellen Gilchrist, born in Vicksburg in 1935, delayed the beginning of her writing career until she obtained her bachelor's degree from Millsaps College in 1967. Gilchrist's writing includes two collections of poetry and six novels, but she is best known for her short stories. She first gained attention with her collection, *In the Land of Dreamy Dreams* (1981). Since that time she has published eleven additional short-story collections, including *Victory Over Japan* (1984), which won the National Book Award for fiction that year. Gilchrist is known for her accurate and sympathetic presentation of the struggles of childhood and adolescence and evocations of the sights and sounds of New Orleans.

During the dark days of racial repression of the 1920s and 1930s, a major black literary voice from Mississippi arose. Richard Wright was born in 1908 into a sharecropping family on a plantation near Natchez. After his father deserted the family, Wright went to Jackson to live with relatives. He attended Jim Hill School, where he was valedictorian of his ninth-grade class. He worked at odd jobs, first in Jackson and then Memphis. He left the South for Chicago in 1927 and later signed on with the WPA's Federal Writers Project in New York. Two works that appeared during the World War II era established Wright as one of the nation's most eloquent spokesmen for the plight of black Americans. The first of these was *Native Son* (1940), the story of Bigger Thomas, a young black man confronted with the problems of life in a northern, industrial city. In 1945 Wright's autobiographical novel, *Black Boy,* appeared. Although he continued to produce significant works throughout the 1950s, Wright's affiliation for a time with the Communist party and his self-imposed exile to Paris lessened his influence in the United States until a rebirth of interest in his writings during the 1960s. Two of his books, *Eight Men* and *Lawd Today,* were published after his death.

Another black Mississippi author, raised under rather different circumstances than Richard Wright, is Margaret Walker Alexander, who was born in Birmingham, Alabama, the daughter of a minister. She received her bachelor's degree from Northwestern University in 1935 and her master's and doctoral degrees from the University of Iowa. While most of her adult life was spent as a professor at Jackson State University, she has received wide recognition as a poet. Alexander won the Yale Series for Younger Poets Award in 1942 and also received a Houghton Mifflin Literary Fellowship. Among her books of poetry are *For My People* (1942) and *October Journey* (1973). Her widest acclaim, however, came with the publication of the novel *Jubilee* (1966), which depicts the black struggle in America.

Mississippi is far from Broadway, but among the greatest of American playwrights was Mississippi native Tennessee Williams. He was born in 1911 in the rectory of his grandfather's Episcopal church in Columbus, Mississippi. Both his grandfather and Mississippi would have a lifelong influence on the writing of Williams. Especially in his early plays, during the most creative period of his career, the characters often reflect Mississippi mannerisms.

The characters in Williams' plays, burdened with guilt and fear, attempt to come to terms with their past. Ultimately, they show their innermost selves, as their masks are lowered during the course of the play. Williams' plays that best reflect his Mississippi background are *Glass Menagerie* (1945), *Summer and Smoke* (1948), *A Streetcar Named Desire* (1947), and *Cat on a Hot Tin Roof* (1954). For these last two works, he received Pulitzer Prizes; he also won three New York Drama Critics Circle awards.

Mississippi authors born during and after World War II have also made major contributions to literature. A native of Meridian, Barry Hannah spent most of his childhood in Clinton. After receiving his B.A. from Mississippi College in 1964, he embarked on a writing career. His first novel, *Geronimo Rex* (1972), gained wide acclaim. Throughout his work he presents a highly energetic style. After his next novel, *Nightwatchman* (1973), and a book of short stories, *Airships* (1978), he began a major experiment with language in *Ray* (1981), which was followed by five additional novels and two short-story collections.

Richard Ford was born in Jackson in 1944. He received a B.A. degree from Michigan State University and a M.F.A. from the University of California. *A Piece of My Heart,* Ford's first novel, published in

Beth Henley, Pulitzer Prize-winning dramatist, drew on life in the Mississippi towns of her childhood for locations in her plays, Crimes of the Heart, The Miss Firecracker Contest, *and* The Wake of Jamey Foster. *Born and raised in Jackson, Henley often visited her grandparents in Brookhaven and Hazlehurst, which are named as locales in her work. Photo by Chrissy Wilson*

1976, received critical acclaim. Ford won Guggenheim and NEA fellowships to write his second novel, *The Ultimate Good Luck* (1981). His last three novels, *The Sportswriter* (1986), *Wildlife* (1990), and *Independence Day* (1995), are all set outside the South and have secured Ford's reputation as a major American literary figure, He received the Pulitzer Prize for Literature in 1996.

Beth Henley of Jackson has continued the prize-winning tradition of Mississippi writers. After receiving her B.F.A. degree at Southern Methodist University in 1974, she embarked on a career in acting and playwriting. Her plays include *The Miss Firecracker Contest* and *The Wake of Jamey Foster. Crimes o f the Heart* won the 1981 Pulitzer Prize for drama and other awards. Henley sets her plays in Mississippi locales; *Crimes of the Heart* is set in Hazlehurst, Mississippi. Henley probes deeply into the human condition, especially as manifested in Southern family relationships, and finds humor as well as enlightenment.

Two historians from Mississippi have received the Pulitzer Prize for their biographical work. The late Dumas Malone, born in 1882 in Coldwater, received his B.A. at Emory University and his M.A. and Ph.D. from Columbia University, where he continued his academic career and pursued a lifelong passion for and commitment to his multi-volume biography of Thomas Jefferson. In 1962 he became biographer in residence at the University of Virginia. When the fifth volume, *Jefferson and His Time: Jefferson the President, Second Term, 1805-1809,* appeared in 1974, Malone was awarded the Pulitzer Prize. Technically the prize was for that particular volume, but it also served to recognize a life of devoted scholarship. Malone completed his biography in 1981 with the publication of *Jefferson and His Time: The Sage of Monticello.*

David Donald is the other Mississippi historian who has won the Pulitzer Prize. Donald, born in Goodman in 1920, is a graduate of Holmes Junior College and Millsaps College. He received his doctorate from the University of Illinois. After teaching for twenty years at Columbia and Johns Hopkins, Donald joined the Harvard faculty in 1973. He received the Pulitzer Prize for the first volume of his biography of Charles Sumner, *Charles Sumner and the Coming of the Civil War* (1961). Among his other significant works are the second volume of the biography, *Charles Sumner and the Rights of Man* (1970), and *Look Homeward: A Life of Thomas Wolfe* (1987).

Mississippians have excelled in the world of journalism, from county-seat weeklies to the *New York Times.* In the 1930s Hodding Carter, Jr., and his wife Betty came to Greenville from Louisiana to establish one of the most prominent newspapers in the state, the *Delta Democrat-Times.* Carter's fearless editorials won a Pulitzer Prize in 1946. He was hardly a liberal; nonetheless, he spoke for fair treatment of blacks and moderation in racial matters.

Turner Catledge, a contemporary of Carter, left the hills of eastern Mississippi for New York. By the 1960s he was executive editor of the *New York Times.* He, more than any other national newsman, made sure that the civil rights movement received full, accurate, and fair coverage. When Andrew Goodman, James Chaney, and Michael Schwerner were murdered near his native Philadelphia in 1964, Catledge turned the focus of national publicity on local law enforcement officials and held them accountable.

During the 1960s there were many white Mississippians who sought to be voices of moderation. Coming to the fore were Oliver Emmerich of the *McComb Enterprise-Journal* and Hazel Brannon Smith of the *Lexington Advertiser.* For her efforts in Holmes County during a most difficult time, Smith won a Pulitzer Prize in 1964.

In that special genre of literature and of history, autobiography, twentieth-century Mississippians have given us insights from a number of perspectives. In addition to Richard Wright's *Black Boy,* which told of his boyhood and transitions from Mississippi to the North, four autobiographies are especially noteworthy.

William Alexander Percy will always be remembered for *Lanterns on the Levee: Recollections of a Planter's Son* (1941). In a poetic style that is almost lyrical at times, Percy paints a picture of turn-of-the-century Mississippi from the perspective of the planter class. From descriptions of sharecropping to an account of his father's campaigns for the United States Senate against Vardaman, this book is a clear portrayal of the Delta aristocracy.

Writing from the other end of the social spectrum is Anne Moody, a black woman who grew up in southwest Mississippi during the 1950s. During her years at Tougaloo College, she was deeply involved in the civil rights movement. Much of *Coming of Age in Mississippi* (1968) reflects her frustration with the failure of America to keep the movement alive. In spite of her anger—or maybe because of it—the reader gains valuable insights into what it was like to grow up poor and black in the Mississippi of that era.

For the most part, little attention has been given by scholars to the other underprivileged segment of the Mississippi poor, low-income whites. In his autobiographical writing, Will D. Campbell has assisted us in gaining a better understanding of that significant portion of Mississippi's population. In *Brother to a Dragonfly* (1977), Campbell discusses growing up during the 1930s in Amite County. He also takes us into the civil rights movement during the 1950s and early 1960s, when he turned his ministry toward America's "hidden minority," poor whites. This unique personal odyssey touches on so many aspects of Mississippi society from the 1930s onward that it is like a roadmap marking the significant events in the state during that period.

Representing those who have sought opportu-

Toward Home (1967), an autobiography of a Mississippian in New York, expressing his mixed feelings toward his native state and region. In 1980, Morris returned to Mississippi, living and writing there until his death in 1999.

Since World War II, much of Mississippi's popular culture has been reflected in the citizens' love of athletics. Football dominates Mississippi's spectator sports scene, as fans avidly follow both high school football and their favorite college teams. The wealth of gridiron talent within the state has had an impact on professional football. The National Football League's all-time rushing leader is Walter Payton of Columbia, who played at Jackson State University; the league's all-time pass receiving leader is Jerry Rice of Crawford, who played his college ball at Mississippi Valley State University; and the league's only three-time Most Valuable Player, Brett Favre of Kiln, is a former University of Southern Mississippi quarterback.

Mississippians have also found success in television and film. Oprah Winfrey, a native of Kosciusko, is both an accomplished actor and one of the most popular nationally-syndicated talk show hosts in the history of television. Jim Henson, creator of the Muppets and the characters on the popular children's television show, *Sesame Street,* spent his early years growing up in Leland. He named his best-known puppet creation, Kermit the Frog, after a childhood friend in Mississippi.

Over the last century, Mississippians have excelled in many American art forms. That talent has ranged from the blues of the Delta to the country music of the hills. Mississippi musicians have performed from Parchman prison in Sunflower County to the New York Metropolitan Opera House. Mississippi writers have won every major literary award.

As young people grow up in a state that appreciates and rewards its artists, Mississippi will

continue to be a leader in the production of the one product that will not diminish in its importance and relevance to human beings: its art. Mississippi artists celebrate to the rest of the nation and to the world those values of the state they revere: its rich history, its dramatic landscape, and its diverse people.

Hugh White combined Mississippi's penchant for beauty queens with his BAWI program to launch a major public relations effort to support the plan. A caravan of five Mississippi floats were driven to the 1938 national American Legion Convention in Los Angeles to dramatize Mississippi to the nation. Elaine Russell of Vicksburg accompanied the caravan as Gov. White's personal representative. Courtesy, Mississippi Department of Archives and History

CHRONICLES OF LEADERSHIP

Ever since its entry into the Union in 1817, Mississippi, the Magnolia State, has been a "nativist" state while continually open to new people, crops, industries, and economic advances. For more than two centuries prior to statehood, the indigenous Indian population interacted with first the Spanish and then the French explorers. The 1699 settlement of the French on the east shore of Biloxi Bay marked the first permanent settlement of the entire Mississippi Valley.

Throughout the eighteenth century the French (from their outpost at Natchez), the British (through their British West Florida possessions), and the Spanish (who retained control of Natchez briefly in the 1780s) left their respective imprints on what is today Mississippi. The Territorial Period, 1798-1817, introduced the influence of the young American nation.

The state's adoption of an improved Mexican variety of cotton in the 1820s opened up a new era of nativism—dependence on cotton as a staple crop. The cheap land, high prices, and easy credit associated with cotton at that time helped foster increased immigration, speculation, and slave labor during the next decade. Despite the Panic of 1837 the Cotton Kingdom entered its golden age in the 1850s, aided by the building of levees and draining of swamplands along the Mississippi and Yazoo rivers in the Delta.

The Civil War years and their aftermath brought economic chaos. Some 78,000 Mississippians entered Confederate service; more than 59,000 of them were dead or wounded by war's end. During Reconstruction the state turned again to cotton as a staple, but with massive unemployment, little capital, and an unskilled work force, the old antebellum plantation and small, independent farms were replaced by the sharecropper/ tenant system.

In the 1880s a new resource was exploited—timber. Northern industrialists expanded railroad spurs into the state, establishing Mississippi as the third-largest timber-producing state in the nation for the 1904-1915 period. Unfortunately, these virgin forests were virtually stripped by the 1920s, leaving in their wake erosion-ridden cutover areas.

Most political leaders in the early twentieth century tended to exhibit an anti-industrial bias. A distinct shift came with Governor Martin Sennett Conner's (1932-1936) sound fiscal reform of state government and public education. Governor Hugh Lawson White, who followed Conner, offered the progressive Balance Agriculture With Industry program, which allowed local governments to issue public bonds to secure sites and erect industrial buildings for private enterprise.

Today the state's economy is more balanced. Mississippi still boasts numerous agriculture-related enterprises, including poultry, timber, cattle, soybeans, sweet potatoes, and pecans. The natural gas and oil industries are also important, but the state also relies on a more urban, business, and industrial-oriented culture, as well as tourism, to complement her agricultural heritage.

From the defense contract projects at the Ingalls Ship-building facility on the Gulf Coast to the interregional Mississippi ports along the Tennessee-Tombigbee Waterway in northeast Mississippi, the economy is continually undergoing changes. The firms represented on the following pages are part of this progress. They illustrate the variety of ways in which businesses, learning institutions and individuals have contributed to Mississippi growth and development.

BELLSOUTH-MISSISSIPPI

BellSouth is both a pioneer and a modern-day leader in the telecommunications industry. Headquartered in Atlanta, BellSouth operates in nine states, including Mississippi, North Carolina, South Carolina, Georgia, Kentucky, Louisiana, Florida, Alabama and Tennessee .

BellSouth-Mississippi is based in Jackson and services more than 1.3 million access lines throughout the state. Once primarily known as the company behind the phone on the kitchen wall, BellSouth has evolved into a technology company that provides a full array of broadband data and e-commerce solutions to business customers, including Web hosting and other Internet services. In the residential market, BellSouth offers Digital Subscriber Line (DSL) high-speed Internet access, advanced voice features and other services. BellSouth also offers business and residential customers a variety of calling plans for nationwide and international long-distance service. Whether business or residential, BellSouth has been consistently recognized for its high customer satisfaction.

A Technological Leader. Ever since Jackson's first telephone was installed in the mayor's office in 1882, the company that would eventually be known as BellSouth has worked to provide a reliable communications system for every residence and business in Mississippi. BellSouth is committed to maintaining its position as a leader in communications, continually bringing new technologies and opportunities to its customers.

BellSouth's state-of-the-art network is second to none. The company has invested approximately $3 billion in Mississippi's telecommunications infrastructure, including fiber optics, digital connectivity, and Integrated Services Digital Network (ISDN) lines.

Fiber-optic cables allow fast, error-free transmission of high-tech signals. Made of hair-thin glass

filaments, fiber optics transmit large amounts of data—including voice, video and computer signals—at the speed of light. Mississippi has more than 92,000 miles of fiber-optic cable in place, with more being put into the ground every day.

BellSouth was among the first to offer ISDN, the technology that allows the integration of voice and data signals over a single telephone line. ISDN makes videoconferencing, PC-to-PC file transfer, and long-distance medical imaging possible.

Recent technological innovations include SmartRing, Zip-Connect and a high-speed broadband network. SmartRing is a rerouting service that provides an alternate path when the primary route is

interrupted by broken or damaged cable. This innovative network design utilizes fiber optics facilities to reduce and often eliminate service interruptions.

ZipConnect allows callers to dial a single number for a multilocation business and become automatically connected to the office nearest the caller's zip code. This technology saves time that would otherwise be spent searching through multiple listings in a telephone book.

BellSouth's sophisticated Asynchronous Transfer Mode-Synchronous Optical Network Transmission (ATM-SONET) high-speed broadband network offers business customers two-way interactive video services for distance learning, videoconferencing and high-resolution medical imaging. The

South as a leader among the largest telephone companies in customer satisfaction.

In addition to superior customer service, BellSouth-Mississippi stresses community involvement. The company supports a number of charitable causes and donates its employees' time and expertise to telecommunications and education-related projects, including wiring Mississippi schools for Internet access, painting playground maps of the United States at elementary schools, and providing Web-based, curriculum-enhancing programs. BellSouth Pioneers, the corporate volunteer organization for Bell-South, consistently donates more than 400,000 hours of community service across the state each year.

"Communication services are an integral part of people's lives at home and at work," said John McCullouch, BellSouth-Mississippi president. "BellSouth is proud to operate the most reliable network available at competitive rates. We think of ourselves as *the* communications provider in Mississippi."

broadband service is an integral part of the Mississippi Information Superhighway, which is designed to connect schools, universities, community colleges, hospitals and other public sites.

Since 2000, BellSouth has rapidly expanded the number of Mississippi markets where the company's high-speed DSL service, BellSouth FastAccess® Internet Service, is available. With FastAccess, customers can access the Internet at lightning-fast speeds. FastAccess allows business and residential customers to maximize their Internet usage with faster downloads, real-time interactive multimedia and voice-on-demand. This DSL service provides a dedicated line that is on 24 hours a day, seven days a week—with no dial-up wait time or busy signals.

Customer-Friendly Solutions. The first U.S. telephone company to establish 24-hour customer service, BellSouth is customer focused, creating products and services that make advanced communications easy to use. National studies conducted by J. D. Power and Associates continually rank Bell-

ALCORN STATE UNIVERSITY

Alcorn State University (ASU) was founded in 1871 as the first land-grant institution for African Americans in the United States under the Federal Morrill Act. Alcorn State University was created as a "seminary of learning" and was originally named Alcorn University of Mississippi by the state legislature in honor of Governor James L. Alcorn for his recommendation that the university be established.

Alcorn has a rich and illustrious history. It is located on the original site of Oakland College, which was a Presbyterian school for the education of white males, founded in 1830. Oakland College closed its doors at the beginning of the Civil War so that its students might answer the "call to arms." Upon failing to reopen after the war, the state purchased the college for the education of its African-American citizens. The Honorable Hiram R. Revels, the first African American to serve in the United States Senate, resigned his seat in the U.S. Senate in 1871 to become the first president of the newly established institution.

The university was given $50,000 per year for 10 years (the same as

Center for Academic Excellence.

Mathematics and Science Complex.

the University of Mississippi) when it first opened its doors as a state institution. Alcorn State University also received three-fifths of the proceeds from the sale of agricultural scrip under the provisions of the Morrill Land-Grant Act of 1862. According to the Alcorn State University catalogue of 1872, "the fund amounted to $189,000, three-fifths of which, or $113,400, became the property of Alcorn University, the income from which is to be devoted to the agricultural and mechanical department of the institution."

Alcorn State University's land-grant status was reaffirmed in 1890, when the state of Mississippi accepted provisions of the 1890 Morrill Act specifically providing for the establishment of separate land-grant institutions of higher education. Hence, although created under the 1862 Morrill Act, Alcorn State University is often referred to as an 1890 land-grant institution. Thus, from its beginning, Alcorn State University has been one of Mississippi's land-grant institutions.

In 1878, the Mississippi State Legislature changed the name of the institution to Alcorn Agricultural and Mechanical College. Recognizing the tremendous growth and impact of the institution during its more than one-century existence, the Mississippi State Legislature changed the name of the institution to Alcorn State University in 1974.

Today, Alcorn State University is a diverse equal opportunity institution. It admits students without regard to age, race, creed, color, national origin, religion, gender or physical disability. Its student body and faculty are literally from all over the world.

Alcorn State University is located

Historic Oakland Memorial Chapel, circa 1830.

near Lorman, Mississippi, 80 miles southwest of the capital city, Jackson, and 35 miles north of Natchez, Mississippi. The campus rests on 1700 acres of land, lending itself to a serene learning environment and unique opportunities for outdoor recreation. Scattered among the university's buildings are giant moss-draped trees and scenic lakes. The 172-year-old Oakland Memorial Chapel, the surviving landmark of the original Oakland College, has been designated a national historic site and is one of the leading tourist attractions in southwest Mississippi.

Oakland Memorial Chapel, like the other four original buildings remaining from Oakland College, was built in 1830 by slaves of the Presbyterian founding fathers. The beautiful wrought-iron stairs leading up to the chapel came from Windsor Castle, once a splendid antebellum home nearby, which was destroyed by fire in 1890. The

six cast-iron baluster panels are also from Windsor. Originally, the chapel was used for a prayer hall, classrooms, study rooms and laboratories.

After more than one-and-a-half centuries, the building remains almost unchanged and serves as a campus symbol of dignity. This beautiful structure of Greek revival architecture offers a sanctuary for quiet meditation and currently houses an art gallery on the ground level.

Alcorn State University is the epicenter for higher education in southwest Mississippi and has been recognized by the United States Department of Agriculture as a Center of Excellence for Rural Development. Alcorn's Master of Business Administration Program and School of Nursing are located in Natchez, Mississippi. Several computer science, nursing and teacher education classes are offered in Vicksburg, Mississippi.

Alcorn is affectionately known as the "Academic Resort," and is committed to academic excellence and the holistic development of the person. During the decade of the nineties, Alcorn State University consistently sustained the following national rankings: one hundred percent of the teacher education graduates passed the National Teacher Examination; one hundred percent of the nursing students who took the state licensure examination passed on both associate-degree and baccalaureate-degree levels; awarded the greatest number of master's degrees in teacher education to African Americans; number one among the nation's one hundred institutions in producing African-American graduates with agriculture business and production degrees; number six in African-American baccalaureate graduates in the biological sciences; number seven in African-American baccalaureate graduates in engineering-related technologies; number nine in African-American baccalaureate graduates in agriculture sciences; and number ten in African-American baccalaureate graduates in mathematics. These rankings are according to the U.S. Department of Education (2000 statistical report).

Alcorn State University prides itself on being a "communiversity," an institution that melds academic excellence with meaningful and effective community interaction. The university and the community are working together as true partners for the mutual benefit of both. Under the communiversity concept, Alcorn State University is engaged in a variety of activities to educate the next generation of citizens and to build communities in a changed world. Among the most successful programs is the Saturday Science Academy. The program provides a rewarding experience that is educational and motivational for the surrounding communities. Through the program, students in grades five through eight are introduced to the disciplines of chemistry, biology, physics, mathematics and computer science. Each three-hour Saturday session includes a scientific lecture and a hands-on activity. Parents participate in the various activities with their children, thus broadening the university's community impact.

Another noteworthy program is Alcorn's telemedicine project. The ASU Nursing School and the University of South Alabama, as partners, are utilizing a portable computer monitoring device called a Vital-Link to bring medical services to rural citizens. In complicated medical cases, doctors in different locations can view a patient's scans or X-rays, discuss what they see, and come to a consensus on treatment. Telemedicine brings immediate medical expertise to patients in rural areas who might be unable to travel to specialists for consultation.

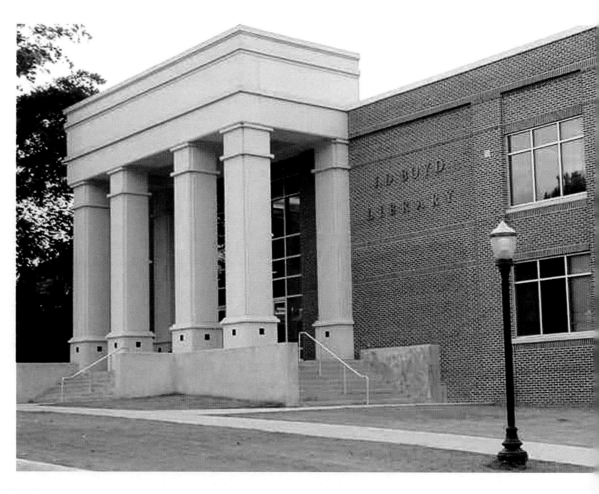

The J.D. Boyd Library.

Alcorn's unique research is focused on feeding the world and lighting the world. The ASU School of Agriculture is a national leader in nutrition and assisting Mississippi small farmers in growing and marketing alternative crops with high economic value, e.g., sweet potatoes. Through its unique fuel cell research, Alcorn generates electricity by converting animal waste and biomass into electrical energy without combustion. This technology has national and international applicability.

Alcorn's future will be as glorious as its past through its general research programs and continuing research in the life sciences, particularly biotechnology. Alcorn State University has grown from a small center of liberal arts preparation to an agricultural and mechanical college of wide recognition—and has emerged as a multifaceted university.

Lastly, the university has had sixteen presidents, all of whom have been prominent. Of special note, however, are Hiram R. Revels for his service as a U.S. Senator, Dr. Walter Washington for his twenty-five years of service, and Dr. Clinton Bristow, Jr., for his transformation of the university into the epicenter of southwest Mississippi, a communiversity, and reforming its academic agenda.

MISSISSIPPI HISTORICAL SOCIETY

The Mississippi Historical Society was organized in Jackson in November of 1858 under the leadership of B. L. C. Wailes, an Adams County planter and naturalist. The new society survived less than two years and was reorganized in 1890. By 1898 under the editorship of Franklin L. Riley, the Society had published the first of fourteen volumes of the *Publications of the Mississippi Historical Society,* a notable series that was to set the tone for other distinguished society publications during the next century.

The Society led efforts to establish the Mississippi Department of Archives and History in 1902, and the executive committee of the Society became the first board of trustees of the Department. Dunbar Rowland, the Department's first director, edited the *Centenary Series* of the *Publications* in five additional volumes between 1916 and 1925. In 1939 Department director William D. McCain founded the *Journal of Mississippi History,* a quarterly journal that has been jointly published by the Department and the Society since that date.

The Society had once again become dormant, but a reorganizational meeting in 1952 reactivated the group. Since that date the Mississippi Historical Society has held regular annual meetings at different locations around the state and has continued the Society's tradition of publishing books on the history of the state, including the 1964 reprint of J. F. H. Claiborne's *Mississippi as a Province, Territory, and State;* the 1987 popular illustrated history, *Mississippi: An Illustrated History,* by Edward N. Akin; and other books, maps, and brochures. The Society has also supported the establishment of Junior Historical Society chapters in Mississippi schools in cooperation with the University of Southern Mississippi.

The Society has initiated a major book series, the *Heritage of Missis-*

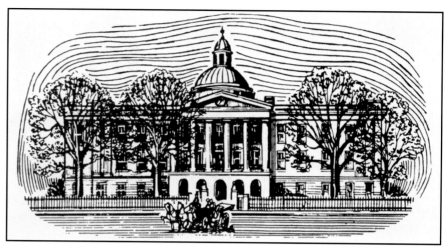

The Mississippi Historical Society was organized in the House of Representatives chamber of the Old Capitol in Jackson on November 9, 1858.

sippi series, covering the history of the state, with special focus on those subjects and periods in need of new and fresh scholarship. The books will be published over a period of about 20 years. The first volume, *Art in Mississippi, 1720-1980,* by Patti Carr Black, was published in 1998 jointly by the Society, the Mississippi Department of Archives and History, and the University Press of Mississippi. The second volume, *Religion in Mississippi,* by Randy J. Sparks, was published in 2001 for the Society by

B. L. C. Wailes, founder of the Mississippi Historical Society.

the University Press of Mississippi.

The Federation of Mississippi Historical Societies, organized by the Society in 1996 to provide support to local historical societies, sponsors popular annual workshops on topics relevant to the membership.

In 2000 the Society, with the help of the Mississippi Department of Education, corporate sponsors, and interested individuals, launched an Internet publication for students, teachers, and the general public: *Mississippi History Now* (http://mshistory.k12.ms.us). The site features illustrated essays by historians, along with useful lesson plans.

Today, the Mississippi Historical Society has approximately twelve hundred members. Members receive the quarterly *Journal of Mississippi History,* and the monthly *Mississippi History Newsletter,* which reports news and activities from the Department of Archives and History.

The annual meetings of the Society feature distinguished speakers, tours of historic sites, and social events. Awards are presented to scholars, lay historians, teachers, and others who have made outstanding contributions to the study of Mississippi history.

In short, the Mississippi Historical Society is an active group of people who share a common interest in the history of a fascinating state.

BALCH & BINGHAM LLP

Balch & Bingham LLP is a full-service firm that strives to be a proactive partner in its clients' businesses rather than a reactive legal adviser. The firm's attorneys, numbering over 180, as well as its support staff, realize that today's consumer of legal service needs more than just outstanding legal results. Clients expect and deserve outstanding service as well, including prompt responses and efficient and cost-effective legal services delivered with courtesy. The firm's individual attorneys strive to meet these expectations and promote this policy collectively.

The founder of Balch & Bingham LLP, William Logan Martin, joined his brother in opening a law practice in Montgomery before serving as the State's Attorney General and as Judge of the 15th Judicial Circuit. In 1922, he moved to Birmingham and established the law firm that is today Balch & Bingham LLP. The tradition of integrity and unparalleled service to its clients, which Judge Martin infused into the law firm he established over 80 years ago, continues today at Balch & Bingham LLP.

Balch & Bingham LLP's office in Gulfport began as Eaton and Cottrell, P.A. Since its beginning,

Balch & Bingham LLP's Gulfport office.

Eaton and Cottrell has been a presence in the civic and business affairs of the Gulf Coast. It has provided leadership in all aspects of community life. Barney Eaton, Sr., founding partner of Eaton and Cottrell, came to the Coast in 1909 as legal counsel to the Gulf and Ship Island Railroad Company, then formed the law firm in 1932. In addition to his duties as general counsel for the railroad and his active law practice, Barney Eaton, Sr., also served as the first president of Mississippi Power Company, from 1924 until his death in 1944. David Cottrell, from West Point, Mississippi, joined James Eaton in

the practice of law after the death of his father, Barney Eaton, Sr., thereby forming Eaton and Cottrell. James Eaton and David Cottrell remained active members of the firm until their deaths in 1994 and 1995, respectively.

In January 2001, Balch & Bingham LLP and Eaton and Cottrell merged to form the Gulfport and Jackson offices of Balch & Bingham LLP, and currently maintain offices in Birmingham, Huntsville and Montgomery Alabama—and Washington D.C. From these centers, Balch & Bingham LLP attorneys serve a varied and diverse range of clients throughout the U.S. and abroad. Businesses and individuals from the private and public sector—including profit and non-profit corporations; limited liability companies; federal, state and local governments; and quasi-governmental entities—have turned to Balch & Bingham LLP for their experience and service-oriented philosophy. Balch & Bingham LLP is known for its deep involvement with the various industries it serves. The firm is active in writing and lobbying for key legislation and actively participating in trade associations. The firm's attorneys view

Balch & Bingham LLP library.

their role as counselors who not only assist clients in times of crisis, but also play significant roles in a planning and preventative capacity to help them avoid potential legal problems. The firm provides newsletters, updates, and seminars to keep clients apprised of changes in law that could affect their businesses, their industries, and their legal well-being. Periodic reviews soliciting client feedback assist the firm's attorneys in monitoring their client's level of satisfaction with the service they receive.

The firm's commitment to serving its clients also extends to serving the communities in which Balch & Bingham LLP maintains offices. Attorneys and staff members are involved in a broad range

Balch & Bingham LLP's Gulfport office atrium.

of community projects individually and as a firm. Those projects range from serving meals at area homeless shelters to serving on the boards of directors for many non-

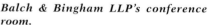

Balch & Bingham LLP's conference room.

profit and charitable organizations.

In 1991, Balch & Bingham LLP joined Samford University's Cumberland School of Law in sponsoring an Explorer post through the Boy Scouts of America. The firm continues this program today, providing scholarship information pertaining to a career in the legal profession by the Boy Scouts, for inclusion in its master scholarship database.

From the earliest days, the Gulfport office has contributed to the growth, prosperity and the quality of life on the Mississippi Gulf Coast. Today, the firm provides a broad range of services to commercial clients in many fields. Besides traditional professional services in litigation and commercial transactions, the firm also represents clients in environmental, international commerce, gaming, and labor matters. The firm's locations in Gulfport and Jackson allow them to provide legal services anywhere along the Mississippi Gulf Coast and throughout the state.

No representation is made that the quality of legal services to be performed is greater than the quality of legal services performed by other lawyers.

DELTA STATE UNIVERSITY

Located on a picturesque campus in the heart of the Mississippi Delta, Delta State University is an active and integral part of the community and region. Known for its superb teaching, exciting and award-winning athletics, and effective administration, this unique institution provides an educational environment in which students can learn, discover, create, and grow in service to humanity.

Starting as a Teachers College, Delta State now offers a broad range of programs through its Colleges of Arts and Sciences, Business and Education, and the Schools of Nursing and Graduate Studies, including the educational specialist degree and doctor of education degree. It has the only commercial aviation program in the state offering both bachelor's and master's degrees, a state-of-the-art aquatic center, and the state's only swimming and diving program.

Bordered on the west by the Mississippi River and located within the boundaries of an 18-county area of northwest Mississippi, the Mississippi Delta has come to represent much of what people love about America. Known worldwide for its richness of cultural expression, Delta music, literature, art, and

The entrance to the University is lined with majestic oak trees planted by President Kethley.

Students have benefited from a Delta State University education since 1924.

food all send a message as to the area's special sense of place.

The Delta was mostly virgin wilderness and swamp at the turn of the 20th century, cleared for cotton through the 1930s, dominated by politically powerful gentleman planters, peopled by African-American sharecroppers, Italian immigrants, Chinese, Lebanese, and Jewish merchants. It is home of the Blues, Gospel, soul food, and the civil rights struggles of the 1950s and 1960s. It was home to Tennessee Williams, Eudora Welty, Clifton Taulbert, Shelby Foote, and Hodding Carter. It is where Teddy Roosevelt saved the original "Teddy Bear," and the area that inspired the blues renderings of Charlie Patton, Robert Johnson, Muddy Waters, John Lee Hooker, and B. B. King.

It was in the early 1920s that a few leading citizens proposed a need for a college in this, the richest agricultural region of Mississippi. At that time Bolivar County was one of the most populated and wealthiest counties in the state, and its leaders wished to see it progress educationally and culturally, as well as economically.

In 1924, the legislature passed Senate Bill No. 236, entitled "An Act to Create and Maintain Delta State Teachers College." Bolivar County residents offered to provide the Bolivar County Agricultural High School plant of three two-story buildings and 120 acres to house the college. Impressed by this offer, the Legislative Site Committee recommended that the newly created school be located in Cleveland.

Governor Henry Whitfield signed the bill creating Delta State Teachers College on April 9, 1924. Dr. James Wesley Broom was named the first president and immediately began planning for the college's first year of classes. He selected a faculty of 11, including Dr. William Zeigel as dean. In what the *Bolivar Commercial* called the "the most important educational undertaking in Mississippi in the past twenty years," the first regular session opened on September 15, 1925, with 97 students enrolling for the fall quarter.

Unfortunately, Broom's untimely death kept him from completing the first year, and Dr. William Marion Kethley was named Delta State's second president. Kethley faced obstacles ranging from the Great Depression to World War II. The enrollment during that fall quarter of 1945–1946 was 185, but had increased to 596 by the fall of 1947. The postwar boom had started. Recognition of the expanding educational programs for its students came in the institution's name change to Delta State College in 1955.

Kethley resigned due to health reasons after three decades of service to Delta State, and the board of trustees chose Dr. James Milton Ewing as his successor. Ewing's tenure was to last for 15 years, during which time the institution grew not only in enrollment but also in academic programs and physical facilities.

In 1971, Dr. Aubrey Keith Lucas became the fourth president of Delta State College. Under his leadership the campus and academic programs experienced continued growth, with emphasis given to developing a strong faculty. To reflect this growth, Delta State College was designated a "university" in 1974.

Dr. Forest Kent Wyatt became the first alumnus to be named president in 1975. During his 24 years as president, the university experienced dramatic growth, becoming a multi-disciplined university.

Following Wyatt's retirement, Dr. David Leigh Potter was named the university's sixth president. Upon his arrival in the summer of 1999,

Dr. David Potter, the sixth president of Delta State, is continuing to build the University's reputation for academic excellence through the personal interaction between faculty and students.

Potter found a university with a distinguished past. Enrollment had grown to more than 4,000, and all of the academic programs had earned national accreditation, a distinction shared by only one other public university in Mississippi.

Realizing that the future would require Delta State to meet the challenges of the region, Potter began immediately to define a

A state-of-the-art, Olympic-size pool is the focal point of the newly constructed $7 million Natatorium that is the home of the Swimming and Diving team, the only collegiate team in the state of Mississippi.

strategic planning process to guide the future development of the university. His goal was to draw upon the qualities that distinguish a Delta State education, such as that recounted by Dr. Patricia Thrash, former dean of women at Northwestern University, and retired executive director of the North Central Association of Colleges and Schools Commission on Institutions of Higher Learning. A 1950 graduate, Thrash credits guidance and instruction from caring professors as crucial to a successful career in higher education. "I consider Delta State to be a truly outstanding regional university with a totally unique learning environment," she says. "Delta State offered me an unparalleled opportunity for friendship, for academic challenge, for support, and for personal growth. It changed my life. That's what a college should do!"

In the fall of 2000, Potter introduced a strategic plan featuring commitment to serving the Delta region—drawing upon its rich traditions and history, and responding to its needs. He encouraged faculty and staff to continue their traditional contributions to the region, while developing new initiatives to help ensure a bright future.

Delta State has built its reputation for academic excellence through the personal interaction between faculty and students and

Personal interaction between faculty, staff, and students is a hallmark of a Delta State education.

The center of campus, The Quadrangle, has seen over 21,000 students earn a degree since 1924.

the standards of achievement that its faculty demands. Both the university and its faculty place the highest value on teaching and learning. In addition, the faculty takes pride in their involvement with students outside the classroom—as mentors, advisors, and counselors.

The university places much of its emphasis on graduate programs that advance its regional mission. Extensive programs that prepare advanced practitioners for work in K-12 schools are central to this effort. Master's degree programs are also offered in Criminal Justice and Community Development. The Community Development program addresses social and economic problems of the Delta, while the Criminal Justice program prepares a highly trained workforce for law enforcement and corrections for the region.

Delta State is committed to extending the preparation of its students beyond the classroom. The university is a member of Campus Compact, a coalition of colleges across the nation who have committed to civic engagement as

an educational goal. The university also participates in Lighthouse Project, a service-learning project designed to link community engagement projects with academic outcomes.

Volunteerism in experiential projects such as Habitat for Humanity is emphasized through the curriculum in the Social Work Department.

The importance of exposing students to diverse cultures is supported through the recruiting and advisement efforts of the International Student Office. In 2002, 53 students representing 26 countries attended Delta State. Students are also encouraged to include a study abroad component in their schedule, with faculty and student exchange, being promoted through the university's membership in the Magellan Group.

Built upon the ideal that you can challenge and win national championships without sacrificing the central mission of the university, Delta State's athletics program provides an experience that unites Statesmen and Lady Statesmen fans—and inspires enthusiasm among students, alumni, parents, and friends.

Since 1975 when the Lady Statesmen basketball team won the school's first national championship, DSU teams have won seven national titles, with women's basketball earning six and the 2000 football squad capturing its first. Delta State athletic teams have excelled throughout the university's history with men's basketball and baseball programs having made multiple appearances in the National Tournament and World Series. Individual national titles have been recorded in track and

field and swimming. A member of the Gulf South Conference since 1970, DSU teams always compete at the highest level, and have won more than 30 conference championships.

In response to the university's challenge and mission to serve as the intellectual, cultural, and public service center for the region, "centers for excellence" have been established to address the needs of Delta residents. The university also created a stronger educational presence in the region by strengthening its commitment to continuing education and offering a variety of programs at educational centers in Greenville, Clarksdale, and Grenada.

To monitor the broad-based regional needs, the mission of the B. F. Smith Chair for Regional Development was expanded to better allow Delta State to monitor economic, health care, K-12 education, and community development issues. Other business-related centers making positive contributions are the Small Business Development Center and Center for Business Research which provide counseling and analytical services for area businesses, enhance faculty teaching and research, and give students research experience.

As one of Delta State's "centers for excellence," the Center for Community Development brings together persons of diverse backgrounds in a variety of programs in a non-traditional learning process. The Center provides a point of focus for Delta State's outreach by partnering with regional organizations, community leaders, faculty, and students to develop practical programs that address community needs.

The Center for Science and Environmental Education provides outreach services to residents, schools, and other organizations within the region. It is charged with coordinating existing science and environmental programs offered by

Since its 1995 opening, the remarkable growth of the Bologna Performing Arts Center's programming continues to meet the need and desire for arts experiences for all ages to celebrate the human spirit and strengthen the roots of the region.

Delta State and implementing programs that provide training to regional elementary and middle school teachers in the classroom use of instructional materials.

The Delta Center for Culture and Learning exists to promote an understanding of the history and culture of the Mississippi Delta, and its significance to the World. It fulfills its mission by promoting scholarship and engaging the academic, cultural, religious, business, and political communities of the region. Founded in 2000, the Center presents experiential classes about Delta issues to its students and universities beyond Delta State.

The Madison Center—named for chief architect of the U.S. Constitution, James Madison—focuses upon students having an understanding and appreciation for the Constitution and issues surrounding it. The Center adds to the curriculum by supporting scholarship and internship opportunities and providing civic education for area residents.

Emphasis given to development of a federal relations program has resulted in federal funding support for two significant programs: the Delta Education Initiative (DEI)

and the Delta Health Alliance (DHA). The DEI is a rewarding collaborative project undertaken by Delta State with the Mississippi Congressional Delegation in Washington, D.C., the Delta Council, and a consortium of 34 Delta school districts known as the Delta Area Association for Improvement of Schools. The initiative provides services and professional development for school personnel of member schools and educational opportunities for their students.

In January 2002, under the leadership of President Potter, the DHA —a major proposal to strengthen the health of the Delta region and its citizens—was launched. It is an alliance among Delta State, Mississippi State, Mississippi Valley State, the University of Mississippi Medical Center, and the Delta Council,

a creative partnership focusing on access, research, and education, with a goal of providing adequate health care for all of the citizens of the Delta.

The Bologna Performing Arts Center serves as a dynamic cultural organization, having earned state and national recognition for its contributions to the region and state. Since its 1995 opening, it has significantly impacted the quality of life within the region with its cultural offerings and education programs. The power to change lives is evident in the Center's Arts Education Program. A School Matinee series for grades K-12 reaches more than 14,000 students each year, while the Summer Arts Institute attracts aspiring youth from across the state to explore and participate in the visual and performing arts.

Through its strong faculty and staff, excellent academic programs, and "centers for excellence," Delta State University is committed to serving the Delta region—recognizing the strong attachment people have to this place, the Mississippi Delta.

Eleven collegiate sports are offered with a total of 340 student athletes participating. Caring passion-ately for sports is an experience that unites Statesmen and Lady Statesmen fans and inspires enthusiasm among students, alumni, parents, and friends.

GULFPORT-BILOXI INTERNATIONAL AIRPORT

What today is known as the Gulfport-Biloxi International Airport was originally constructed in 1942 to train B-25 and B-29 flight crews for battle in World War II. Originally known as Gulfport Field, the airport was passed on from the War Department to the City of Gulfport in 1949 to be used as a civil airport. Upon its conveyance, Gulfport signed contracts in the early 1950s with Southern Airways and later National Airlines to provide passenger and cargo service to the Mississippi Gulf Coast. Air service evolved along a normal trend until 1992, but with the advent of the casino industry and an accompanying 190 percent increase in the number of Coast hotel rooms, passenger boardings grew 400 percent during the 1990s. In short, the Airport grew from a local service airport with one airline providing connections to a handful of cities into an international airport in 2001 offering daily, nonstop jet service to seven major airports connecting to over 2,000 flights throughout the United States and the world.

Over the same 50-year time frame, the Air National Guard developed a major military presence

The Air National Guard's high-tech Combat Readiness Training Center is on airport grounds.

An eight-gate terminal handles traffic from around the world.

on the east side of the Airport property, which has since grown into a high-tech Combat Readiness Training Center, one of only four in the nation. Today more than 20,000 Air Guard and Reserve flight personnel train at the base annually. A 10-minute flight is all it takes for supersonic fighters and in-flight refuelers to simulate combat environments over the Gulf of Mexico or at Camp Shelby near Hattiesburg, Mississippi. The Army National Guard has also established the Aviation Classification Repair Depot operation, which repairs several types of combat and transport helicopters for military activities throughout the Southeast and Puerto Rico.

In 1977 Gulfport and Biloxi joined with Harrison County to establish the Gulfport-Biloxi Regional Airport Authority, which is a three-member board of commissioners appointed by the cities and county. These entities tasked the Airport Authority Commissioners to manage airport facility development. During the following two decades, passenger growth increased fourfold and the Airport Authority completed $46 million in capital improvements. Eighty percent of the money for the improvements came from the Federal Airport Improvement Program, and the balance was provided through airport revenues and subsidy from the cities and county. Key projects completed include construction of a new mid-field terminal in 1981; two major terminal expansions in 1994 and 1997; and complete rehabilitation of two runways and related taxiways.

The master plan for the Gulfport-Biloxi International Airport provides a comprehensive development plan for the entire airport over the next 20 years to meet the future needs of the Mississippi Gulf Coast. The plan provides for expansion of commercial airlines, general aviation development, air cargo facilities and military activity. With

In 2001 the airport served 840,000 passengers.

nearly 1,600 acres of property, Gulfport-Biloxi has the land area, airspace and land use zoning, and approaches to accommodate a total of three runways, a terminal area that is expandable up to 80 gates, and a new site for general aviation, which is currently under construction. The Airport also has a large area for development of multi-modal cargo in Foreign Trade Zone No. 92 and a new area for expansion of military missions. At 9,000 feet, Gulfport-Biloxi International Airport has the longest runway in the region and routinely accommodates the largest aircraft in the world, including the Antonov 124, C-5A, and B-747 aircraft. The alternate runway, currently 5,000 feet, will be extended to 7,000 feet in 2005.

The mission of the Airport Authority is to provide a high quality, safe public airport so that Coast citizens receive a sustained and superior return on their investment. In this regard, Gulfport-Biloxi is one of the fastest growing airports in the United States. But that's not all. It was also one of the most efficient airports in 1999 and received the FAA Southern Region Airport-of-the-Year Award. Having handled 840,000 total passengers in 2001, the Airport forecasts over 1 million total passenger movements in 2005. An eight-gate terminal complex is in place to accommodate the new passenger demand.

The future for the Gulfport-Biloxi International Airport is very promising. With continued resort development and the near term potential for a cruise ship homeport on the Mississippi Gulf Coast, more growth is anticipated. Studies have shown that with every new first-class hotel room built, 100 new passengers are generated through the Airport. Based on the expected resort development, the Airport could realistically double its current passenger boardings by 2010. The Airport Authority also has marketing partners that assist with the promotion of the Airport and its airlines. Those marketing partners include: area businesses and industry, casino resorts, the Harrison County Tourism Commission, the City of Biloxi, the City of Gulfport, Harrison County, the Port Authority, the Convention Center, and the State of Mississippi.

The Gulfport-Biloxi International Airport has provided vital economic stimulus for the Mississippi Gulf Coast. While the Airport Authority employs 36 people, when the tenants from all of the different facets of the airport are added, the total is more than 1,300 employees working on the grounds of the Airport. The economic impact of the Airport now exceeds $600 million annually.

Serving as one of the area's most valuable economic tools, the Gulfport-Biloxi International Airport remains critical to the expansion of the community's existing businesses and the catalyst for attracting new businesses to the Mississippi Gulf Coast.

World-class air cargo facilities support a growing Coast economy.

HANCOCK FABRICS

Only the true historian of Hancock Fabrics understands the significance of the phrase "under the cottonwood tree," which refers to the legendary birthplace of the 45-year-old Tupelo-based fabric company—where it had its beginnings as a traveling sundries store on Tupelo's Gloster Street. The story of Hancock Fabrics plays out in three distinct 15-year parts and, like most true adventures, is more about the journey itself than the destination.

When Hancock Textile Company was founded by Lawrence Doyce Hancock in 1957, even one of Mississippi's greatest visionary entrepreneurs couldn't have foreseen the trip that was ahead. After all, this company began in a panel truck peddling pencils, razor blades, and candy, among other things. Lawrence Hancock, though, was a dreamer, and he had the tenacity and business instincts to make his dreams come true. Maybe more important was his ability to make others believe—if not in the dream, then in the man.

Hancock, known by most as simply "L. D.," liked to tell the story of borrowing five dollars from his father to buy the fourth tire for his van. Even then, he was a master at juggling finances. Later on, he grew the fledgling textile company by

Founder of Hancock Fabrics, Lawrence Doyce Hancock, 1913–1998.

CEO and Chairman of the Board, Larry Kirk.

leveraging other people's money—giving 60-day terms to wholesale customers, while getting 120-day dating from his own mill suppliers.

The move to a future in fabrics was actually more significant than it was intended to be. Hancock traveled to Atlanta to bid on a small part of the inventory of a distressed textile distributor. When he returned to Tupelo, he owned it all—rather, he and the bank owned it all. He needed a distribution infrastructure quickly for all those goods, and he didn't have one. Using the lures of business ownership, credit, and a single source for product, Hancock recruited friends, relatives, and acquaintances to his network of wholesale independent customers. A concept was born atop display fixtures that were only a degree above two saw horses and a sheet of plyboard. Later on, that concept would have a name—"category killer." To L. D. Hancock, it was simply a store dedicated to doing one specialized thing and doing it better than it had ever been done. Selection and price were the cornerstones of a large store dedicated exclusively to fabrics. Hancock described it as "piling it high and selling it cheap." His favorite business axiom was at work:

"It's better to get a quarter from four customers than a dollar from just one." He didn't use retail jargon like traffic counts, velocity, turns and frequency, but he knew perfectly well how to get them.

Consumer response to a full-size, full-line retail fabric store was exciting and, with the vast supply of overruns and mill closeouts available at the time, the temptation to expand rapidly was often greater than the cash flow needed to fund it. The explosive growth of Hancock's business in fabrics and notions (buttons, zippers, thread, etc.), resulted in 80 company-owned stores and over 200 wholesale independent customers by the arrival of the 1970s. By private company standards, the far-flung collection of retail operations was now sizeable and increasingly difficult to fund and manage. Consumer demand for polyester double-knit fabrics was at a fever pitch with no apparent end in sight, but the 58-year old founder felt that the time had come to sell the business to a better capitalized organization that could realize the untapped growth possibilities. In 1971, L. D. Hancock commissioned a business matchmaker in Minneapolis to find a buyer for Hancock Textile Company and the 26 separate retail corporations operating under the Hancock Fabrics umbrella. With the Company's annual sales volume then at $90 million, the era of the founding entrepreneur was drawing to a close.

In late 1971, Lucky Stores, the second company to conduct acquisition-due-diligence on the Hancock companies (Beatrice Foods in Chicago was the first) struck a deal with L. D. Hancock to acquire the business for about $51 million in stock. The California-based food retailer typified the diversification mentality of the '70s, acquiring a number of businesses ranging from auto parts to jewelry to restaurants—and then fabrics. It was official on February 1, 1972,

Hancock Fabrics today—not just a sewing store anymore.

with "the Boss" agreeing to stay on for one year in a transition role.

The Lucky era was one of continuing change for Hancock Textile Company. In hindsight (some say it was foresight by at least one individual), the inevitable bust of polyester double-knits came soon after Lucky acquired the company. It wasn't pretty or gradual. Some Hancock veterans, with only slight sarcasm, recall that the double-knit crash occurred "one Thursday afternoon" in 1973. So swift was the plunge in the value of double-knits that sales and margins dropped precipitously, and inventories of unsaleable fabrics were bloated for several years. Robert

"Under the cottonwood tree"—the first building used for textile goods, Gloster Street, Tupelo, Mississippi.

Tedford, Mr. Hancock's long-time enforcer, took the reins in early 1973 following the agreed-upon transition and ran the company until 1980. He was a terse, fiery operator who subscribed completely to the "push theory" of product distribution, and his chore was to work out of the near-worthless knits and find something else to sell.

Although Lucky did instill some structure into its new subsidiary, and upgraded the almost non-existent information systems, it allowed quite a lot of autonomy to Hancock. With so much of its inventory in overvalued double-knits, Hancock struggled to purge itself of millions in dead merchandise. Fortunately, from a competitive standpoint, most of the company's rivals had virtually *all* of their eggs in the polyester basket, and several fabric chains even larger than Hancock melted down like the

cheap synthetics they stocked.

In 1980, Morris Jarvis, a licensed mortician who had been lured like many other north Mississippians by L. D. Hancock's promise of wealth in the budding fabric business, became the company's third president. Jarvis had started with the company in the late sixties in the Tupelo warehouse and later opened the first retail store in the Ft. Worth, Texas market. He had no previous retail experience and recalled that Mr. Hancock met only briefly with him at the store before "pitching me the keys" and returning to Tupelo.

Over the next five years, growth was steady and profitability improved somewhat, but the fabric business was clearly not a priority with Lucky. Jarvis had to pester the parent relentlessly for the go-ahead to acquire Minnesota Fabrics, a 100-store fabric chain in the midwestern region of the country. Eventually, the deal was done in 1985 for $42 million, bringing the total number of stores to 320 with annual sales at $280 million. The cash generation of the company was more impressive than its book profits, and cash accumulated during the slower growth period of the late eighties. Unfortunately for Lucky, the California tax laws made it too expensive for the parent to upstream the cash to headquarters, so it resided on the books and in the banks of the Hancock subsidiary.

In late 1986, Lucky came under a takeover attempt by a New York investor named Asher Edleman, one of many activists at the time who were challenging large,

At the very beginning, Houston, Texas, early 1960s.

underperforming companies to create more value for shareholders. Some, like Edleman, extracted greenmail in exchange for going away, but the more significant result for Lucky was a restructuring back to its core food business and the disposition of its non-food operations. In Hancock Fabrics' case, it was a spinoff of new common stock to Lucky's shareholders as a separate publicly traded company listed on the New York Stock Exchange. The second 15-year phase of Hancock Textile Company, and the name itself, ended on May 4, 1987, when Hancock Fabrics, Inc., shares traded on the Big Board for the first time under the symbol, HKF.

So, what happened to the cash? Lucky took it, all $80 million of it, plus another $32 million in proceeds from bank debt that became the obligation of the new company, Hancock Fabrics, Inc. Not so high a price for freedom, one might argue, if being a public company exposed for all to see can be described as freedom. The $32 million of debt was certainly manageable, and a new banking syndicate was formed

within the mahogany walls of J. P. Morgan Bank in New York City in April 1987. As for the local banks, it must have been a surprise when they learned from the spinoff announcement that $80 million in Hancock cash had been, for years, invested somewhere else.

To say the least, life as a public company was eye-opening. After 30 years of discretion, dropping the financial and operational drawers for all who cared to look was quite an adjustment for a north Mississippi-based company, only the second in the state at the time to be listed on the New York Stock Exchange. And, realizing that the SEC was not your favorite college football conference was even more sobering.

On the other hand, public company life was invigorating. The pride and challenge of competing on the financial world's stage was clearly felt by Hancock's entire management team who, for the first time, had an opportunity for ownership with a broad-based stock option program. The company and the industry were poised for growth, and Wall Street demanded it. Hancock, as well as the six other large U.S. fabric chains operating at the time, launched a

period of aggressive store growth in the late 1980s and early 1990s. By that time, the fabric section in department stores had disappeared, and the mall-based chains realized the need for larger stores in less expensive strip shopping centers. The race was on.

Unfortunately, industry capacity was increasing at a time when consumer demand had peaked and started to decline. Cheaper ready-to-wear clothing from abroad took its toll on the home-sewing of clothing. Industry balance sheets came under intense pressure as well, resulting in a wave of store closings and bankruptcies that would not subside completely until the late '90s.

In early 1996, Hancock's leadership changed for only the third time. Larry Kirk, President/Chief Financial Officer and 25 years with the company, was named CEO and was elected chairman of the board a year later. Kirk may well have been the last employee that L. D. Hancock personally hired before leaving the company.

At the time, the company operated over 500 retail stores across the U.S. with annual sales of $364 million. The new management group embarked on a three-pronged strategy to reposition the store base, to re-merchandise the product mix, and to market and advertise to a new, younger customer demographic. Today, after 250 store closings or relocations, two acquisitions and 110 new store openings, the company has reinvented itself once more to appeal to a broader base of customers; yet, it has still managed to stay true to the fabric business. In 2002, Hancock Fabrics is on pace to do $425 million in annual sales and about $20 million in net earnings, and the company is essentially debt free. Hancock employs 7,000 people in 42 states with an annual payroll of $73 million.

Although the four administrations were very different in their strategies and approach, some common threads, if a pun can be

Hancock's "store-within-a-store" for home decorating.

forgiven, can be found throughout the company's existence. A strong work ethic carries over from the early years when long days, tiring trips, and working weekends were the norm. When scheduling an out-of-town trip, Mr. Hancock would admonish the crew to "meet at the warehouse at 4 a.m. and be done 'et." It was a favorite colloquialism of his, meaning that the group would be starting early and would not be stopping along the way for breakfast. The expression is still used today when travel plans are made, often by employees who never actually met "the Boss."

Cost consciousness is also a carryover from the company's fragile beginnings. Even today, employees, including executive management, split a motel room to save travel expenses . Coach airline tickets at the most economical fares are standard operating procedure. The company pays the salaries—and bonuses when it produces well—but nobody expects to be put up at the Ritz when they're out on company business.

Financial stability continues to be the mantra of Hancock Fabrics. Over the years, the inevitable ups and downs of business flushed out several fabric chains who didn't maintain enough financial capacity to see them through unforeseeable turbulence and industry cycles. By contrast, Hancock was in position to survive the downturns and even acquire competitor casualties in strategic markets on three occasions. Some outstanding people came to Hancock in those acquisitions and are now a part of a story whose best chapters are still ahead.

Perhaps the most basic and valuable cornerstone of Hancock's success and longevity has been its commitment to the core business of fabrics while continuing to reinvent itself within that specialty business. Hancock was intent on concentrating on one thing and trying to do it better than anyone else—a category killer before the term was even coined.

If it really is about the journey and not so much about the destination, one of the most gratifying stops along the way for the people of Hancock Fabrics was at St. Jude Children's Research Hospital in Memphis, Tennessee. Since becoming a St. Jude sponsor in 1996, Hancock employees, suppliers, and customers have raised over $1 million for the hospital.

Throughout its existence, the company has drawn from its own ranks for its leadership at virtually every level, believing it to be both proper and profitable to "dance with the one who brung ya." It's still early, but it's been quite a dance so far.

Robert Tedford, second president, is the man in the foreground on the right, talking to the shorter lady with glasses.

ISLE OF CAPRI CASINOS, INC.

Bernard Goldstein, a man often credited with the title of Father of Riverboat Gaming, authored a book in 1998 entitled *Navigating the Century*. It can be safely said that Goldstein has done just that.

Current chairman of the board and chief executive officer of Isle of Capri Casinos, Inc., characterized by *Casino Journal* as "one of the fastest growing mid-cap gaming companies in the country," Goldstein grew up in Rock Island, Illinois on the banks of the Mississippi River. Interest in the family business, Alter Trading, led him in 1957 to become the first person in the Quad Cities of Iowa and Illinois to move scrap along that same river. Goldstein greatly enlarged upon the scrap metal company, which had been established in 1898, and in 1960 created Alter Barge Lines. Both companies continue to flourish under the management of Goldstein's sons. Their father, however, took a different route, one that would diverge pretty wildly from the business of scrap metal.

In 1991 the state of Iowa legalized riverboat gaming. Goldstein, a graduate of the University of Illinois College of Law, followed the legislative process closely, and in that same year, Alter Barge Lines established Steamboat Companies as the new owner of two riverboats. *Diamond Lady* took to the water

The first roll for the first property. Left to right: Isle chairman and CEO Bernard Goldstein, and State Senator Tommy Gollott.

A player's paradise: the Isle of Capri Casino Resort & Hotel—Biloxi, located on the Mississippi Gulf Coast.

on April 1, 1991, with the cameras from *Good Morning America* celebrating Goldstein's christening of Iowa's first riverboat casino.

When Mississippi legalized gambling in 1992, Goldstein moved his business south, and Steamboat Companies became Casino America, Inc., the first publicly traded riverboat casino operator in the country. Goldstein, who had traveled to the state's barrier islands during his honeymoon, was seeking a symbolic link to local history in the site for his new casino. He found it in the Isle of Caprice, a 1930s Prohibition-era casino, located on Dog Island eight miles south of Biloxi. When a forward-thinking local lawyer pointed out that the name "Isle of Capri" would require two less letters in its sign, Goldstein resigned himself to the abbreviated form. He honored the past by installing in the Isle of Capri-Biloxi, flagship for the current Isle of Capri enterprise, an antique roulette wheel salvaged by local fishermen.

Inspired by the tropical climate and culture on the Mississippi Gulf Coast, the midwestern entrepreneur decided to incorporate lush tropical themes into his riverboats and casinos, a rare departure from form in an industry that relies mostly upon Southern plantation frippery, Victoriana, and Western motifs to create an authentic gaming atmosphere. The strategy proved successful: Goldstein's enterprise has grown into a billion-dollar company that currently operates 13 recreational properties, including riverboats; dockside and land-based

Island Gold Members Club Card. The company is very strong in their database and member-tracking efforts, and they have a cutting-edge program.

casinos in Iowa, Mississippi, Colorado, Missouri, and Louisiana; and a harness racing track in Pompano Beach, Florida. When Casino America, Inc. became the Isle of Capri Casinos, Inc., on September 28, 1998; it marked the formalization of the company's brand.

Company president and chief operating officer John M. Gallaway credits much of Isle's success with a management tool he calls "Islestyleazation"—an approach to operations and marketing that allows the company to compete effectively against larger casinos by supplying a consistent product, thereby keeping down costs and increasing efficiency. This strategy, which standardizes all elements of the resorts to provide a level of comfort and familiarity to guests, provides defined operational templates to all staff for procedures as diverse as cooking a steak and keeping the books. The management plan, with its emphasis on efficient training, also allows Isle to hire as much as 90 percent of its staff locally.

The South greets gambling Isle style: The Isle of Capri of Biloxi opens its doors on Saturday, August 1, 1992, as the region's first casino. Thousands of guests wait in line for their turn to board the Isle and be a part of gaming history.

Time magazine emphasizes the resort management company's regard of that staff in an April 2002 article titled "Wanted: Complainers." The article notes that Isle employees are encouraged to e-mail concerns to top management through "Speak-Up" computer terminals located on the casino floors, and are guaranteed a response in 48 hours. Messages include complaints, suggestions and cost-cutting. Gallaway credits use of the speak-up system with a reduction in worker turnover. Leslie Yerkes includes Isle of Capri Casinos in her book *Fun Works: Creating Places Where People Love to Work*, which also includes such companies as Southwest Airlines and One Prudential Exchange.

The Isle of Capri has grown to operate four casinos in Mississippi in the last 10 years. Properties are currently located in the state in Biloxi, Vicksburg, Natchez and Lula. Each of these Isle of Capri Casino operations brings with it an abundance of benefits to its com-

Vicksburg, Mississippi exterior was the second casino to open—Biloxi was first.

munities. The tone is always set at the top, and Goldstein ensured from the beginning that the Isle would always be a good corporate citizen, giving back to the communities which the company calls home. The Isle focuses on benefiting civic, non-profit and local charities and organizations.

The company has centered its cultural roots around its superior guest satisfaction. Exceeding customers' expectations is the number one goal of the more than 10,000 employees. In fact, every staff member is required to participate in customer service training. The company recently introduced a program called "One Customer at a Time," which encourages a personalized approach to extending great service.

Goldstein guides the company with a mission statement that is more than words on paper, it is a way of life at the Isle. It was written by Goldstein himself: Isle of Capri Casinos, Inc., is to be the best gaming entertainment company— best for its guests, best for its employees, best for its communities, best for its investors . . . not the biggest, but the best.

Awards such as Ernst and Young's Louisiana's 1999 Entrepreneur of the Year; the National Rivers Hall of Fame Achievement Award; and the Simon Wiesenthal Center Distinguished Community Award honor Goldstein's business acumen and support of the communities in which he invests. His expertise, entrepreneurial spirit and vision will navigate this company well into this new century.

JACKSON STATE UNIVERSITY

Jackson State University is the only comprehensive, four-year university based in Jackson—the state capital and the largest metropolitan area in the state of Mississippi. Situated less than one mile from the downtown business district, Jackson State is the cornerstone of one of the most historic neighborhoods in Mississippi—the starting place for civil rights groups, notable writers and renowned statesmen. Medgar Evers, Margaret Walker Alexander and Richard Wright all rose from the roots of the Jackson State community. The University continues to promote a climate of cultural awareness and civic responsibility, particularly with respect to global concerns and modern social issues.

In 1877, Jackson State University opened its doors in Natchez, Mississippi, operating as Natchez Seminary, a private school, under the auspices of the American Baptist Home Mission Society of New York. Its purpose was to educate newly freed slaves between Memphis and the Mississippi Gulf Coast.

B. Baldwin Dansby served as the fourth president of Jackson College from 1927 to 1940. Under his administration, the school transferred from the private auspices of the Baptist Home Mission Society to state control.

Historic Ayer Hall, constructed in 1903, is the oldest structure on the University's main campus today.

Serving primarily as an educational institution to train ministers and teachers, the fledgling school enrolled 20 students.

Dr. Charles Ayer, a trained theologian, served as the first president, and the school prospered and grew. In November 1882, the society moved the school to Jackson, the site where Millsaps College now stands. A part of this transition was the renaming of the school to Jackson College, in recognition of the institution's new, central location in the city of Jackson. At the close of the 1894 school year, Dr. Ayer resigned, and Dr. Luther G. Barrett, the second president, was appointed to fill the vacancy. Jackson College relocated from its original site in north Jackson to a tract of land in the southwest section of the city. Construction on the new site began in 1902, and the University remains on this site today.

On October 1, 1927, Dr. B. Baldwin Dansby was appointed the fourth president of Jackson College. During this period, the major educational activities were directed toward teacher education for in-service teachers. When the American Baptist Home Mission Society withdrew its support from the institution in 1934, it became apparent that state support was needed to sustain the school. A hallmark of the Dansby Administration was the transfer of the school from the pri-

vate control of the church to the state education system.

Dr. Jacob. L. Reddix took office in 1940 and was the first president to serve under the mandate of the state. Initially, the school had been specifically designated by the state to train rural and elementary teachers. The curriculum was reorganized to suit that purpose and subsequently granted two years of college work. The first four-year graduating class under state support received their degrees in May 1944. A Division of Graduate Studies was organized during the summer of 1953, and the program of Liberal Arts started in the fall of that year.

Dr. John A. Peoples, Jr., was appointed as the sixth president of Jackson College on March 2, 1967. He was the first alumnus to serve in that capacity and embodied a new spirit of pride and freedom for the students and faculty. This spirit resonated through the new institutional motto: "You shall know the

Jacob L. Reddix was the first president of Jackson State to serve under state mandate. Under his tenure, the first four-year graduating class received degrees in May 1944.

truth, and the truth shall make you free." Under Dr. Peoples' administration, the academic program of Jackson College was greatly expanded and strengthened. The entire curriculum was reorganized, and the Schools of Liberal Studies, Education, Science and Technology, Business and Economics and the Graduate School were established. Dr. Peoples enhanced the faculty in quality and quantity. By the conclusion of his 17-year tenure, the faculty tripled in size, and the faculty members with graduate degrees increased eightfold in ten years.

One of the most profound accomplishments of the Peoples administration was the designation of Jackson College to Jackson State

The Class of 1926. Jackson State University was established in 1877 to educate newly freed slaves. The University soon developed a mission to produce qualified, socially conscientious teachers for the African-American community in Mississippi.

University on March 15, 1974. Through a legislative act signed into law by Governor William Waller, Jackson College gained university status in accordance with the expanded breadth and quality of its academic programs. In 1979, the University was officially deemed the state's Urban University by the Board of Trustees, State Institutions of Higher Learning.

It was also during Dr. People's tenure at Jackson State that the University sustained one of its most tragic losses. In the spring of 1970, state troopers fired into a girls' dormitory injuring several students, two of whom were fatally wounded. Mr. Phillip Gibbs, a senior French major, and Mr. James Earl Green, a local high school student who crossed the campus on his way home from school, were both killed at the scene. Just ten days after the Kent State shootings, the incident at Jackson State has often been eclipsed by the event in Ohio. Since 1970, Jackson State students have celebrated the memory of these two young men,

Class of 2002—Today, Jackson State University's enrollment is nearly 8,000 strong. Of approximately 400 faculty members, 70 percent have terminal degrees.

and in 2001, the University dedicated a full week of activities to commemorate this tragedy. Gibbs/Green Week is now an annual event featuring lecture series, performances, plenary sessions and other activities to recognize this pivotal moment in the University's history.

Jackson State University's Sonic Boom of the South is a constant crowd pleaser. It is one of the largest college marching bands in the region and has won numerous awards and accolades.

The H. T. Sampson Library at Jackson State is an exemplary modern facility with state-of-the-art resources for faculty and student research. The library has a database of more than 250,000 on-line journals and publications.

In 1975, a class action lawsuit was filed against the state of Mississippi, charging racial discrimination in the operations of the state's eight institutions of higher learning. Mississippi's three historically black colleges and universities were named as plaintiffs in the court case. The Ayers Case, as it is popularly known, is similar to those which have been litigated and settled by courts for educational institutions in other states, as a means to eradicate racial discrimination in the allocation of state resources to public institutions. Twenty years after the initiation of the lawsuit, a district court, upon remand by the U.S. Supreme Court, determined that the state of Mississippi had not erased all remnants of racial inequality in its higher education system. Consequently, the state of Mississippi, under

mandate from the court, embarked upon a plan to remedy constitutionally suspect policies in the higher education system. Several changes, concomitant with the state ruling, have given Jackson State greater capacity to better fulfill the larger aims of its academic mission and fully serve its constituency.

The legacy of social awareness and exemplary leadership at Jackson State University continues with the February 1, 2000, appointment of Ronald Mason, Jr., Esquire, as the ninth president. In addition to his extensive experience in higher education, institutional management and community development, Dr. Mason has invested the presidency with a renewed spirit of advancement and excellence that will propel Jackson State University to unprecedented heights in the New Millennium. He christened his administration with an innovative financial plan that maintained current levels of fiscal operation in spite of state mandated budget cuts. He has also established the Blue Ribbon Commission—a panel of local, state and federal leaders who directed the

Current Jackson State President Ronald Mason, Jr., and President Emeritus John A. Peoples, Jr., work together on the University's strategic plan.

most comprehensive strategic planning process in the University's history. "Beyond Survival: Jackson State University's Millennium Agenda" provides a blueprint for how the University will position itself as a world class institution of higher learning in the 21st century. The Faith Fund—an alumni-driven campaign to reconnect graduates with the university—and the Payton Family Student and Athletic Complex, in memory of Jackson State alumnus, Walter "Sweetness" Payton, are also important developments underway at Jackson State.

Dr. Mason recognizes Jackson State's unique opportunity to make a substantial contribution to the region, not only in producing effective, competent graduates, but also in furthering the overall economic prosperity of the region. "There has been a wall of racial perception that is based on the University's history but is no longer an accurate portrait of what Jackson State is today," Mason says of the misconception many people have about historically black colleges and universities. Jackson State University has partnerships and memoranda of understanding (MOUs) with the Mississippi Technology Alliance, the National Aeronautics and Space Administration, the National Oceanic and Atmospheric Administration, Livermore National Labs, the Office of Naval Research and numerous other entities. The University is the only HBCU with two supercomputers and has technology infrastructure that rivals many larger and wealthier institutions. "Globally, we can see the importance of technology not only with respect to industry and commerce but also in its ability to transcend numerous social and cultural problems," Mason said. "At Jackson State, technology

is more than a trend; it is our key to success for the future." In addition to fortifying the school's technological infrastructure, Dr. Mason's administration is dedicated to focusing on community service, furthering the diversification of the student population and solidifying Jackson State University's role in the advancement of the city of Jackson and the state of Mississippi.

In 2000, Jackson State finalized an agreement with the Allstate Corporation to assume ownership of their 33-acre facility in south Jackson. The University has converted the site into the Mississippi e-Center—a multifaceted hi-tech park that houses a business incubator, a

The Dollye M. E. Robinson School of Liberal Arts Building was completed in 2001. It features computer labs, student classrooms, a complete art gallery and a 200-seat auditorium.

Jackson State awards a number of degrees to African Americans in the sciences. It ties with Howard University among all historically black colleges and universities in producing the most African Americans with master's degrees in biology. The University ranks third in the nation in producing African Americans with Ph.D.s in all disciplines.

commercial data center, an access grid node, classrooms, technology development research and other commercial and economic resources. The e-Center is designed to be the cornerstone of e-City, a five-square-mile community surrounding Jackson State and linked through technology and telecommunications infrastructure. Included in e-City is the Mississippi Learning Institute (MLI), a collaborative partnership between Jackson State and a Jackson Public School feeder pattern. The MLI is a reading-based initiative that promotes proficiency in math, science and technical literacy. It also features a lab school and professional development program that links the Jackson State University School of Education directly with teachers in the public school system.

A comprehensive University with the programs of large schools and intimacy of smaller colleges, Dr. Mason has deemed Jackson State, "the best kept educational secrets in the South." The University consists of eight colleges that offer 43 undergraduate and 53 graduate degree programs, more than 100 student clubs and organizations and on-campus chapters of 22 national honor societies. The W.E.B. DuBois Honors College was established in 1980 and has an impressive record of graduating students of exceptional talent. The Honors College has a 100 percent rate of placing students into some of the top graduate and professional schools in the country. Jackson State ranks third in the nation among historically black colleges

and universities in awarding African Americans Ph.D.s in all disciplines, and is 11th in the nation in awarding baccalaureate degrees to African Americans. The University ties with Howard University among all HBCU's in producing the most African Americans with Masters degrees in Biology, and has an internationally renowned department of Computer Science. Jackson State is the only university in Mississippi with a Ph.D. program in meteorology and the only undergraduate program in professional meteorology in the state. Along with a rigorous academic schedule, Jackson State is known for its solid foundation in the humanities and liberal arts. The internationally renowned poet Margaret Walker Alexander taught at Jackson State until her death in 1986. Jackson State is home to the legendary "Sonic Boom of the South"—one of the most celebrated and award-winning marching bands in the area.

In October 2002, Jackson State celebrates its 125th anniversary. Currently in the midst of one of the largest facilities expansion programs in the school's history, Jackson State recently completed construction on a new School of Liberal Arts building and two new student residences—and is in the process of developing a pedestrian mall, a new School of Business building and a student health and recreation center. The University's enrollment is nearly 8,000 strong, with students from almost every state in America and from over 40 countries. With more than 400 faculty members, Jackson State provides academic opportunities to develop knowledge and skills that will empower students to succeed in an increasingly complex and technologically advanced world.

MASONITE INTERNATIONAL CORPORATION

Mississippi has been bountifully blessed with natural resources, not the least of which are its forests of the Long Leaf Pine Belt physiographic region in the southern part of the state. Lumber and pulpwood mills buzzed continuously until the 1930s, when sawmill production outstripped the supply of trees. Fortunately, a concerted tree-planting campaign turned the tide, replacing the cutover and wastelands by World War II.

To most observers at the turn of the century, a tree's usefulness was served once furniture and paper products were turned out. Wood scraps were just excess waste. William H. Mason, a former associate of Thomas A. Edison and an expert on wood derivatives was not, however, an average observer. Mason had gone to Laurel, Mississippi in 1920 to pursue his work on wood extractives for Wausau Southern Lumber Company, and had become convinced that there must be a profitable use for the vast amounts of wood trimmings and other waste being burned by the sawmills.

In 1924, in what turned out to be one of the all-time accidental discoveries in lumber history, he successfully perfected a process for turning raw wood chips into wood

Old portrait of William H. Mason, 1877–1940.

fiber insulation board. A leaky valve on the press in his laboratory allowed excessive heat and pressure on a wood fiber mat for a prolonged period, producing a thin, tough sheet of "hardboard," much more dense and durable than insulation board.

At first Mason did not know the marketable value of his new discovery. Through his wife's uncle, Walter Alexander, his product was presented to the Wausau Group, a loosely organized association of Wisconsin manufacturers who specialized in products made from wood. Alexander and the other investors of the group had previously

financed Mason's short-lived turpentine extraction projects and were, at least initially, hesitant to invest in the new venture.

However, their visit to the Laurel plant ended with a $50,000 commitment and the formation of a syndicate to pursue product development and patent protection. The syndicate members included Ben Alexander, Walter Alexander, D. Clark Everest, William H. Mason, John F. Ross, Charles J. Winton, Aytch P. Woodson, Cyrus C. Yawkey, and the W. H. Bissell Company.

In 1925 the syndicate committed to go forward with a complete insulation board unit and, after some initial reservations, with room for the still-unvalidated hardboard production. On September 1 of that year, the Mason Fibre Company was formed. The name was changed three years later to Masonite Corporation.

The new company sought to raise $1 million through the offering of preferred stock—even to non-group members such as the friendly competitor and Laurel neighbor, Eastman-Gardner Lumber Company. Outsiders held temporary membership, choosing to sell back their shares in the difficult early years. With the Wausau Group owning most of the preferred and common shares by 1927, the young company survived in the next few years, to a large degree, through the intervention of several members who personally guaranteed notes. Budding success became evident in 1935 when, with 266,689 shares outstanding, Masonite's common stock was listed on the New York Stock Exchange.

A successful product inevitably brings imitators. Although securing 34 patents relating to hardboard production machinery, the company faced its stiffest competition patenting hardboard itself. A legal battle with the insulation board manufacturing pioneer, Celotex Company, ensued in the late 1920s, resulting in a lower court favoring

The Mason Fibre Company plant in Laurel, as it was in 1926, showing the original woodroom (right), production unit one (center), and warehouse (left).

Mason Fibre Company   Laurel, Miss.

Aerial view of the Laurel, Mississippi facility.

Line 1 Molded Doorfacing press began manufacturing operations in 1991.

chanical process was developed in the early 1930s that produced fiber at higher yields than before. This so-called Asplund method, incorporated by plants worldwide, ended Masonite's monopoly by the 1950s.

Masonite's contributions to World War II were quite impressive. Practically all of Masonite's production went into supplying the military with essential materials. The versatile hardboard could be found almost everywhere there was a GI; from liners of Quonset huts—housing an estimated 3 million soldiers—to Red Cross ambulances and PT boat circuitry. Even volatile landmines were topped with the product. The company received several Army-Navy "E" awards.

To alleviate the pent-up postwar demands unleashed on the Laurel

Line 3 Molded Doorfacing press, constructed in 1995.

Celotex, but a court of appeals siding with Masonite. The battle was costly to both firms.

Out of the litigation, however, came an agreement—known as a del credere factor contract—whereby Celotex would become Masonite's agent, but could not take title to the board it sold. This arrangement allowed Masonite to control the pricing structure of its product. Other building materials manufacturers soon followed suit with similar arrangements. These contracts were challenged in 1940 by the U. S. Justice Department's Anti-Trust Division, and the U.S. Supreme Court ruled that such price fixing constituted a restraint of trade. Consequently, Masonite cancelled all of them in the early 1960s.

The defiberization method developed by Mr. Mason became known as the "gun" or "explosion" process, since it involved subjecting wood chips to steam under high pressure and releasing the pressure suddenly, producing an explosion of wood fiber and steam. Through the experimentation of Arne Asplund, a Swedish chemical engineer employed at one time by Mason, a new, continuous, thermo-me-

plant, the company purchased 86,000 acres of prime Douglas fir and redwood in an area of northern California and built a new plant at nearby Ukiah, connecting the plant and timberland with a road over the coastal range. In the mid-1960s a new plant was established in the Appalachian foothills of northeast Pennsylvania. Manufacturing centers in Australia, Italy, Canada, and South Africa, through their various legal agreements with Masonite, transformed the company into a truly international enterprise.

To counter its lost markets in the postwar period due to competitors entering the market, Masonite turned to extensive product development. Taking the lead from its Canadian affiliate, the corporation, in 1957, offered consumers Misty Walnut, a mass-produced pre-finished panel for use as an interior wall lining. Subsequent refinements of the interior paneling line included hundreds of different combinations of wood grains, colors, groove designs, and embossed textures. Interior paneling production continued into the 1990s.

Responding to the demand for exterior products in the early 1950s, a variety of new offerings were introduced to the marketplace during that decade, including some pre-primed items. Then, in 1960, Masonite led the industry with an innovative new generation of exterior products, the X-90 family. Many product variations of patterns, textures, grooves, and colors followed during the next four decades. Some were pre-painted with long-term finishes.

Management in the postwar period also successfully handled the problem of its overextended work force. From being one of the least efficient operations in the late 1940s, the Laurel plant—through layoffs and renegotiated labor agreements—was recognized as one of the industry's most efficient by the late 1960s.

Timber management has long been a priority with the company. Since the 1930s it has sought to educate farmers to view this renewable resource in the same vein as other agricultural pursuits. Fully developed tree stands, ready for harvest, were thus available in 10- to 15-year cycles.

In 1935 the firm's Forestry Division began complementing its program of direct assistance of seedling plantings with the start of a concentrated reserve acreage accumulation, now surpassing 380,000 acres in the Laurel area

Control Room for the Line 3 Molded Doorfacing press, constructed in 1995.

alone, exclusive of the aforementioned Douglas fir and redwood holdings in California. Management decisions in the 1980s led to the separation of some 467,000 acres of southern and western timberland from the company into a partnership. In any event, credit must be given to these conservation efforts—which included an aggressive pulpwood purchasing policy—for saving southern Mississippi from economic catastrophe.

Research and development programs, an ongoing tradition for Masonite, centralized at the John M. Coates Technical Center in West Chicago, Illinois for the past 40 years, have produced a stream of creative product innovations as the industry has evolved—always at the forefront. The continuous parade of new and advanced interior and exterior products released during the 1950s, 1960s, 1970s, 1980s, and 1990s bore witness to the company's continuing, long-term commitment to research and development. That commitment continues today.

In 1972, a pre-finished doorfacing product with an embossed

oak texture, in three color tones, was introduced to door manufacturers by Masonite for their use in making flush doors. The success of this product prompted experimentation with molded thin hardboard. As a result, in the fall of 1974, a pilot line was installed at the Towanda, Pennsylvania mill utilizing a new die-form process to produce molded panel doorfacings, which could be used by door manufacturers to produce doors that look like the popular wood panel doors, using their conventional flush door manufacturing techniques. These doors have become the most popular style of doors in North America and many parts of Europe and continue to grow rapidly in other international markets. Masonite manufactures the dies for pressing molded doorfacings in-house.

Masonite became the takeover target of several companies in the early 1980s. To ward off a possibly unfriendly takeover, an agreement was reached with United States

Masonite's two-panel, smooth-molded door unifies contemporary and traditional design elements and complements all interiors.

Gypsum Company for their purchase of Masonite Corporation. Masonite became a wholly owned subsidiary of USG in the spring of 1984. The relationship with USG was very compatible, since company philosophies were quite similar. Also, because of the similarity of products, USG's Wood Fiber Division became part of the Masonite organization.

Then, in 1988 USG became the target of the take-over artists and, in their strategy to avoid the raiders, it was necessary that they divest business units that were not part of their core business. In this process Masonite was purchased by International Paper Company in the fall of 1988. Masonite melded well into the IP organization, contributing significantly to its segment growth. Molded doorfacings were a strong contributor to that growth.

International Paper rewarded Masonite's contributions with substantial investments in new equipment and modernization of several facilities. As siding demand decreased significantly in the early 1990s, molded doorfacing capacity was installed in the Laurel mill. Doorfacing demand had been increasing at double digit rates annually. By 1995, Laurel had three production lines to produce molded doorfacings. The number of patterns and sizes offered had been increased substantially. By 2000, Masonite had produced enough molded doorfacings to outfit 20 million U.S. homes.

Business was growing in other parts of the world, as well, and to meet that challenge, Masonite built a molded doorfacing mill in Ireland, which began production in 1997, and one in Korea in 1998.

Although Masonite had experienced considerable changes in its operations during the 1990s, the end of the decade foretold another. International Paper announced that it would sell some of its businesses in order to focus more

The sophisticated continuous arch of Masonite's two-panel, Roman smooth-molded door lends elegance to any space.

directly on papermaking and related businesses. Masonite would be sold. The agreement to sell to Premdor, Inc. was announced in October 2000, although it was not finalized until August 2001.

In order to insure a competitive, independent source of supply for molded doorfacings to independent U.S. door manufacturers, the U.S. Department of Justice and Premdor entered into an agreement, which required the divestiture of Masonite's Towanda, Pennsylvania mill. That sale was finalized in March 2002.

The new parent company was Masonite's largest molded doorfacings customer. In addition to Premdor's North American operations, it has facilities in South America, Europe, Asia, and Africa, employing more than 10,000. Its principal business is the manufacture of doors for new residential construction, home repair, renovation and remodeling, and commercial use. In fact, Premdor is the world's leading manufacturer of doors.

Premdor demonstrated its pride and confidence in its acquisition by changing its name to Masonite International Corporation. Masonite International's CEO, Philip Orsino best described the new company: "The choice of the Masonite name for our combined operations builds on the strengths of two great companies and sets the stage for a new era of growth."

Masonite International Corporation is optimistic as it views its future. As Jim Morrison, Masonite Corporation's president, wrote in the 75th anniversary commemorative book: " . . . Masonite will approach this new opportunity with the resourcefulness and resiliency that is part of the company's heritage. The legacy of innovation and entrepreneurship that began with Bill Mason will continue. The qualities of operational excellence, customer attention, and excellent people for which the company has come to be known during its 75 years will continue. Together these form the core of Masonite's strengths. These strengths will nurture the Masonite of tomorrow as new chapters in the company's growth and success are written."

SOUTHERN IONICS INCORPORATED

Southern Ionics Incorporated (SII) is an innovator and leading manufacturer of specialty and intermediate inorganic chemicals—with products based on aluminum, magnesium, sulfur and zirconium. Founded in Mobile, Alabama in 1980 by Milton O. Sundbeck, the company is active in both business and community projects. Sundbeck, who was born in Austin, Texas, is also SII's president. He received his chemistry education at the University of Texas and was first employed with Hercules and American Cyanamid.

Along with Sundbeck, Joe Stevens, vice president of SII, plays an integral part in the success of the company. Stevens, who received his education at Millsaps College and has been with the company since he was a teenager, oversees product development, purchasing and manufacturing. He also serves on the Board of Directors for the Tennessee-Tombigbee Waterway Development Council.

SII, which started out with only ten employees, is known for pioneering a method for acquiring its key raw material, aluminum trihydrate (ATH) filtercake, by barge. Through cooperation with its alumina suppliers, SII was able to access ATH filter cake prior to drying in the bauxite refineries. This resulted in lower costs and a

Operator unloading supersacks of zirconium at SII's Pasadena, Texas plant.

President and CEO Milton Sundbeck, right, with Sales Manager Dan Sundbeck, left, and Vice President Joe Stevens, in the center.

dust-free material that could be transported by barge and truck to various locations. The company also utilizes co-produced streams of sodium aluminate, aluminum sulfate, sulfuric acid and sodium bisulfite as replacements for purchases of virgin raw materials where feasible.

The company is proud of its expansion over the past years and is committed to continued growth. Its product line has increased from one product to over fifty different products, and the success of the business is found in its commitment to quality.

SII's quality management system is certified to meet ISO 9002:1994 standards. Seven of the ten plants are ISO certified, and all potable water treatment products are National Sanitation Foundation (NSF) certified for use. Many of their

products meet the FDA GRAS (Generally Recognized As Safe) requirements.

The safety of its employees and the community is an important concern. The company's quality policy is to direct all their efforts toward total customer satisfaction, which is achieved by exceeding customers' expectations, preventing deficiencies in products and services—and continuing to improve processes which are focused on satisfying customers' key measures.

In order to succeed, SII believes that companies must continue to diversify their product lines. SII's product line offers diverse applications in many markets, such as pulp and paper, water and wastewater treatment, titanium dioxide and catalysts.

In the pulp and paper industry, SII's aluminum chemicals are used to reattach wood rosin released in the thermo mechanical pulping of southern pine used to make newsprint and light weight magazine grade coated paper. Southern Ionics became a leader in this technology to the extent that most southern newprint production uses this technology. Sulfur chemicals are used as pulping and brightening aids in chemi-mechanical pulping, provide efficient bleach vent gas scrubbing, and maintain pH control. Recently, SII developed a patented de-inking product for paper mills. The SI-SOLV™ de-inking process significantly improves effective residual ink concentration (E.R.I.C.) values at lower costs.

Another important market for SII is water and wastewater treatment. SII's sodium bisulfite is used as a dechlorination agent as well as a safe replacement for sulfur dioxide. Its aluminum sulfate is used in water treatment as a coagulant to remove suspended solids and TOC. Many municipalities currently use aluminum sulfate as a coagulant for water treatment. SII's municipal customers include the city of Houston, Texas; Mobile Water &

Sewer Board in Mobile, Alabama; and the city of Fort Worth, Texas. Additionally, many small towns in the Southeast (including its hometown of West Point, Mississippi) purchase SII's chemicals for water and wastewater treatment.

SII's products also have a significant application to the cement industry. SII has developed a new technology for recycling dust generated in cement kilns, which has been granted a patent. The dust is typically disposed of in a landfill or quarry. Recycling the dust allows a cement plant to recover costs and eliminate waste products.

SII's AQUA-CAT™ aqua ammonia is the latest addition to its diverse product line. AQUA-CAT™ aqua ammonia is known as ammonium hydroxide or ammonia solution. The main uses for AQUA-CAT™ aqua ammonia are SCR (selective catalytic reduction) and SNCR (selective non-catalytic reduction) for removal of nitrous oxides in stack emissions, catalysts manufacture, pharmaceuticals, water treatment, and fiber manufacturing. AQUA-CAT™ aqua ammonia is manufactured at SII plant sites in Tuscaloosa, Alabama; Pasadena, Texas; and Lake Charles, Louisiana.

Of high importance to SII is its commitment to build a team of motivated individuals who can advance the technology of its business, manufacture quality products and provide its customers with the service and know-how to maximize the products' value. For its clients, the company provides comprehensive technical service and application assistance through engineering, technical sales and R & D personnel.

Customer satisfaction is SII's number one priority. The company has a centrally located Customer Service Department, with toll-free telephone and fax numbers—and an 800 number for after-hours and emergencies. The department can

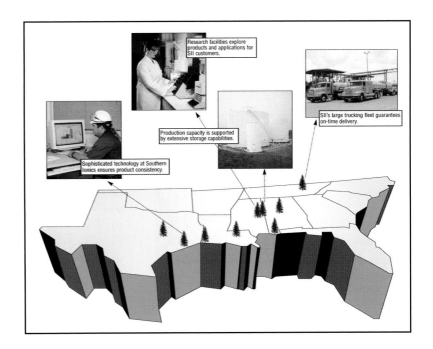

handle every customer's request each day, at any hour.

Inventory management is likewise available. SII staff members contact customers via an electronic dial-up remote tank-level monitor system. SII then schedules delivery based on the customers' inventory targets and usage rates. Customer contacts for inventory management are also made by scheduled phone or Internet queries.

Southern Ionic's rail and truck loading facility in Pasadena, Texas.

Map of SII's nine plant locations in Alabama, Louisiana, Mississippi, Tennessee and Texas.

In 1982, the corporate headquarters moved to an 8,000-square-foot building in the center of downtown West Point, Mississippi, which is a small town with a population of a little over 20,000. West Point is also known as one of the "Top 100 Small Towns of America." This small-town atmosphere was a contributing factor to Sundbeck's relocation from Mobile.

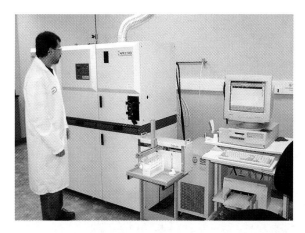

Southern Ionic's ICP spectometer used for metals analysis. Inductively coupled plasma.

The West Point corporate office —which has 11,000 square feet and room for growth—houses the accounts payable, accounts receivable, human resources, customer service, transportation, safety, marketing, manufacturing and purchasing divisions. In 1996, the corporate office headquarters was expanded into the building next door, which was an old JCPenney department store. After renovation, both buildings were connected by a skywalk. SII's first plant is nearby and manufactures an aluminum chemicals product line, as well as a slurry thinner product, used by Holcim. (Holcim, formerly known as United Cement, was SII's first customer— and remains loyal today.) Construction of a new zirconium sulfate plant in West Point was established in 1995.

In 1999 West Point hosted the Women's U.S. Open at Old Waverly Golf Course. This tournament was historical for West Point and SII. For seven days, it drew over 100,000 people—which had an economic benefit of almost $100 million for the area. Employees interested in volunteering to help did so for that entire week.

SII has slowly, but steadily, continued its growth. As expansion became crucial in SII's development, so was the objective of having multiple manufacturing

facilities strategically located on or near inland waterways. In 1986, its largest production plant opened in Pasadena, and a transloading facility opened in Midlothian, Texas. Three years later, production at the Baton Rouge, Louisiana plant began. Then, in 1993, SII expanded further by forming Tenn-Tom Tank, Inc. (TTT). TTT (now known as the SII Columbus facility) is located in Columbus, Mississippi on the Tennessee-Tombigbee Waterway. It consists of a tank farm and a barge unloading facility. Raw materials used by SII and other customers of SII are delivered to the Columbus facility by barge and unloaded there. Product is then distributed to customers in northeast Mississippi by SII trucks and trailers.

In 1994, SII built a new plant in Calhoun, Tennessee, approximately 30 miles north of Chattanooga on the Hiawasse River. The plant was originally built to be in close proximity to Bowater, a newsprint manufacturer and SII customer. The following year, another plant was built in Chickasaw, Alabama, which is part of the greater Mobile

SII's pre-delivery checklist performed by SII personnel prior to delivery.

area. The plant was strategically placed to pipeline sodium aluminate to UOP, another SII customer.

SII purchased the Tuscaloosa sodium bisulfite plant from Indspec Chemical Corporation in 1995. This investment strengthened the company's position in the markets they served and provided opportunity for growth in areas surrounding the plant. With this expansion, SII hired fifty-eight new workers, which increased the total number of employees to 162.

The year 1997 saw SII expand its sulfur chemicals business with the addition of a new product and manufacturing facilities in Baton Rouge and Pasadena, where state-of-the-art sodium bisulfite, sodium sulfite and sodium thiosulfate units were constructed. The Baton Rouge manufacturing expansion included manufacturing capabilities for sodium thiosulfate and sodium sulfite, and served as a distribution location for sodium bisulfite manufactured at the Tuscaloosa and Pasadena plants.

In 1998, an additional location was added in Lake Charles, Louisiana. The plant was purchased from Alcoa and was relocated on twenty-one acres to the west of Lake Charles in Carlyss, Louisiana. In 1999, this Lake Charles facility started up a new high-purity aqua ammonia (ammonium hydroxide) unit. Also in 1998, the Pasadena plant began its zirconium chemicals operations. The plant was designed to produce high-purity zirconium chemicals for demanding applications in automotive catalytic converters, oil refining catalysts, ceramics, pulp and paper, molecular sieves and ion exchange.

In 1999, the Research and Development Center was moved to a newly constructed 7,600-square-foot building near Columbus, Mississippi, fifteen miles from the corporate office in West Point. The R & D Center is a modern, state-of-the-art

SII's barge terminal in Tuscaloosa, Alabama.

research laboratory for product development, manufacturing support, application research and customer service. Dr. Joe Steelhammer, manager of the R & D Center, received his degrees from the University of Houston, the University of Minnesota and Yale University.

Although there have been hardships, SII has been fairly recession-proof. For the most part, SII has been able to grow business more in times of recession than in times of prosperity. SII chemicals go into fundamental products such as newsprint, paint, gasoline production and bar soap. Water treatment is also a significant business sector. Water treatment and pollution-control chemicals historically do not suffer too much during recessions.

When there were recessions, though, SII limited capital projects and did not expand its workforce. New customers were hard to come by—and, therefore, SII made every effort to service its customers and maintain the business volume that they had. Sundbeck said, "I always like to remember something my Grandpa White used to tell us. If a man can live on one sweet potato root a day, he can learn to live on

half a root a day." Milton's grandfather was a rancher and farmer in west Texas and saw a lot of good times and a lot of bad times, but he was always able to sustain his family with wisdom and courage that, in the end, provided plenty for all.

Besides business, SII is devoted to philanthropic causes within the community. This company believes in reaching out to help its neighbors—particularly children. After developing caring relationships with the West Point Public School

SII's sodium bisulfite production facility in Pasadena, Texas.

District, for example, SII now participates in the district's Partners in Education program. This partnership increases student motivation, encourages and enables teachers, provides joint community services and builds positive images of participants.

Partners in Education builds stronger schools and better prepares students to become responsible citizens—and increases community/business cooperation, collaboration and understanding. In order to be a partner, businesses must submit an annual plan implementing at least one activity a month in the following program areas: student motivation, teacher appreciation, community service and partner appreciation. SII has been a partner since 1997, and for the past two years has received the Golden Achievement Award for setting a standard for a successful partner program.

SII is also active in the West Point School District's mentoring program. Each school year, SII encourages two to three employees to leave the workplace once a week to volunteer as mentors. The mentors then meet with students for activities such as arts and crafts, cooking, computer games, etc., which, SII hopes, will help the children to see good role models in action.

Lastly, SII is dedicated to help state highways remain litter free. The company has been in the "Adopted Highway" program for the last three years—so that the roads near West Point remain beautiful and clean.

After twenty-two years in business, SII now has ten facilities, employs over 230 employees, and averages over $80 million in annual sales. The company is strong and continues to strive in a market that is always changing—and realizes that its accomplishments have been the result of hardworking employees, who have dedicated their lives to help the company succeed.

STYLE-LINE FURNITURE, INC.

On July 19, 1952, Billy Anderson, 17, joined the United States Navy; however, because of the untimely death of his father on January 19, 1955, he received an honorable discharge. After coming home, Billy began his career in furniture at Futorian/Stratford in New Albany, Mississippi. On April 21, 1956, Billy Anderson and Margie Scruggs were united in marriage and began their incredible journey together.

Between the years of 1957 and 1958, Billy worked for other furniture upholstery manufacturers, while he and Margie prepared to begin a family. With great joy, they welcomed the birth of their first son, Philip, in 1958. From 1959 to 1961, Billy worked for a commercial lighting company, while also working in the garage of their home at night, re-upholstering furniture and auto seats. After Philip's first birthday, Margie began her career in furniture at Futorian/Stratford, while continuing to sew upholstery for Billy during the late evening hours. Their second child, Tina,

A sample of the many fine pieces and styles of furniture that is manufactured by Style-Line Furniture, Inc.

Billy and Margie Anderson.

arrived on the scene in 1961. One year later, with great vision, they expanded to a small building next to their home, and produced brand new furniture.

In 1963 the Andersons took on a business partner and relocated to Tupelo, Mississippi. The following year, their third child, Mark, was born. In 1965 they bought their partner's interest, becoming the sole owners of Anderson Upholstery, with two employees. In 1969 the company became Anderson Manufacturing Inc., and moved into an 8,000-square-foot facility

with 20 employees. While purchasing frames and poly foam from an outside source, the company manufactured swivel rockers and chairs. During this time, they also did sub-contract work for Relax-O-Lounger.

In 1973 they purchased 7.8 acres in the Lee Industrial Park in Verona, Mississippi as a future building site. Realizing that their dream of a new manufacturing facility would have to wait a few years, they moved into a 33,000-square-foot temporary building in 1975. Two years later, they added an additional 33,000 square feet, and for improved quality, and to meet the needs of anticipated growth, they purchased $60,000 worth of equipment for foam fabrication purposes in 1980.

The Anderson's dream became a reality in 1981 as construction began on a new facility. The 40,000-square-foot facility was built on the property purchased in 1973, with production beginning on March 8, 1982. Less than one month later, however, the Anderson family was given devastating news: their new building was on fire. This horrific fire caused a total loss of the building, as well as the loss of skilled production labor, equipment, and a growing customer base. In May 1982 they placed orders with another upholstery manufacturer to help their customers meet the demands of furniture sales. This was not in the best interest of Anderson Manufacturing Inc., because the furniture was not produced with the same quality. After all the insurance claims were settled and all outstanding accounts paid, there was no money left.

Undaunted, the Andersons would not let the fire destroy their "American dream." After hearing that a local company filed

The first shop next to the Anderson's home.

for bankruptcy, they purchased its equipment with the help of the local bank—and the bank loaned the Andersons enough money to rebuild. The company had only been out of business for nine months when, in February 1983, production resumed under the new name of Style-Line Furniture, Inc., in a new 40,000-square-foot facility. Billy and Margie felt the name change was necessary because of the change in the style and price line of their new products—which were moving up to the mid-price range.

By the end of the year, Style-Line Furniture, Inc., had sales of $2,500,000, with 85 employees. Continued growth with double the amount of sales blessed the company in 1984. In 1987 sales had reached $12,870,000, with a payroll of $2,648,000. "With an eye to the future," the Andersons purchased state-of-the-art equipment and built top-notch manufacturing facilities, the first of which was the Foam Fabricating addition in 1995. The year 2000 saw increased sales reach $25,000,000, with a payroll of $5,810,500. Over the years, there were eight additions made to the Style-Line Furniture facilities since re-opening in 1983, with a grand total of 360,000 square feet.

The Anderson's built the com-

pany with high standards of quality and integrity. While understanding the needs of busy families today, Style-Line continues to give great value, service and style in every piece. Their commitment to provide customers with a product of unsurpassed quality has paid off through repeat business. Style-Line takes great pride in providing its customers with a high-end look at affordable prices.

A strong sense of family is evident through the entire operation because of loyal, dedicated employees. Mark Anderson joined the Style-Line team in 1986. As vice president today, Mark carries on the legacy that began so many years ago, along with the help of his sister, Tina. Style-Line's greatest assets are its employees—and it makes sure that each one feels appreciated. If, for example, an employee suffers a devastating loss because of sickness or fire, the company steps in to help. It also throws annual picnics and holiday meals for its employees, and makes time for reflection, as when employees were moved to pray for the nation after the tragic events of September 11, 2001.

The hard work down through the years in making Style-Line what it is today paid off when it caught

the attention of Kathy Ireland Worldwide, which asked it to produce a home-collection brand. Style-Line, being a family owned-and-operated company, felt that partnering with Ireland was a great fit. Since Ireland is known to be a friend to families, Style-Line expects her home collection to be the most popular brand.

In the early days, when Billy and Margie worked late into the night to build their business, neither of them dreamed the company would become what it is today. The Andersons attribute their company's success to hard work and the grace of God. They realize how blessed they are and always give back to the community through charities such as Feed the Children, Habitat for Humanity, the American Cancer Society's Relay for Life—and scholarship programs such as the Mary Kirkpatrich Haskell Scholarship Foundation. They also contribute yearly to the local fire department, sheriff's department and the Verona Police Department.

Style-Line marches into the future with great anticipation and excitement, and expects sales to increase to $40,000,000 in 2003.

Part of the Style-Line Furniture, Inc., manufacturing facilities. Missing from this photo is another 127,500-square-foot building completed in January 2002.

WATKINS & EAGER

For four generations, the law firm of Watkins & Eager has excelled in the representation of clients throughout the state of Mississippi and beyond. Based in the historic Emporium Building at the corner of Congress and Capitol Streets in downtown Jackson, the firm has a rich history, a diverse and talented membership, and a demanding and dynamic practice.

The firm's founder, William ("Will") Hamilton Watkins, was the son of a Jefferson County farmer and grandson of a pioneer Methodist circuit rider. In 1895 Will Watkins became the twentieth member of the Jackson Bar. He established himself in private practice, opening a modest office on Capitol Street. The influential career of Will Watkins spanned sixty-four years, during which he argued over twenty cases before the Supreme Court of the United States.

Pat H. Eager, Jr., joined Will Watkins in 1916 and practiced with the firm until his death in 1970. He was recognized as a premier trial lawyer who served as president of the International Association of Defense Counsel from 1943-1944, and who was Mississippi's initial invitee into the American College of Trial Lawyers.

Elizabeth Watkins Hulen was the first woman in Mississippi history to argue a case before the Supreme Court of the United States.

Bill Goodman, grandson of the firm's founder and senior partner, is in his fiftieth year of distinguished practice. He is a member of both the American College of Trial Lawyers and the American Academy of Appellate Lawyers.

For several decades, the image of the firm was heavily influenced by two children of Will Watkins. Elizabeth Watkins Hulen, an outstanding appellate advocate, was the first woman in Mississippi history to argue a case before the Supreme Court of the United States. Thomas H. Watkins earned a national reputation in the representation of corporate and governmental clients.

Will Watkins' grandson, Bill Goodman, is in his fiftieth year of distinguished practice and is the firm's senior partner. He has argued three cases before the Supreme Court of the United States and is a member of both the American College of Trial Lawyers and the American Academy of Appellate Lawyers. The fourth generation of the Watkins legacy is represented by Will Goodman, Bill Goodman's son and the great-grandson of the firm's founding partner.

Watkins & Eager is a "family firm" in the sense that four generations of the same family have maintained leadership roles and a continuous presence within the organization. In a broader sense, however, everyone who works with

the firm, in whatever capacity, becomes a member of the Watkins & Eager family. Many talented people, past and present, have contributed to the growth and progress of the firm, which now enjoys an extensive corporate and business practice in addition to its long-established premier trial and appellate practice. As a result, professional publications throughout this century have recognized Watkins & Eager as a firm composed of preeminent lawyers. One example is the firm's selection for almost sixty years to author the annual digest of Mississippi law in *Martindale-Hubbell*.

Today sixty-six lawyers practice with Watkins & Eager. Seventeen of these lawyers are women and three are African-American. From Elizabeth Watkins Hulen's admission to partnership in the 1930s, Watkins & Eager has developed a strong reputation for recruiting, retaining, and promoting women and minority lawyers and staff. Firm lawyers possess a variety of academic backgrounds, with graduates in law from the University of Mississippi, Mississippi College, Florida State University, New York University, Tulane University, the University of California, Hastings

Pat H. Eager, Jr., who joined the firm in 1916, was Mississippi's initial invitee into the American College of Trial Lawyers.

The influential career of William Hamilton Watkins, the firm's founder, spanned sixty-four years during which he argued over twenty cases before the Supreme Court of the United States.

College, the University of Florida, the University of Virginia, Vanderbilt University and Columbia University. The firm is assisted by a staff of over eighty support personnel, and the special work environment led to the firm's recognition in *America's Greatest Places to Work with a Law Degree.*

The Emporium Building, home to Watkins & Eager, PLLC is listed on the National Register of Historic Places.

The firm is proud of the academic achievements and honorary qualifications of its lawyers. The distinguished senior United States Senator from Mississippi, Honorable Thad Cochran, is a former member. One of the firm's active members, Charles Clark, is the retired chief judge of the United States Court of Appeals for the Fifth Circuit and is also a member of both the American College of Trial Lawyers and the American Academy of Appellate Lawyers. One of our senior partners, Nick Harkins, served in 2001-2002 as president of the Defense Research Institute, the nation's largest organization of defense lawyers.

Individual lawyers are associated with recognized civic, industry and professional organizations. Members belong to the Defense Research Institute, the International Association of Defense Counsel, the Product Liability Advisory Council, the American College of Trust and Estate Counsel, the American College of Employment Lawyers, and the

American Academy of Appellate Lawyers. Since the formation in 1950 of the prestigious American College of Trial Lawyers, seven Watkins & Eager partners have been inducted as fellows of that college: Pat Eager, Tom Watkins, Bill Goodman, Vardaman Dunn, Hassell Whitworth, Mike Ulmer and Nick Harkins.

Watkins & Eager has traditionally engaged in a general civil practice with an emphasis on

Charles Clark (left) is a member of the firm and retired chief judge of the United States District Court of Appeals for the Fifth Circuit.

litigation. Today, the firm continues to enjoy both a broad-scale trial practice in state and federal courts and before administrative agencies, and a comprehensive appellate practice at both the state and federal levels. The firm continues to expand upon its historic position as a leading litigation law firm in Mississippi. In recent years, our lawyers have tried cases in a number of other states, including California, Connecticut, Florida, Louisiana, Pennsylvania and Tennessee. Today, the firm serves certain major clients as regional or national coordinating counsel.

The firm's practice encompasses diverse non-litigation matters as well. Watkins & Eager is privileged to repre-

sent, among others, banking and financial institutions, manufacturers, oil and gas producers, telecommunications providers, investors, insurers, institutions of higher learning and governmental agencies at the municipal, county, state and federal levels.

The current members of Watkins & Eager are fortunate to have inherited a legacy of excellence, and they strive to continue to merit the reputation that the firm has long

The foyer of the Emporium Building, renovated in 1988.

enjoyed. The firm's goal is to attract individuals to its ranks who have keen intellect, logical reasoning power and high ideals—men and women who possess potential to deal with the complex problems which arise in every community and state.

While the bulk of the firm's work is in civil and corporate litigation, its membership undertakes to be at home in all aspects of the law. Watkins & Eager is attentive to both the technicalities of everyday practice and to those higher phases of the legal profession involving its philosophy and ethics. In this firm's view, capability not only

requires legal expertise, but it also demands analytical power, experience, and an instinctive respect for justice.

To balance its perspective, the law firm must also be a valuable citizen. Watkins & Eager's diverse practice has kept it in close contact with business and government as well as minority leadership. The firm's sixty-year liaison with Millsaps College, and its involvement with public institutions, has provided an ongoing relationship with Mississippi's educational community. Work for agencies of various churches has enabled the firm to keep in contact with much of the area's clerical leadership. Firm lawyers are closely involved in leadership roles

The firm has a reputation for recruiting, retaining, and promoting minority lawyers and staff.

with many local charitable organizations, arts groups and educational institutions.

Senator Cochran offers this assessment of his former firm: "It is a unique place and a place that is respected and individual lawyers are respected. The firm is looked up to by those who have dealings with it, and it's just as true today as it was when William Watkins and Pat Eager were in their heyday."

Watkins & Eager is a professional limited liability comapny

Members Nick Harkins and Bill Goodman are joined by Senator Thad Cochran (center) who was associated with the firm prior to his entering public service.

THE GADDIS FARMS

J. L. Gaddis, Sr., was born in Scott County, Mississippi in 1860. He moved to the Bolton area in 1874 and went to work for his uncle, Robert Crook, who was involved in the mercantile and farming business. In the early 1890s J. L. Gaddis, Sr., began acquiring several thousand acres of farmland in northwest Hinds County. His son, J. L. Gaddis, Jr., and son-in-law, F. M. Greaves, became involved in the business as it continued to grow, and on December 3, 1936, The Gaddis Farm was incorporated and acquired all of the assets of a partnership, trading in the name of Gaddis Farms.

During the first half of the 20th century, tenant-raised cotton was the main cash crop. These tenants farmed with mules and hand labor. At one time there were three cotton gins operated by The Gaddis Farms. Some cattle were raised during this period, but the main crop was "King Cotton."

After World War II a transition in agriculture began, and, over a period of 25 years, the old system for raising cotton disappeared as mechanization took over with the advent of diesel tractors and mechanical cotton pickers.

During this same period, beef cattle became a much more important part of The Gaddis Farms as the herd was increased and pastures improved.

J. L. Gaddis, Jr., passed away in 1959; F. M. Greaves retired; and the management fell to Ted Kendall III, a great-grandson of the founder. He was assisted by his cousin-in-law, Pat McCain. His father, T. H. Kendall, Jr., and his uncle,

D. W. Graham, both of whom were bankers, assisted—along with his uncle, H. M. Kendall, an attorney.

Today, The Gaddis Farms is a family-owned corporation consisting of over 20,000 acres of land in the Brown Loam section of Mississippi, stretching from the Big Black River to Raymond in Hinds County. Ted Kendall III, Mary Anna Kendall Garraway, Kay Graham Townes, Frances Graham McCain and their 10 children currently own the company. These shareholders are all direct descendants of J. L. Gaddis, Sr.

Timber and wildlife management have become very important parts of the

Left to right: Kendall Garraway, Ted Kendall IV and Ted Kendall III.

J. L. Gaddis, Jr.

operation. A long-range timber plan has been developed that provides for timber harvest and reforestation on a perpetual basis every year. Cotton, cattle, corn and soybeans continue to be profit centers for The Gaddis Farms. Oil was discovered in the 1950s and continues to contribute a small amount to the company.

The Gaddis Farms office is located in Bolton, but the main farm headquarters is located approximately three miles north of Bolton on a tract of land acquired in 1923. During the Civil War, Joe Davis, brother of Jefferson Davis, owned this tract.

Ted Kendall III and fifth generation descendants of J. L. Gaddis, Ted Kendall IV and Kendall Garraway, currently manage the company.

BLUE MOUNTAIN COLLEGE

Blue Mountain College was founded in 1873 by Civil War General Mark Perrin Lowrey. A village preacher before the war, General Lowrey was a man of vision, who saw the importance of providing a thorough education for women. Exchanging his farm in Ripley with a friend for the old Brougher mansion, General Lowrey renamed the site Blue Mountain after the bluish tint of the trees on the pine-covered knoll. During the summer of 1873, the first classroom building with a moveable partition was constructed for the fall session. He and his two oldest daughters, Modena and Margaret, comprised the faculty at what was first known as the Blue Mountain Female Institute. Despite the fact that the South was poor, and the education of women was not very popular in 1873, fifty students were enrolled for the first session.

In 1876, Modena Lowrey married the Reverend W. E. Berry, who immediately joined in the family endeavor by purchasing a half interest in the school and serving as a longstanding college advisor and faculty member. Serving as Lady Principal, and then as vice president from 1873 to 1934, a tenure perhaps unequaled by any other

Blue Mountain College is located in a small, safe community yet accessible to the city of Tupelo and the metropolitan area of Memphis, Tennessee.

Students listen to the psychology professor in the new Fisher-Washburn Hall.

woman college official, Modena Lowrey Berry was affectionately known as Mother Berry. She was the second woman in the state's history to be named to the Mississippi Hall of Fame, and she and her father, General Lowrey, are the only father and daughter to be thusly honored.

Between 1873 and 1960, three generations of the Lowrey family, including the general; his sons, Dr. W. T. Lowrey and Dr. B. G. Lowrey; and his grandson, Dr. Lawrence T. Lowrey, presided over the college. In 1960, Dr. Wilfred C. Tyler, longtime professor of Bible at the college, accepted the presidency

and served until his death in 1965. Dr. E. Harold Fisher became the sixth president on July 1, 1965, and served until his retirement on June 30, 2001. On February 23, 2001, Dr. Bettye Coward was unanimously elected by the Board of Trustees as the seventh president of the college and was the first woman to serve as its president. She assumed her official duties on July 1, 2001.

Blue Mountain College was independently owned and administered until 1920, when it became affiliated with the Mississippi Baptist Convention. In 1955, Blue Mountain College began offering a coordinate academic program for men preparing for church-related vocations. For those men who aspire to careers as pastors, music directors or missionaries—or for careers in other types of Christian service—the ministerial education program offers a strong Christian, liberal arts foundation in preparation for further study in seminary or graduate school.

Today, the curriculum is organized around six academic departments with majors being offered in twenty-one fields. The academic program also provides for pre-professional preparation for students interested in pursuing careers in health and law. A medical technology program is available through an arrangement with the school of medical technology at the North Mississippi Medical Center. The following three degrees are available at Blue Mountain College: Bachelor of Arts, Bachelor of Science, and Bachelor of Science in Education.

Initiated in 1987, the teacher assistant program at Blue Mountain College is widely recognized as one of the most innovative and successful continuing education programs in the state. A teacher assistant can earn a degree in education while continuing to work full time in the classroom. Classes are arranged to accommodate most work and personal schedules. Even without prior college experience, a person can complete the program in five years, taking two courses each semester and four courses during the summer.

Having a small, student-centered campus and a committed faculty and staff, the college exhibits a climate of personal attention, respect, and inclusion. While the development of the mind is a major focus, students are challenged to develop physically, socially and spiritually. Inspired by the Lowrey's chapel talks, Dr. Bettye Coward continues the tradition of investing time with students during chapel through Coward's Chapel Chats. The college motivates students to passionately pursue intellectual growth, developing a joy in knowing and a commitment to lifelong learning. Students are encouraged to think in order to resolve life's challenges—so that knowledge gained will result in their making positive choices for their lives.

Blue Mountain College continues to be distinctive in the student population it serves—for both women, for whom the college was founded, and men who are preparing for ministry. The atmosphere of Blue Mountain College is attributable to a blending of several factors: the college's sense of its mission as a Christian—and, specifically, a Baptist—institution; the traditions

Graduation at Blue Mountain College.

created by a distinguished founding family and Christian educators; career preparation grounded in the liberal arts; a special kind of student life with a system of student government and honor uniquely available in a small college for women; and a family-like environment where students, faculty and administrators genuinely believe in the worth of the individual.

Blue Mountain not only offers one of the best private educations that money can buy, but, more importantly, is committed to making it possible for students to afford this enviable college experience by helping them finance their education. Scholarships, grants, loans and work study opportunities based on financial need are determined by an analysis of the Free Application for Federal Student Aid (FAFSA) form of the College Schol-

arship Service. Through federally funded programs such as the Pell Grant and Stafford Loan programs, a financial aid package can be tailored to meet each student's needs. Merit scholarships are also offered based on academic performance and/or ability.

Ultimately, the graduates of the college will leave its gates prepared for successful careers—and, more importantly, they will leave the institution as people of Christian character, equipped with a passion and commitment to a life of service to others and with a resolve to make a difference wherever they may go, in whatever they do. Since 1930, a plaque on the entrance gates has read "Enter to grow in wisdom . . . Depart to better serve."

The 2002 Blue Mountain College Lady Toppers Basketball Team was recognized as a Champions of Character Institution by the National Association of Intercollegiate Athletics.

CHAMBERLAIN-HUNT ACADEMY

The Academy's foundation is linked inextricably with the demise of Oakland College, not in the least because both of its namesakes are connected with that institution. Founded by the Presbytery of Mississippi in 1830, Oakland College survived until after the War Between the States. Dr. Jeremiah Chamberlain was its first president, and Mr. David Hunt was a generous benefactor, giving $175,000 over the course of his life to the institution.

After the War, the Synod of Mississippi could no longer afford to operate the College, and decided to close it, selling the property in 1871 to the State of Mississippi which in turn opened Alcorn State College. The Synod, in order to carry out the wishes of the original donors to Oakland College, transferred the funds to the Presbytery of Mississippi with the condition that they be used to endow "an institution of liberal Christian learning" close to the site of Oakland College.

In October 1877 the Presbytery of Mississippi chose Port Gibson as the home of the new institution, to be named Chamberlain-Hunt Academy. The Academy was originally housed in the old Brashear Academy building adjacent to the First Presbyterian Church of Port Gibson. It was slated to begin operation in fall 1878, with Dr. J. W. Kerr as its first principal, but a yellow fever outbreak prevented students from attending.

This photo was taken circa 1915-1920. Notice the beauty of the architecture and design of the original McComb building. It's said that the bell tower on the left hand side reached five stories and its turrets on either side gracefully embrace the skyline. Historical records show that over 1,000 people came from Mississippi and Louisiana to celebrate the cornerstone laying.

The school actually opened in the fall of 1879, with Mr. John H. Leckey as principal and professor of mathematics and ancient languages. Reverend David A. Planck, pastor of the Presbyterian Church in Port Gibson, served on the Board of Trustees and also taught english literature and history. Mr. Thomas Norwood rounded out the faculty teaching modern languages (French and German) and the natural sciences.

In the fall of 1883, Mr. Walter C. Guthrie assumed the title of principal and he would hold that position until spring 1907. During his administration, Reverend Planck continued as in-

structor in Bible history, a position he would occupy until Reverend Hervey H. Brownlee, the next pastor of the Presbyterian Church of Port Gibson, succeeded him.

The Academy and the Presbyterian Church has thus always been closely linked. Many presidents and professors of the Academy have served as elders and deacons of the church. In addition, Reverend M. E. Melvin served as pastor of the church from 1904 until 1908 and as president of the Academy from 1908 until 1914. Many other pastors have served on the Academy's Board of Trustees or have taught classes.

Cadets have always worshipped at the Presbyterian Church. The very first catalog of the Academy states that "On Sabbath, pupils are expected to attend Divine Service with the principal or some one of the assistants." Today, all the boarding cadets worship weekly in the same spacious sanctuary, built in 1860, which also housed daily chapel exercises in the Academy's earliest years.

Daily worship remains a part of the Academy's life. Cadets are given opportunities to sing God's praise, to lead in worship and to hear visiting speakers. Cadets also study the Bible daily. The Bible Department offers a three-year Bible curriculum, as well as studies in the Westminster Standards and in the

One of Chamberlain-Hunt's earliest baseball teams. Circa early 1900s.

analysis and application of the Christian Worldview.

During Mr. Guthrie's tenure the Academy incorporated what was to become one of its most important defining features: the Military Department. Milling M. Satterfield, an 1889 alumnus of the Academy, became the first Commandant of the Cadets in 1895. At first voluntary, by 1905 all students were required to be members of the Corps of Cadets. Chamberlain-Hunt continues to use military discipline to shape Christian character today. To quote from the 1905-1906 catalog: "The prime essentials of Moral Development are respect for authority, habits of obedience, order, punctuality, system, self-control and a feeling of individual responsibility. Experience has established the fact that these can best be secured in school life under a military system."

In 1900 the Academy moved about a mile south to its current campus. After Mr. Guthrie's retirement, the dormitory was named for him. The main classroom and administration building was name McComb Hall to memorialize Mr. J. J. McComb of New York, who gave generously for the new buildings and who personally supervised their design. This building was gutted by fire in 1924, but was immediately rebuilt using the original masonry walls, although without its elegant Victorian spires. McComb Hall today houses classrooms, computer labs, office space and the campus chapel.

The fire required a new dormitory to be built to replace space lost when McComb Hall was remodeled. As a result, Redus Hall was built and named in honor of Dr. W. D. Redus, chairman of the Board of Trustees from May 1902 until his death in April 1924. In 1948, Gage Hall was built and named in honor of Robert D. Gage, who had

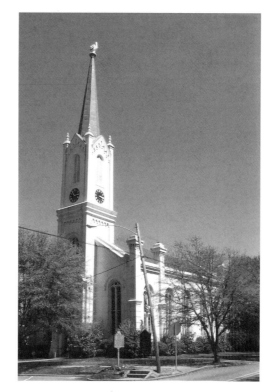

The First Presbyterian Church in 2002.

also served as chairman of the Board of Trustees. In the fall of 2002, Gage Hall reopened after a year-long, $800,000 renovation project. When full, it will house 50 boys.

The Academy has continued to grow and expand, benefiting greatly from the generous support of Presbyterians from all over the Synod of Mississippi. Synodal funds began to dry up in the early 1970s however, because of the disruption of the Presbyterian Church

The school today.

in Mississippi, as many congregations withdrew to become part of the newly formed Presbyterian Church in America. As a result, capital improvements came to a halt, and the school began to incur debts which would, after only a few years, become crippling.

By 1998 the Board of Trustees of the Academy had run out of money and out of options. They approached French Camp Academy, another academy that had been founded by Mississippi Presbyterians in the late 19th century, and asked their Board of Trustees to assume control of Chamberlain-Hunt. French Camp agreed to do so, and in the years since, amazing things have been accomplished on the campus in Port Gibson.

Of course, many buildings have been refurbished which have needed attention for years. French Camp has undertaken an ambitious $20 million capital funds drive in order to provide even better facilities at Chamberlain-Hunt, and to increase the number of scholarships that can be provided to needy cadets.

But the most important improvement that French Camp has brought to Chamberlain-Hunt is the reinforcement and reinvigoration of the Christian mission that was the very reason that Chamberlain-Hunt first came into being. New faculty and staff have been hired who give evidence of both a warm and genuine Christian faith and the ability to integrate that faith into all aspects of campus life.

Guided by its traditions, trusting in the Lord Jesus Christ and remaining committed to the development of the leaders of tomorrow, Chamberlain-Hunt is stepping forward into a new century, striving towards Knowledge and Wisdom in Submission to God.

COOKE DOUGLASS FARR LEMONS, LTD.

The founders of Cooke Douglass Farr Lemons, Ltd. were William H. Cooke, Jr.; Nelson L. Douglass, Jr., and Robert E. Farr. Both Cooke and Farr were employed by N. W. Overstreet, A.I.A., prior to his merger with Joseph Ware and John Ware to form Overstreet, Ware & Ware. Nelson Douglass joined the firm in January 1960.

During 1960 these three worked together at Overstreet, Ware & Ware Architects & Engineers. The three decided to become partners and form their own firm, which would offer architectural and engineering services. Robert Farr is an architect, William Cooke is a civil engineer and Nelson Douglass is a mechanical engineer. During 1960, Douglass visited his parents in Grenada, Mississippi. Their next-door neighbor was John McEachin, the city manager of Grenada. Mr. McEachin asked Douglass if he would be interested in designing a new city hall for the town of Grenada. Douglass consulted with

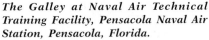

The Galley at Naval Air Technical Training Facility, Pensacola Naval Air Station, Pensacola, Florida.

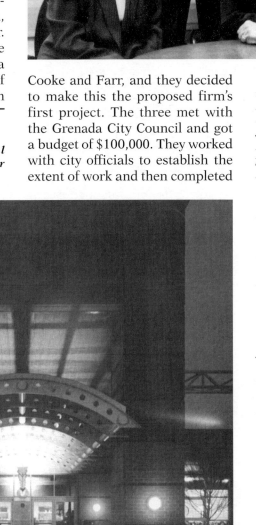

Cooke and Farr, and they decided to make this the proposed firm's first project. The three met with the Grenada City Council and got a budget of $100,000. They worked with city officials to establish the extent of work and then completed

The CDFL principals are, from left to right, sitting: Ann Somers, Nelson L. Douglass and David A. Lemons. Standing, from left to right: Gene Crager, Jody Coleman, Robert O. Byrd, Robert E. Farr II and Jesse Browning. Missing from the photograph is Steve Phyfer.

contract documents, took bids and awarded the contract to the low bidder for approximately $90,000.

Several months later on a Saturday, Cooke and Douglass were in Grenada inspecting the project with the contractor and the city manager, when Joseph Ware came into the building. He had been told that Cooke Douglass Farr had a project in Grenada, and he was there to verify the fact. The three men were fired on Monday, but they had already rented office space and were only waiting a few weeks to make their announcement, which was done for them in May 1961.

Even though the Wares expressed their dissatisfaction with the three, they nevertheless asked Douglass to continue performing mechanical design on their projects throughout 1961and 1962. Douglass worked for Overstreet, Ware & Ware during this period, and these funds helped to support Cooke Douglass Farr initially.

By 1962 Cooke Douglass Farr had been hired to design several schools in Montgomery County, Mississippi. This project had a budget of $400,000. With a design fee of $24,000, which was quite good in 1962.

Since Douglass was going to North Mississippi all of 1962 and 1963, he also pursued other work there. The best job they acquired was a large retirement home in Tupelo from the North Mississippi Conference of the Methodist Church. This initial project has led to several additions and numerous other projects for the Methodist conferences. This work has also led to many new contacts throughout the state of Mississippi.

Through the years, the firm developed many governmental clients because of the ability to provide both architecture and engineering with an in-house team. These clients include the following: the Department of Defense, the Department of Energy, the General Services Administration, the U.S. Postal Service, the Department of Labor, the U.S. Corps of Engineers, the Naval Facilities Engineering Command, the Veterans Administration and the U.S. Department of Corrections.

The firm has also worked for a number of agencies in the state of Mississippi, including the Bureau of Buildings, the Department of Transportation and the State Department of Health—as well as the University of Mississippi, Mississippi State University and numerous community colleges.

The firm does most of its work in Mississippi, but it has performed numerous projects outside the state, including recent projects at Auburn University and Baylor University.

The firm continues to offer both architecture and engineering, and today this includes electrical engineering as well as landscape architecture and interior design.

David Lemons joined the firm in 1981 as a project architect, and he was made a partner in the firm in 1992. Robert E. Farr II acquired his father's stock in the firm in 1992. Since the retirement of William H. Cooke and Robert E. Farr, the firm has taken on a number of additional partners besides Nelson Douglass, Robert E. Farr II and David Lemons. New partners in-

Thad Cochran Center for the Development of Natural Products, University of Mississippi, Oxford, Mississippi.

clude: Steve Phyfer, A.I.A.; Jody Coleman, A.I.A.; Jesse Browning, P. E.; Robert O. Byrd, P. E.; Gene Crager, A.I.A.; and Ann Somers, A.I.A.

All of these partners regularly participate in civic, community, church and professional activities. This firm is fortunate to have had so many good years, but it takes a lot of effort by everyone for continued success.

EDUCATION SERVICES FOUNDATION

Education Services Foundation (ESF) is a non-profit organization based in Jackson, Mississippi, with the sole purpose of "Making College Possible" for students in the Mississippi area. ESF seeks to fulfill its vision by means of free college planning resources and services provided by ESF CAPP (College Access Planning Program); a mentoring program for under-served students in the Mississippi Delta provided by ESF Delta Scholars; annual scholarships; and low-cost student loans with industry-leading borrower benefits.

The history of ESF actually begins with the Mississippi Higher Education Assistance Corporation (MHEAC), a nonprofit corporation started by a group of concerned educators and businessmen in 1980 to help students get a college education. The corporation was organized at the request of the board of trustees of State Institutions of Higher Learning (IHL) of the state of Mississippi, the Post-Secondary Education Financial Assistance Board of the state of Mississippi, and the Division of Federal-State-Local Programs within the Office of the Governor of the state of Mississippi for the exclusive purpose of acquiring student loan notes so that lenders could reinvest the proceeds to provide future student loans. Serving as a secondary market for student loans, MHEAC helped ensure adequate funds were available to all Mississippians in-

From left to right: Vernetta P. Fairley, Ann G. Hendrick.

terested in pursuing higher learning. Since its inception, MHEAC has assisted more than 200,000 students.

In 1995, many of those who founded MHEAC, along with others, established Education Services Foundation (ESF). With more flexibility than MHEAC, ESF was able to help students in new ways.

First, ESF provided a new college access planning program, ESF CAPP, designed to help students make better decisions before they began their college experience. The five pillars of ESF CAPP are vision development, skills assessment, career selection, school choice, and financial aid. This flagship program served more than 25,000 students in 2001, and the number increases dramatically each year. Services are provided onsite at two resource centers; through presentations in schools and communities, and via Mississippi Educational Televi-

sion Interactive Video Network; on the foundation's Web site, www.esfweb.com; and by a toll-free hotline. To further expand its reach, ESF CAPP partners with prestigious organizations such as IHL, Mississippi Counseling Association, Junior League of Jackson, Fellowship of Christian Athletes and Parents for Public Schools. History has shown that students helped by ESF CAPP were, across the board, more likely to have a successful college experience and be better prepared to accomplish their life goals. Further, students engaged by ESF CAPP were less likely to default on their student loans. Best of all, ESF CAPP services are free to students, parents, and educators.

Next, the Delta Scholars program was initiated to mentor Delta area students with less opportunity and provide them with a vision for their future. The Delta Scholars

From left to right: J. Herman Hines, Alvis T. Hunt, William M. Jones and Dr. Thomas D. Layzell.

From left to right: Dr. Jayne B. Sargent, Tom B. Scott, Jr., Sid J. Sims and Kenneth L. Smith, Jr.

program begins working with students in the ninth grade with after-school workshops and study sessions. The favorite annual event is the college tour, where many students who have never been outside their county visit college campuses throughout the Southeast, awakening their minds to educational possibilities.

ESF expanded its vision by making student loans available in 2000. ESF is able to offer, without question, the most economically beneficial borrower benefits available on loans originated by ESF and by lenders using MHEAC as their secondary market. In simple terms, this means with an ESF loan the student has the potential to keep more money at disbursement and during the repayment period. ESF loans are marketed not only through the foundation, but also in partner banks throughout the state,

J. C. Whitehead on the left, and Jack L. Woodward.

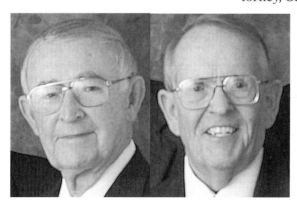

providing convenient hometown access for students. ESF firmly believes that the foundation's vision is being accomplished by helping students get the lowest-cost student loans available.

To ensure students and parents receive the best possible customer service during the loan process, ESF provides origination and in-school servicing for not only ESF, but a number of other lenders.

ESF has made scholarships for students available through several venues since its inception, increasing the scope each year to a total of more than $60,000 to be awarded in 2003. In 2002, nearly 800 wrote essays for $15,000 awarded, and $25,000 will go to the winners in the 2003 essay contest.

The MHEAC and ESF directors and officers are comprised of a distinguished group of outstanding leaders in the community and business arena:
• Tom B. Scott, Jr., MHEAC and ESF board chair and director, attorney, Scott & Scott.
• Jack L. Woodward, MHEAC and ESF board vice chair and director, retired dean of Student Aid Financial Planning, Millsaps College.
• J. C. Whitehead, MHEAC and ESF secretary/treasurer and director, chairman emeritus, BancorpSouth.
• Vernetta P. Fairley,

MHEAC and ESF director, director of Standards of Excellence Review Program, National Association of Student Financial Aid Administrators.
• Ann G. Hendrick, MHEAC and ESF director, dean of Admissions and Financial Aid, Millsaps College.
• J. Herman Hines, MHEAC and ESF director, retired chairman and CEO, Deposit Guaranty National Bank.
• Alvis T. Hunt, MHEAC and ESF director, vice chairman emeritus, Trustmark National Bank.
• William M. Jones, MHEAC and ESF director, retired senior vice president, Deposit Guaranty National Bank.
• Dr. Thomas D. Layzell, MHEAC director, commissioner of higher education, Board of Trustees of State Institutions of Higher Learning.
• Dr. Jayne B. Sargent, MHEAC and ESF director, retired superintendent, Jackson Public Schools.
• Sid J. Sims, MHEAC and ESF director, senior vice president, AmSouth Bank.
• Kenneth L. Smith, Jr., MHEAC and ESF executive director.

Led by these stellar directors and officers, ESF's vision for the future is to grow and expand the ESF CAPP, the ESF Delta Scholars, the ESF Scholarship Program, and the student loan programs. All four of these programs are making college possible for students in the Mississippi area.

HEARTLAND BUILDING PRODUCTS

The Little Heart That Could. Booneville, Mississippi didn't become a major center for the production of vinyl siding overnight. That heartbeat started small and faint. An afterthought in the mind of a local producer of PVC pipe products called H & W Building Products. But, that tiny heartbeat has steadily grown into becoming one of the single, largest volume manufacturing facilities for the production of vinyl siding in the world and is still located in the same small Prentiss County town, in Northeast Mississippi, about halfway between Tupelo and Corinth on Highway 45.

In 1981, Randy Heath, the owner of H & W Building Products and several other PVC pipe producing operations around the country, observed with great interest the rapid growth being exhibited by the still fledgling vinyl siding industry. What particularly interested him at the time was the impressive profit potential available to a pipe producing company which was already buying in large quantity and successfully extruding Polyvinyl Chloride (PVC) resin, the main ingredient in vinyl siding.

So, he diverted one of his Booneville PVC pipe extruders to the project and hired two employees to set it up in a back area of the pipe production facility and put together a production team to start running vinyl siding. In fact, two of those

Aerial view of the Heartland manufacturing facility taken in 1989. The operation currently occupies 25 acres of land at the same location.

original employees still work for the company—Donald Harris, Heartland vice president of manufacturing and Dewayne Morgan, Heartland continuous improvement team manager. This original mono-extruding operation could produce 1,200 square-feet of vinyl siding an hour — enough for about half of a modest-sized home. But, the H & W marketing strategy was to capture market share by significantly underpricing the more established competition and selling only to independent wholesale distributors around the country. These stocking distribution outlets would, in turn, resell the product to siding contractors, remodelers, and builders in their market areas.

By 1987 the upstart H & W operation in Booneville, Mississippi was producing $36 million in sales annually and had grown from the one, simple mono-extrusion line into a battery of 13 state-of-the-art vinyl siding production lines, including six co-extrusion lines that were each producing over 1,800 square feet of vinyl siding an hour. The original backroom operation in the PVC pipe plant had long before been traded-in for a nearby, brand-new 100,000 square-foot production facility with 160,000 square feet of product warehouse space and 50

Heartland employees gather in 1985. Twenty-six percent of the current workforce have been with the company 10 years or longer.

employees. According to Mr. Heath, "the best vinyl siding production facility in the whole country was located in Booneville, Mississippi in 1987."

However, the pounding heartbeat of the miracle growing in Booneville did not go unnoticed. In 1987, a 133-year-old Canadian conglomerate, Redpath Industries, with vinyl siding holdings in Canada, saw an opportunity to enter the lucrative U.S. vinyl siding marketplace. Redpath paid Mr. Heath $33.3 million for his siding operation. They brought in experienced vinyl siding manufacturing and marketing managers; and, they changed the name of the company, to avoid confusion with the original PVC pipe plant, to Heartland Building Products. They added a unique heart-shaped weephole to every piece of siding produced as Heartland's "signature of quality and pride" and began creating the marketing concepts and in-home selling tools that would power the company's growth in future years.

They also changed the product-selling proposition from "cut-rate, low-cost" to "value-added quality."

The Redpath years for Heartland were to be short. In 1989, just a little over a year later, the rumbling heartbeat in Booneville attracted the attention of yet another, even larger Canadian company. Jannock Ltd., with roots in the building industry going back to 1893 and vast holdings in brick production and steel fabrication, acquired Redpath Industries to help complete its desire to serve all major segments of the home construction industry in the U.S. The result for Heartland was a very opportune infusion of dollars for needed capital improvements to the physical facilities in Booneville that would be necessary if the company was to continue its remarkable growth.

Jannock's deep pockets produced amazing results. In 1989, when Jannock purchased Redpath, Heartland was producing 72,500,000 square feet of vinyl siding for the U.S. building and remodeling marketplace—all from Booneville, Mississippi. The available plant capacity at that time was 100,000,000 square-feet of vinyl siding from this same location. The company had five Heartland salesmen in the field and was also handled by four additional independent manufacturer's representatives. The Booneville workforce had grown to 140 people, and Heartland was the eighth largest producer of vinyl siding in the world.

By 1996, "the little heart that could" was the fourth largest producer of vinyl siding with $86 million in annual sales. The company's product was being stocked in 290 distribution locations around the country and was being exported to China, Japan, Russia, Poland, and Korea. The Heartland sales force now numbered 23, and the Booneville workforce had expanded to 278 local employees.

Jannock's willingness to put dollars into their investments had made it possible for Heartland to increase the Booneville plant facility to 320,331 square feet with another 150,000 square feet of nearby leased warehouse space to help handle the demand for product needed to load-out anywhere from 17 to 30 truckloads of product a day. Four high output extrusion lines were added, each capable of producing 4,000 square feet of vinyl siding per hour; and, the company had its own 15-car railroad spur capable of holding up to 3 million pounds of PVC resin at a time.

A new employee center had been constructed in 1993, an important improvement for a workforce that was maintaining 12-hour shifts, 24 hours a day, 365 days a year with few breaks in production. In 1994, a modern, fully automated and computerized $2 million blending and material handling facility—a four-story tower—had been added,

Heartland's $2 million raw materials handling and blending facility, constructed in 1994, utilizes computerized automation to deliver precisely mixed and measured amounts of its Super Polymer Vinyl Siding formulation to the extrusion lines.

which would enable even faster, more efficient control and delivery of raw materials to the humming Heartland production lines. The office space had been expanded to over 6,000 square feet to accommodate the growing need for administration to keep up with production. Rotary embossers, a closed-loop chilling system, dual-manifold die innovations, rotary-cam slotter/cutter/pullers, automated packing tables, a palletizing facility, shrink-wrapping equipment and a complete quality testing facility and materials laboratory each had

Extruded Heartland Super Polymer Vinyl Siding panels are 12' to 12' 6" in length when they arrive at the jobsite for application to the home.

made its beneficial impact on the Heartland system and had increased the company's ability to do and be more to its customers.

Heartland had also become known for its marketing and manufacturing innovation. High speed extrusion technology and the unique skills developed by the local workforce were allowing the temperature and production speeds needed to operate under strict production tolerances that would deliver an unmatched quality of product to the field. Heartland's recipe for making vinyl siding became known as "Super Polymer." On-line colorization and computer color-matching allowed product of different colors to be produced without halting the production process to make changes. Concentration of anti-weathering materials at the surface of the siding, in a "Weather Barrier Shield," as well as throughout the panel, found favor with customers. SPX-2000 UV Blocker And Sunscreen Protection, (Infra Red) Tri-Pigment Technology, Natural Patina Low Gloss Finishes, Authentic Woodgrain Impressioning. The combining of marketing and manufacturing concepts to improve production, to give its products a uniqueness in the marketplace, and to increase product visibility, proved to be very successful.

Actually, the key to Heartland's climb from obscurity in the rough-and-tumble world of vinyl siding production was first, and foremost, its people. From the very beginning, in 1981, the company's dedicated Booneville, Mississippi workforce was challenged to constantly analyze the operation's current and future needs; and, fortunately, they were empowered by each successive ownership group to do whatever it took to be "the best vinyl siding production facility in the whole country." Management held the tiller, but the wind in the sails of this success story came from every level of employee participa-

tion. This special ongoing employee-management relationship produced a loyalty within the workforce that has resulted in a large core of technically experienced employees staying with the company over the years. In fact, at this writing, over 26 percent of the Heartland workforce had been with the company for over 10 years and several employees had 18 years of service or more.

In 1996, Heartland became one of the first in the vinyl siding industry to successfully pursue certification as a Quality Management System under the International Standards Organization (ISO) 9002 program. The Heartland effort was totally accomplished through an employee-driven initiative to create a Quality Policy with set standards, procedures, and work instructions for every department in the facility. Heartland was successfully updated and re-registered to the newer 9001:2000 ISO standard for quality management in 2002.

Employee-monitored process control strategies to improve production efficiencies began to be introduced at Heartland, in 1997. These were soon followed by completely employee-driven continuous improvement teaming to identify and attack specific areas within the operation that might

Heartland vinyl siding products, made in Booneville, Mississippi, can be found on homes throughout the U.S. and in several foreign countries.

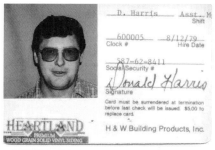

Original photo ID badges of two members of the 1981 vinyl siding production team at the H & W pipe plant in Booneville, Mississippi—Donald Harris, current Heartland vice president of manufacturing, and Dewayne Morgan, current Heartland continuous improvements manager.

reduce overall efficiency and profitability.

By 2002, Heartland Building Products had grown from the most humble of beginnings in a small Mississippi community, basically as an experiment, to become a modern, large capacity producer of vinyl siding products for the U.S. and foreign markets. The "little heart that could" had grown from blind ambition with cast-off resources to the realization of an ongoing vision closely held by its loyal and industrious Booneville employees.

Say what you do and do what you say. Strive for success and accept nothing less. Give "quality from the heart" in all that you do.

The "heart" in Heartland lies not in any one place or in any one person. It lies in every employee . . . in every manager, supervisor, and executive. It lies in the fathers and sons and daughters that have maintained its machines, packed its product, loaded its trucks, guided its success, and powered the vision from the very beginning. It lies in Booneville, Mississippi.

Among the new companies that have flourished in Mississippi over the last thirty years is Howard Industries of Laurel, a manufacturer of computers, ballast equipment, and distribution transformers. The company's 1.6 million-square-foot transformer facility is the largest such plant in the world. Courtesy, Mississippi Development Authority

MISSISSIPPI UNIVERSITY FOR WOMEN

When Mississippi University for Women was chartered in 1884, it made educational history as the first state-supported college for women in America. MUW's founding mothers had been persistent and tireless in their efforts, which had spanned over 20 years. Energetic campaigning in the 1860s and 1870s by activist Sallie Eola Reneau of Grenada had resulted in legislative approval, but no appropriations. A decade later, Olivia Valentine Hastings of Copiah County and Annie Coleman Peyton of Claiborne County joined forces to lobby legislators and journalists in support of a public women's college. Mrs. Hastings' friend, legislator John McCaleb Martin of Claiborne County, drafted the original bill to create a state college for women. Strong political support from a few key representatives, combined with the backing of Governor Lowery, aided the passage of the Martin Bill, although by only one vote in the Senate and two votes in the House.

Originally known as The Industrial Institute and College (II & C), this new institution provided a

A view of front campus from the 1898-1899 annual catalogue.

unique hybrid: a high quality collegiate education for women coupled with practical vocational training. As one legislator said, it was a "Godsend" for the "poor girls of Mississippi." In a time when intellectual training for women was considered by many to have disastrous consequences, Mississippi had the foresight to recognize that its young women were going to have to be taught not only to think for themselves, but also to support themselves. The innovation and the historical value of the II & C's curriculum is illustrated by the other state-supported women's colleges which patterned themselves after the Mississippi prototype: Georgia State College for Women (1889), North Carolina College for Women (1891), Alabama College (1893), Texas State College for Women (1901), Florida State College for Women (1905), and Oklahoma College for Women (1908).

The first session began in October 1885 in Columbus, a city that had won the college by virtue of its early interest in women's education and its willingness to commit both property and cash to the endeavor. The city donated to the state the buildings and grounds of the Columbus Female Institute, a private school founded in 1847, in addition to city bonds in the amount of $50,000 for any

needed improvements to the property. That October, 341 blue-uniformed girls embarked on this new educational experiment. Four years later, the first graduates received their diplomas.

The first president, Richard Watson Jones, who also taught physics and chemistry, presided over an all-female faculty, women who influenced the political and educational life of Mississippians for many decades to come. Pauline Orr, Mistress of English; Mary Callaway, Mistress of Mathematics; and Sallie McLaurin, Mistress of Industrial and Decorative Arts became powerful mentors for the young women who began leaving the II & C to attend graduate schools, to teach, or to find their places in the business world as bookkeepers or telegraphers. Miss Orr was active in the women's suffrage movement and urged her students to press for the vote for women. After her retirement from teaching in 1913, Orr became a full-time suffragist, serving as president of the state association and speaking up and down the eastern seaboard, using her connections with former students and faculty to further the cause. Most historians agree that Governor Henry Whitfield, sixth president (1907-1920) of the II & C—which became Mississippi State College for Women (MSCW) at the end of his tenure—

Turn of the century II & C basketball team (from the 1902 yearbook): Bennie Will Gibson, captain, Annie Perkins, Mattie Thornton, Almira Pardee, Carrie Lee Crisler, Ruby Johnson, Mary Ellen Herrin, Mary Ella McFarlane, Mamie Weems, Zula Morris, Pearl Turner, Jean Oliver.

was elected governor of Mississippi through the efforts of the newly-enfranchised MSCW alumnae who campaigned for him all over the state.

Other early faculty members became household names in Mississippi because of their innovative teaching and their passion for their disciplines. Emma Ody Pohl, legendary physical education teacher from 1907 until 1955, brought mandatory physical education courses to all students and created some of the most distinctive campus traditions: the Junior-Freshman Wedding and the Zouave marching drill. Weenona Poindexter, music faculty member from 1894 until 1945, initiated the diploma in music and began decades of highly-successful concert series by personally guaranteeing the funding for an Ignace Paderewski concert on campus in 1905. Mabel Ward, the first home economics professor in Mississippi, created innovative programs, such as her Home Management Practice House, which set precedents for home economics departments all over the country.

Many of the early graduates embarked on prestigious and long-lasting professional careers. Eula Deaton ('89) became a prominent educator in Chicago; Blanche Colton Williams ('98) was head of the English department at Hunter College for many years and a member of the founding committee of the O. Henry Short Story Awards; Rosa Peebles ('91) chaired the Department of English at Vassar; Frances Jones Gaither ('09) became a best-selling novelist; Helen C. Carloss ('13) earned a law degree and served on the U.S. Court of Appeals; Dr. Marietta Eichelberger ('12) was for a time Director of Nutrition for the Evaporated Milk Corporation of America, while her sister, Lillian Eichelberger ('14), became the first female member of the University of Chicago School of Medicine; Dr. Elizabeth Lee Hazen ('10) became a scientific researcher

Mississippi University for Women, front campus view.

who isolated the antibiotic nystatin; and Fannye A. Cook ('10) founded the Mississippi State Wildlife Museum in Jackson.

In 1920 when The Industrial Institute and College became Mississippi State College for Women, the new name more clearly reflected the institution's merging of all professional training with four-year collegiate degrees. By 1974, as all eight universities in Mississippi began adding and strengthening graduate programs, MSCW became Mississippi University for Women. In 1982, The Supreme Court, in a split vote of five to four, ordered MUW to admit male applicants to the School of Nursing. To avoid further litigation, the board of trustees then directed MUW to open all academic programs to men. Shortly afterward, however, the IHL board reaffirmed the original mission focused on women's

education, and the campus welcomed its first woman president, Dr. Clyda Stokes Rent, in 1989.

Mississippi University for Women still provides a high-quality liberal arts education with a distinct emphasis on professional development and leadership opportunities for women. Regularly ranked as one of America's best colleges by the prestigious *US News and World Report*, MUW is also ranked in the top 100 "best public colleges in America" by *Kiplinger's Personal Finance*. MUW scholar athletes are nationally recognized for their high graduation rate by the *USA Today*/NCAA Foundation Academic Achievement Awards. MUW Nursing graduating classes regularly receive a 100 percent pass rate on national licensure examinations. MUW remains an educational model and pioneer not only in Mississippi, but in the nation.

Callaway Hall and Orr Chapel at Mississippi University for Women.

PARKWAY PROPERTIES, INC.

Started in 1971 in Houston, Texas, as the Texas First Mortgage REIT, the company became The Parkway Company when it moved its headquarters to Jackson, Mississippi, in 1980. In 1996, the company moved its public stock listing to the New York Stock Exchange under the symbol "PKY" and changed its name to Parkway Properties, Inc. Parkway President and Chief Executive Officer Steven G. Rogers stated, "I was attracted to the company because of the promise I saw and the values that were readily apparent in my first visit with then President and Chief Executive Officer Leland Speed in 1983." Values and promise have been a hallmark of Parkway from the beginning. The company has been praised by industry experts, analysts and investors for its customer orientation, industry-leading tenant retention, innovation and total return performance. It has also been noted for its community spirit, employee excellence, buying discipline and adherence to its core values.

Unlike other real estate investment trusts, the company defines its business as the Tenant Retention Business and focuses on keeping customers happy rather than the transactional nature prevalent in the real estate industry. "We work hard to provide great service for the customers in all of our properties," Rogers emphasizes. "We recognize that satisfied tenants are the key to our company's operating success; therefore, we want our customers to enjoy their office space. With high occupancies in our buildings, our biggest risk is that our customers will become unhappy and move out; so all of our actions are oriented toward making their stay in a Parkway property a pleasant experience."

The responsibility to its shareholders runs deep, but it is not Parkway's singular mission. It serves many constituencies, including our employees, customers, communities and shareholders, to

name a few. Rogers stated, "We do not have an organizational chart in our company, but if we did these four groups would be at the very top."

One of the secrets to its success, is hiring, training and retaining great people. Parkway treats people with respect and expects a lot from them. The reason it does so well in other areas of the company is because of the strength and determination of our people. It promotes a customer-service mentality at all levels of the company through teamwork and open communication, as evidenced by weekly local team meetings, Parkway University and our monthly Parkway Connection lunches—in which every employee attends in person or via a conference call. It believes in matching responsibility and authority by empowering its people

Parkway's officer team consists of experienced people from various disciplines of asset management, leasing, customer advocate, accounting, finance and administration. The team operates in a collegial setting from its headquarters in the One Jackson Place building in downtown Jackson. The nine senior officers of Parkway have an average of over 20 years of real estate industry experience and have worked together at Parkway for an average of over 14 years.

to take care of the customer. Parkway identifies great people through an active college internship program with Mississippi colleges and universities, as well as through regional and national institutions such as Harvard Business School, which has been ongoing for the past 20 years. We have a lot of MBAs and CPAs on staff, but what we really seek in new employees is well-rounded men and women who

Parkway Realty Services, founded in 1988 as a wholly-owned subsidiary of Parkway Properties, and provides highly specialized sales, leasing and management services to numerous third party clients in Jackson, as well as other cities where Parkway owns property.

show spirit, promise and integrity. We can train anyone on the fundamentals of our business. It's what people come to the company with that matters the most. Everybody in the company is expected to participate and volunteer in our company programs. We believe it is possible to have fun at work and still work hard. This culture has become deeply ingrained in the core values of the company.

The company invests in office properties in markets and cities experiencing significant employment and population growth. "It's

important to understand *why* we are where we are . . . job growth and high employment fill up office buildings," Rogers adds. Parkway's properties are found in Chicago, Houston, Jackson, Phoenix, Atlanta, Winston-Salem, Charlotte, Memphis, Knoxville, Nashville, St. Petersburg and Fort Lauderdale, as well as Columbia, South Carolina and Richmond and Chesapeake, Virginia. Approximately 22 percent of Parkway's total square footage is located in Houston, 11 percent in Chicago and nine percent in Jackson. Parkway's Jackson-owned properties include landmark properties such as One Jackson Place (Parkway's headquarters), the Skytel Centre and SunCom building downtown, and the IBM building on County Line Road/I-55 North, as well as River Oaks on Lakeland

Drive. "Our buying discipline is strict, and we stick to it," says Rogers. "We don't focus on growth of our asset base, rather we focus on growth of our profit and returns to our shareholders." Indeed, Parkway has outperformed its peer group as measured by total return to shareholders consistently for the past ten years, five years and one year.

Parkway is committed to the communities in which it invests, especially its hometown of Jackson. Parkway Chairman Leland Speed is also the head of Jackson's downtown development organization, Downtown Partners. Speed states, "Our commitment to our community is evidenced in many ways, from landscaping to hiring, involvement, leadership and caring. We want to help our cities." As an example of this, the company recently renovated the award-winning Toyota Center, an historic renovation of a 1907 eight-story building in downtown. This development helped initiate the Memphis Redbirds AAA ballpark and numerous other adjacent developments in downtown Memphis. The officers and employees of Parkway hold numerous leadership roles and board seats in volunteer, church and community organizations. Each regional office of Parkway participates in various community events, ranging from raising money for United Way, Muscular Dystrophy and other worthy organizations to hosting blood drives and collecting food, toys, coats and other items for those less fortunate within our communities. Community leadership is an important part of the fabric of our company.

When asked what he wants for the future, Rogers replied, "Our goal is simple. We want Parkway Properties to be the best real estate investment trust in America and for our people to be proud to say they work here."

ROBOT COUPE, U.S.A., INC.

For over 30 years, the Jackson-based Robot Coupe U.S.A., Inc.—which was founded by Jackson residents Rollins Brown, Bill Gilmore and Dan Bounds—has been the food service industry leader in the development and refinement of commercial food processors and vegetable preparation units.

The idea for the company started at LeRuths, an upscale restaurant in New Orleans. While having dinner, Brown and some business associates were joined by Warren LeRuth, owner and chef. When LeRuth discovered that Brown was a manufacturers agent for food service equipment with Marketing Agents South, he promptly showed him the fourteen-quart Robot Coupe food processor—a new machine from France.

LeRuth had discovered the machine—which was developed by Pierre Verdun of Robot Coupe France and produced in Montceau—while dining in four-star restaurants in France, and soon thereafter became the sole importer to America. The Robot Coupe presented a whole new concept in food preparation, because, up until the invention of this machine, slicing, dicing, shredding and grating were all done by hand, which was very labor intensive.

Needless to say, Brown, too, was

Robot Coupe's three founders, from left to right: Dan Bounds, Bill Gilmore and Rollins Brown, in 1998.

amazed by the machine—which was similar to the vertical cutter-mixers (vcm) on the market at that time. He watched as LeRuth prepared pates and mousse effortlessly, and then immediately called Gilmore and Bounds. After seeing the machine in action, the three partners were as equally amazed—and LeRuth, impressed with the enthusiasm and desire of this group, gave them the right to represent the Robot Coupe line in five states and the panhandle of Florida.

Brown, Gilmore and Bounds started selling the machines by demonstrating them at schools, restaurants, conventions and workshops. It was a machine that had to be seen to be believed—and once their audiences witnessed it, everyone wanted one. Sales and demand increased dramatically.

While their sales were skyrocketing, so was the popularity of LeRuth's restaurant. Finding it difficult to manage both the restaurant and distributorship, he contacted Brown and asked if the three men would be interested in buying his inventory—and becoming the sole importer for Robot Coupe machines. Accepting the offer, Brown, Gilmore and Bounds, in conjunction with Robot Coupe

France, soon established a new company, Robot Coupe U.S.A.

Brown, who spoke no French, flew to France to negotiate its distributorship with Pierre Verdun, who spoke no English, with the help of Gilbert Verdun, Pierre's nephew (who had come to America and worked in LeRuth's restaurant to learn English, and who later returned to France.) After a stint in the French Army, Gilbert, who later became general manager of Robot Coupe France, came to America for a number of years to learn about American engineering needs, marketing and generally to get a picture of the American market. He resided in Jackson, Mississippi, and traveled in the United States with Brown, Gilmore and Bounds, demonstrating the Robot Coupe machines and learning about the American food service market.

By the end of its third year, Robot Coupe U.S.A. hired John Holley as its sales manager, and from that point on, the company just kept growing, as it aquired sales reps and held demonstrations—especially in schools, where the company had much expertise. According to Bounds, it was the school market that pulled them through—and enabled them to bring in a professional to help their company with marketing and direction.

Robot Coupe U.S.A.'s booth at the 2001 National Restaurant Show in Chicago.

Brown, Gilmore and Bounds were innovators working at establishing new markets, and although Pierre Verdun had done a marvelous job on the original design of the machine, it needed development to suit the American market—especially the school market. Soon, new machines were manufactured for them in France and shipped to America.

One of Robot Coupe's major achievements was that it was the first to introduce a continuous feed

The Robot Coupe R2N Commercial Food Processor is the best-selling commercial food processor in the world.

table-top unit—where a kitchen staff could continuously shred everything from vegetables to cheese. It was an impressive feature that thrilled everyone, and it was exactly what the marketplace needed.

In its 30-year history, Robot Coupe has grown from four employees—the original three founders and their office manager and secretary, Jo Wilson—to over 40 employees, including Bob Velkey, who was hired to help the firm expand. Today, Robot Coupe is a multi-million-dollar company. From a modest start of only four different food processor models, the Robot Coupe line has grown to

over 68 food processors, vertical cutter-mixers, blixers and power mixers. Its commercial food processor line ranges in size from the R100, 2-1/2-quart unit, to its 60-quart vertical cutter-mixer, the R60TS.

Because of the company's dedication to manufacture the very best product available, its commitment to research and development, and its constant striving to give its customers the best service possible, the Robot Coupe Commercial Food Processor has become the worldwide standard of the industry, for restaurants, schools, corrections facilities, hospitals, nursing homes, cruise ships and delicatessans. They even have a new line of power mixers, which is distinguished from its competitors by its superior clean-ability, power, ease of use and enhanced sanitation.

As Robot Coupe U.S.A. grew, so did its need for additional space. The company is now located in Ridgeland, in a new 30,000-square-foot building, with additional office space, expanded plant facilities for assembly and warehousing, a state-of-the-art test kitchen used for improved dealer/rep training and demonstrations, and a high-tech conference room.

In July 1998 Robot Coupe U.S.A., Inc. moved into its new plant located at 280 South Perkins Street, Ridgeland, Mississippi

Over the years, Robot Coupe has been honored many times by its rep groups for its superior products and excellent customer service. Recently, Robot Coupe was named "Manufacturer of the Year" by the Phil Brant Factory Agents of Jacksonville, Florida. This award was based on sales, service, customer assistance and overall support for customers.

Robot Coupe's roots—past, present and future—are firmly planted in the metropolitan Jackson area, and its management and employees are active in many different charitable and church activities, in and around the Jackson area. Robot Coupe U.S.A. has been good to Jackson, Mississippi, and the people of Jackson have been good to Robot Coupe—which makes for a successful partnership.

In 1998 the staff of Robot Coupe U.S.A. gathered for ground breaking for its present office and warehouse, at 280 South Picken Street, Ridgeland.

THE SUN HERALD

The Sun Herald is "South Mississippi's Newspaper."

Since 1884 *The Sun Herald* has served readers and advertisers in Biloxi-Gulfport and throughout the Mississippi Gulf Coast. Over the years, the newspaper extended its coverage and influence into the six-county South Mississippi region. The story of *The Sun Herald* reflects the growth of South Mississippi.

In October of 1884, George W. Wilkes and M. B. Richmond started a weekly newspaper in the small fishing village of Biloxi. One year later, Richmond sold out to Wilkes, who became sole owner and publisher of the *Herald*.

Despite two fires, the little newspaper thrived and in 1898 became a daily, published afternoons, Monday through Saturday. The first paid editor during the early years was Joseph R. Davis. Davis was the nephew of Jefferson Davis, the first and only president of the Confederate States of America, who lived at Beauvoir in Biloxi.

In 1912, after having editorial offices in Biloxi and Gulfport for two years, the *Herald* moved its printing plant to Gulfport.

George Wilkes died in 1915, and his family inherited the newspaper. His son Eugene, born in 1885, was only 10 years old when he started working for his father. Over the years he held virtually every job there, from carrier to publisher.

Two businessmen passing a **Sun Herald** *news rack in Biloxi.*

Publisher Ricky Mathews.

"Mr. Gene" Wilkes continued for several years as editor of *The Daily Herald* after its purchase by the State-Record Company of Columbia, South Carolina in July 1968.

Gulf Publishing Company was formed as a wholly owned subsidiary of the State-Record Company, and Roland Weeks, Jr., was named president and general manager of *The Daily Herald* in 1968.

Only a few months into his job, Weeks and his newspaper faced their biggest challenge in August 1969 when Hurricane Camille, the worst natural disaster to strike the United States, roared across the Mississippi Gulf Coast. Despite severe damage to the newspaper's printing plant and almost total devastation around them, the staff of *The Daily Herald* continued to photograph and report on the destruction and initial relief efforts around Camille. News and photos were sent to Columbia, South Carolina, where its sister newspaper printed *The Daily Herald* for four days. Free copies of the newspaper were flown to Gulfport and delivered to everyone that the carriers could find in the aftermath of the storm, providing residents with the only source of information available to them. That dedication has enabled *The Sun Herald* to never miss a day of publication or

delivery—in spite of disasters, natural or man-made—which is a record to be proud of.

In early 1970, just five months after the Mississippi Coast began digging out from the destruction of Hurricane Camille, the newspaper launched its Sunday edition. One month later, ground was broken for a new, two-million-dollar plant on DeBuys Road, where Biloxi meets Gulfport. By October 1970 the plant was finished, and operations were moved from the Gulfport printing

Executive editor Stan Tiner.

plant and the Biloxi news office into the new facility on DeBuys Road.

At that same time, the content of *The Daily Herald* expanded, with new features added daily and on Sundays. To keep up with growing readership from a burgeoning population, news bureaus were opened in Ocean Springs in 1969, in Bay St. Louis in 1979, and at the state capital in Jackson in 1973. (*The Daily Herald* was the first Mississippi newspaper to operate a news bureau in the state capital.) Today's *Sun Herald* is served by bureaus in Bay St. Louis, Ocean Springs, Pascagoula, Jackson and Washington, D.C.

Gulf Publishing Company launched the *South Mississippi Sun* on October 1, 1973, as a morning complement to the afternoon *Daily*

Herald. The company continued to publish two separate newspapers for more than a decade.

To better serve the growing Mississippi Gulf Coast, Gulf Publishing Company merged *The Sun* and *The Daily Herald* into an all-day *Sun Herald* in 1984; a year later, the evening edition was discontinued and *The Sun Herald* became a morning daily.

In 1986 the South Carolina-based State-Record Company, with newspapers in Columbia and Myrtle Beach; Alexandria, Virginia; and Biloxi—and with television stations in Charleston, South Carolina and Lubbock, Texas—was purchased by Knight Ridder, Inc., one of America's premier communications companies. *The Sun Herald* joined a network of more than 30 daily newspapers, which extended from Miami to Seattle, and from Philadelphia to Detroit to Kansas City. As proof of the quality of their products, Knight Ridder-owned newspapers have received more Pulitzer Prizes than any other news organization.

The Sun Herald extended its services through the World Wide Web in 1998 by launching SunHerald.com, which quickly became, and still is, South Mississippi's most-used website. As part of the RealCities network, SunHerald.com provides web users with *Sun Herald* coverage of South Mississippi and an easy link to dozens of other news organizations, including partner newspapers in the nation's top 25 markets. Partnering with CareerBuilder, Cars.com, and several home and apartment services, SunHerald.com is South Mississippi's portal to the best the Internet has to offer.

Responding to market opportunities, the newspaper has launched several specialty publications, covering topics from entertainment to the casino industry, for distribution through *The Sun Herald* or outside the market area. Gulf Publishing Company also publishes two military weeklies: the *Keesler News* serves Keesler Air Force Base in Biloxi and the *Seabee Courier* serves Seabees and their families stationed at the U.S. Naval Construction Battalion Center in Gulfport.

In October 2002, Gulf Publishing Company launched *The Journal of South Mississippi Business*, a regional business tabloid serving business and economic development leaders from Hattiesburg to the Mississippi Coast.

The Sun Herald has made several "Nation's Best" lists, and has been a regular winner of the Mississippi Press Association's and the Louisiana-Mississippi Press Association's awards for excellence in writing, editing, design and community service.

Committed to education, *The Sun Herald* sponsors an active Newspaper in Education (NIE) program in more than 150 public and private schools throughout South Mississippi. Students use the newspaper as a "living textbook" to enhance their study of subjects from social studies to fine arts, from math and science to economics and life sciences, as well as history and language arts. The NIE program includes instructor training for teachers and includes such specialized programs as KidsVoting and the Stock Market Game.

The Sun Herald continues to be a leading employer in South Mississippi and one of the area's most active community leaders. Sun Herald executives are active leaders

The Sun Herald *plant and logo.*

in several chambers of commerce and community development organizations, as well as being a United Way pacesetter and major contributor to the Gulf Coast Symphony, the American Red Cross, Christmas in April, KidsVoting, and a host of other programs and organizations.

Today's *Sun Herald* is quite different from the small, weekly newspaper originally cranked out by George Wilkes back in the 1880s—but South Mississippi has changed a great deal, too.

The 21st-century *Sun Herald* is led by publisher Ricky Mathews and executive editor Stan Tiner. Mathews assumed the company's leadership in August 2001 following the retirement of Roland Weeks, Jr. Under Weeks' leadership, *The Sun Herald* grew from a six-afternoons-a-week local paper of less than 30,000 in circulation, to become one of the Southeast's finest newspapers, with more than 135,000 daily and 160,000 Sunday readers. Mathews had almost 20 years of marketing and operations management experience with *The Sun Herald* before being named publisher. He and Tiner lead a management team committed to being "South Mississippi's Newspaper," by providing the news and information relevant to newcomers and long-time residents of the area—and by providing leadership that will keep South Mississippi prospering.

TOUGALOO COLLEGE

A distinctive liberal arts institution located on 500 acres of land in central Mississippi, Tougaloo College is an intellectual, adventurous, enriching and historical indulgence. Tougaloo College has evolved during the course of an amazing journey and has garnered several popular descriptions—a National Historic District, a Mississippi landmark, a cultural homestead, an artistic and academic village, and a resource bank for the global marketplace.

This educational enterprise, established in 1869 by abolitionists from the remains of a slave plantation, stands today as an oasis of freedom and ideas, serving as a major contributor to Mississippi's economy. Boasting of graduating some of the foremost, leading African Americans, Tougaloo College survives because of its rich history, including a renowned tradition of academic excellence and social commitment. The academic offerings are distinct, particularly in the areas of the natural and social sciences, and continue to produce hundreds of scholars in pre-health and pre-law, and a bevy of national

The College's historic Woodworth Chapel served as a strategic platform and safe haven during the Civil Rights Movement.

The Robert O. Wilder Building, commonly known as "The Mansion," is the oldest building on campus. It was designed by J. Lamour of Canton, Mississippi and was constructed in 1848.

talent who choose careers in arts and the humanities. Tougaloo College builds on its deep and strong legacy of educational and political leadership, as it continues to provide quality education and community service opportunities to young men and women, preparing them to become conscientious leaders.

The College has been widely documented and celebrated as the safe haven for the Civil Rights movement, where Freedom Riders and other activists gathered and created strategies during the turbulent '50s, '60s and '70s. Its facilities served as a refuge for those who set out to create some of America's most powerful revolutionary societal changes.

Throughout the 20th Century, the College excelled in its capacity to struggle against the odds by producing leaders in science, medicine, education and law.

Tougaloo, a small city with all its amenities . . .

Mississippi History Notes. Before the turn of the century, despite the late 1800s being an age of uncertainty and fear, students were inspired to test the waters of Tougaloo. To learn to read was dangerous. To speak of going beyond that, to learn math and medicine, law and the arts, definitely could strike the wrong chords

and become life-threatening goals. In spite of those odds and difficulties, Tougaloo stood proud. Nowhere is that more evident than in historian Vernon Lane Wharton's *The Negro in Mississippi from 1865-1890:*

"A much more encouraging story is that of Tougaloo, founded by the American Missionary Association, with the aid of the Freedmen's Bureau. Beginning with a large farm, which included a residence and a number of smaller buildings, the founders immediately erected an auditorium, school rooms, and dormitories for men and women, with a dining hall and kitchen included. Over the next twenty years, a building program gave way to many new structures including a blacksmith shop, carpentry and tin shops, and buildings for the elementary department and industrial department. In spite of new construction and expansion of older structures, accommodations were seldom available for all who sought admission . . . Around 1885, it soon became apparent that Tougaloo was turning out a superior type of teacher. With entrance requirements that were higher than those at Holly Springs or Lorman, [Rust and Alcorn Colleges], a remarkably good faculty, and provisions for practice teaching with supervision and criticism, it sent into the public schools a group of young men and women who, throughout the period, received unqualified praise. By 1890, the College was soundly established, with a student body of 300, and a capable faculty of sixteen members. It had about eighty-six acres planted in a variety of crops, and on its three hundred acres of pasture land, it kept a large herd of cattle . . . The value of the work of its students on the farm, in the public schools, and of their contact with the masses, is beyond calculation."

The transformation. Tougaloo has evolved and remains a critical community anchor. Tougaloo College is a community of learners, teachers and workers, undergirded by its history, environment and promise for powerful potential.

Instead of a farm, many modern architectural buildings are sprinkled among several historically significant structures, along with state-of-the-art fitness and recreational facilities. Students, as well as citizens from area communities, now enjoy wholesome athletic programs that have replaced another era's agricultural activity, which served two purposes—food for the community, and local exercise. Dreams of being literate workers have been transformed into passports and career paths for aspiring trailblazers and pioneers to build and grow a better planet.

Tougaloo is a private, co-educational, historically African-American, four-year liberal arts college that offers choices in 17 major fields of study. It has been recognized and applauded nationally for classroom

Tougaloo constructed and officially opened the long-awaited spacious New Women's Residence Hall in October 2001.

and faculty excellence. With seven applicants for every available space, Tougaloo attracts top students regionally, nationally and internationally. The College's faculty is a diverse group of scholars and teachers committed to the liberal arts tradition and to preparing students for graduate and professional schools. A strong foundation has helped Tougaloo leaders focus today on expanding its resources to forge alliances with business and academe to build stronger outreach components and future business enterprises.

Currently, the College partners with major institutions in Mississippi and across the nation to strengthen student opportunities and bolster local educational, health and recreational facilities for area citizenry. Of particular importance is the unprecedented Jackson Heart Study, initiated in the late 1990s to recruit and study 6,500 African Americans in an effort to decrease the large heart disease and stroke mortality rates in the South. The Jackson Heart Study is not only about clinical trials, but education, research and prevention. Tougaloo's integral role

in building this health legacy is its position as the Undergraduate Training Center (UTC). Located on the campus and working in collaboration with two state institutions, Jackson State University and the University of Mississippi Medical Center, the Heart Study UTC is the first of its kind at a Historically Black College or University (HBCU), with responsibility to help produce the nation's next generation of African-American cardiologists and epidemiologists.

Tougaloo's program also provides summer enrichment classes for high school students. Its programs are designed to help strengthen these students' math and science skills to better prepare them to seek careers in medicine, health and research. The multi-year

In 1910, Tougaloo students made the intricately designed iron-rod gate, which marks the main approach to the campus.

Heart Study is funded by two agencies based at the National Institutes of Health—the National Heart, Lung and Blood Institute, and the Office for Research for Minority Health.

Impacting the nation's workforce. With more than 5,000 alumni living throughout the region, Tougaloo has had a tremendous impact on the pool of professionals in numerous fields. It is best known for producing more than 40 percent of the African-American dentists, doctors, and lawyers who

The George A. and Ruth B. Owens Health, Wellness & Resources Center, named for former Tougaloo president and first lady, was constructed in 1998.

have serviced Mississippi over the past 100 years. Additionally, the College graduated the pioneering Black educators of the Deep South.

Also, Tougaloo's historic alliance with Brown University has been cited as a model among nationally recognized research partnerships. This relationship with Brown, involving students, faculty and staff, dates from the Civil Rights era. A unique and enriching exchange opportunity, more than 200 Tougaloo students have traveled to Providence, Rhode Island to study at Brown, while more than 100 Brown students have traveled south to study at Tougaloo. More than 65 faculty members and adminis-

Historic Holmes Hall, constructed in 1926, was named for the late Rev. William Trumbull Holmes, president from 1913 to 1933.

trators have participated in the program, which was established to combine the academic rigor of an Ivy League institution with community and racial experiences only an historically Black institution could provide. This tradition at Tougaloo resulted in the formation of the The Leadership Alliance, a 23-member institutional partnership among Ivy Leagues, other research intensive organizations and HBCUs.

Mixing art with social issues to foster racial progress. The Tougaloo Art Collections are renowned for history and worth. This resource includes more than 2,000 paintings, sculptures, drawings, collages and various forms of graphic art. It is

Mississippi's most impressive collection of modern Western art and traditional African sculpture. The Tougaloo Art Collections have been cited in numerous publications as collectively being one of the best college art holdings in America.

Also, the campus comes alive each summer with the nationally acclaimed Art Colony. The Colony brings together prominent artists, teachers, scholars, students and adult learners from America and abroad to explore and network. It has grown from a small group of artists and students to more than 100 participants, and is now acknowledged as a "Summer Retreat"—which offers an intensive week-long indulgence in making art and building alliances.

Beside being a favorite and popular tourist attraction in Mississippi, and having a listing in the National Register of Historic Places, Tougaloo received another honor in 1998. The vast assortment of historic buildings, the academic history and legendary economic posture, and, of course, its Civil Rights heritage and significance, led to the College's designation as a National Historic District.

Sharing visions to empower business engines. Even in its early years of growth and slow progress, Tougaloo was driven to excel. Today it enjoys partnerships with businesses such as Kroger, Coca Cola, Nissan, BellSouth and Entergy, and with government agencies such as the U.S. Army, the U.S. Department of Education, and the U.S. Department of Health & Human Services. Business leaders from throughout

the South, and many from across the nation, have helped Tougaloo earn another distinction in the corporate arena. Each February during the Annual Business Luncheon, the College pauses to recognize its donors who have generously supported its financial goals and helped improve life in Mississippi. The occasion has gained popularity and reputation as a premier networking opportunity and speakers' platform for America's top corporate CEOs. The College's employment force, and a student body that exceeds 1,000, provides a healthy supply of eager consumers. Additionally, Tougaloo is an anchor for its immediate business community occupying a location that straddles two bustling economies in swiftly growing Hinds and Madison counties.

Tougaloo student Tara Smith, of Jackson, spent a summer at Western Michigan University conducting scientific research through a grant from the National Science Foundation.

Nissan Motor Company broke ground on April 6, 2001, for a manufacturing plant located just off I-55 N., south of Canton. When completed in 2003, the plant will cover over 3 million square feet. Courtesy, Mississippi Development Authority

A TIMELINE OF MISSISSIPPI'S HISTORY

10,000 B.C.E. The first people, the Paleo-Indians, enter present-day Mississippi.

8,000 B.C.E. The Archaic culture begins to prevail among the native peoples, leading to a less nomadic lifestyle and production of more material goods.

1,500 B.C.E. The Woodland era of North American Indian history is underway. Mississippi Indians adopt agricultural production and populations increase.

700 The Mississippian culture, an infusion of ideas and practices from native American groups in Mexico and Guatemala, takes hold among native Americans in the lower Mississippi Valley, leading to the construction of mounds and plazas, the unification of governmental and religious leaders, and the rise of relatively large urban centers supported by a network of farmers.

1540–1541 Hernando De Soto, Spanish explorer, on a three-year excursion though the southeastern part of North America in search of gold, travels through present-day Mississippi. Though no riches are found, the diseases carried by De Soto and his fellow Europeans decimate the area's native American population.

*Above: **The Great Temple Mound of the Natchez Indians was a center of tribal religious life. Courtesy, Mississippi Department of Archives and History***

*Below: **Jefferson College, the Mississippi Territory's first educational institution, was established in 1803. Named for President Thomas Jefferson, the college struggled for many years after its creation due to inadequate financing, but it continued to operate until 1863. Courtesy, Mississippi Department of Archives and History***

1673 The French explorers, Father Jacques Marquette and Louis Jolliet, on a journey from Canada through the middle of North America travel down the Mississippi River as far south as the mouth of the Arkansas River, near present-day Rosedale.

1682 French explorer Robert Cavelier, Sieur de La Salle, travels the length of the Mississippi River and claims all the land drained by the river and its tributaries for the French king, Louis XIV. La Salle names the region Louisiana.

1691 English traders make contact with the Chickasaw Indians. The British agree to trade goods and money to the Chickasaw in exchange for Indian slaves.

1699 A French expedition headed by Pierre Le Moyne, Sieur d'Iberville and his brother, Jean Baptiste de Bienville, lands on Ship Island and the beach at Biloxi Bay and builds Fort Maurepas near present-day Ocean Springs.

1701 The French move the Louisiana colony to Mobile Bay.

1712–1717 Antoine Crozat holds the royal charter from Louis XIV for the colony of Louisiana. By the end of the period, less than 400 Europeans have settled there.

1716 The French establish a settlement and a fort (Rosalie) at Natchez.

1719 First record of slave traders bringing African slaves to the Louisiana colony.

1720 The "Mississippi Bubble" bursts in France after investors lose confidence in John Law's Mississippi Company to deliver on the promised riches of the Louisiana colony. New Biloxi becomes the capital of the Louisiana colony.

1722 Bienville moves the capital of the Louisiana colony to New Orleans, a town he founded four years earlier.

1724 Bienville enacts a Black Code for the Louisiana colony, outlining proper slave behavior and slave/

JEFFERSON COLLEGE AND MILITARY INSTITUTE, WASHINGTON, SIX MILES FROM NATCHEZ, MISSISSIPPI.
CHARTERED IN 1803.

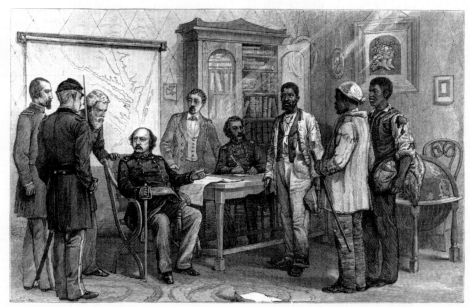

CONTRABAND OF WAR.

Left: As Union armies approached Mississippi during the Civil War, much of the state's slave population fled behind Union lines whenever possible. Union commanders referred to the refugees as "contraband," and their presence forced the Union army and the Lincoln administration to start the process of defining the meaning of black emancipation. Courtesy, Mississippi Department of Archives and History

Below: Jefferson Davis and his family at Beauvoir in the 1880s. After the Civil War Jefferson Davis was imprisoned for two years. He then lived in Memphis for several years until the late 1870s, when he retired to Beauvoir on the Mississippi Gulf Coast. Courtesy, Mississippi Development Authority/Division of Tourism

master relations. Three thousand seven hundred Europeans and 1,300 African slaves live in the Louisiana colony.

1729 The Natchez Indians attack and destroy Fort Rosalie at Natchez and Fort St. Pierre on the Yazoo River.

1736 The French launch a major campaign against the Chickasaw from the Illinois country and newly-built Fort Tombecbee (near present-day Epes, Alabama). The Chickasaw rout the French and their Indian allies.

1739 A second major campaign by the French against the Chickasaw forces the tribe to agree to peace terms.

1746–1750 A civil war within the Choctaw nation pits pro-French Choctaw against pro-British Choctaw.

1763 In the Treaty of Paris that settles the Seven Years War, Great Britain receives all of Louisiana east of the Mississippi and north of Lake Ponchatrain. The area is known as British West Florida.

1775 The British officially designate West Florida as an asylum for loyalist refugees.

1783 In the Treaty of Paris following the American Revolution, Great Britain turns over all land east of the Mississippi River and north of the 31st parallel to the United States, while Spain receives West Florida.

1795 The United States and Spain sign the Treaty of San Lorenzo, in which Spain relinquishes to the United States all claims to land north of the 31st parallel, opens the Mississippi River to American shipping, and allows Americans the right to deposit their freight in New Orleans.

1798 Congress establishes the Mississippi Territory. Winthrop Sargent of Massachusetts becomes the first territorial governor.

1800 Benjamin M. Stokes publishes the short-lived *Mississippi Gazette*,

the first Mississippi newspaper.
1802 The territorial capital is moved from Natchez to nearby Washington.
1803 The Natchez Trace opens as a major overland route between Natchez and Nashville.
1805 In the Treaty of Mount Dexter, the Choctaw cede 4 million acres of south Mississippi land to the United States.
1807 Former U.S. vice president Aaron Burr, suspected of treason, turns himself in to Mississippi territorial officials, but a territorial grand jury refuses to indict him.
1810 The United States annexes Spanish West Florida between the Pearl and Perdido rivers.
1811 The first steamboat, the *New Orleans*, arrives in Natchez. By the next year steamboats run regularly between New Orleans and Natchez.
1817 President James Madison approves the constitution for the new state of Mississippi and admits it as the twentieth state of the Union.
1820 The Choctaw, led by chiefs Pushmataha and Mushulatubbee, sign the Treaty of Doak's Stand, agreeing to give up about one-third of their Mississippi territory in exchange for land west of the Mississippi River. U.S. negotiators are Andrew Jackson and Thomas Hinds.
1821 Jackson, a site at Le Fleur's Bluff on the Pearl River, is selected as the state capital. Franklin Academy, the state's first public school, opens in Columbus.
1823 The Mississippi legislature passes a bill banning free blacks from moving into the state.
1830 In the Treaty of Dancing Rabbit Creek, the last of the Choctaw land is ceded to the state

For much of the nineteenth century, steamboats served as the primary means of transportation linking Mississippi's major commercial centers, Natchez and Vicksburg, to national markets. Though they no longer play any important economic role, steamboats such as the **Delta Queen** *and* **Mississippi Queen** *pictured here still transport passengers up and down the waters of the Mississippi River. Courtesy, Mississippi Development Authority/Division of Tourism*

of Mississippi.
1832 In the Treaty of Pontotoc, the Chickasaw agree to give up their remaining lands east of the Mississippi River in exchange for promised territory in the West. Mississippi adopts a new state constitution, one of the most democratic documents of its day. Property qualifications for voting and officeholding among white adult males are eliminated, and all major public offices, including the judiciary, become elected rather than appointed positions.
1834 Construction begins on the Old Capitol in Jackson.
1837 A financial panic ends the "Flush Times" of the 1830s, wiping out the state's banking system, bursting the public land bubble, and bankrupting many speculators and new settlers. The panic leads to an economic depression that lasts into the early 1840s.
1839 The Mississippi legislature passes the Mississippi Married Women's Property Law, the first state law allowing married women to own property in their own name.
1840 The state's first penitentiary is opened in Jackson.
1843 The Mississippi legislature agrees to repudiate the debts of the state-chartered Union Bank.
1851 Henry S. Foote, running under the banner of the Union party, wins the gubernatorial election, ending the hopes of some Mississippians that the state would reject the Compromise of 1850 and secede from the Union.
1861 Mississippi adopts a secession ordinance, becoming the second southern state to secede from the Union. Jefferson Davis, a Mississippi planter and former U.S. Senator and Secretary of War, becomes president of the Confederate States of America.
1862 During two days of fierce and bloody fighting, Union troops defeat Confederate forces (including many Mississippians) in a crucial battle at Shiloh, just north of the Mississippi border in Tennessee.
1863 Vicksburg, the last Confederate stronghold on the Mississippi River, falls to Union forces led by General Ulysses S. Grant. After the fall of Vicksburg, slaves swarm into Union camps, seeking both liberty and food and clothing. To conduct

the war, Mississippi passes a series of exacting tax measures, including a direct tax on all property, a capital gains tax, and a tax-in-kind on agricultural produce. These policies create resentment on the homefront, especially among poor non-slaveholders.

1865 A constitutional convention writes a new constitution that repudiates secession and accepts the abolition of slavery but limits suffrage to white males. The state legislature adopts a Black Code, which represents an attempt to reestablish the slave codes of the colonial and antebellum periods.

1867 The Mississippi legislature passes a crop-lien law.

1868 A constitutional convention dominated by white Republicans places voting and officeholding restrictions on ex-Confederates while extending the suffrage to adult freedmen.

1870 Mississippi readmitted to the Union. The Mississippi legislature elects Hiram Revels to the U.S. Senate, the first African American to serve in that body.

1875 In a violence-marred election, the Democrats gain control of state politics from the Republicans.

1876 The Democratic legislature impeaches the black lieutenant governor, A. K. Davis. Threatened with impeachment, both Governor Adelbert Ames and the black state Superintendent of Education, T.W.

Cordoza, resign. The Democratic legislature creates a convict leasing system as an inexpensive way to place tougher penalties and controls on blacks.

1878 The state's worst yellow fever epidemic kills more than 3,000. The legislature approves a measure mandating segregation in public schools; the 1870 legislation

establishing the public school system had not required racial segregation.

1888 The state establishes the first of many Jim Crow laws, which require racial segregation in all aspects of public life.

1890 Convention delegates approve a new state constitution, one that severely limits the suffrage, practi-

Above: Legalized racial segregation in Mississippi from the 1880s to the 1960s led to the development of separate institutions and businesses for black Mississippians, such as this black movie house in Leland. Courtesy, Mississippi Department of Archives and History

Right: Vicksburg waterfront, 1890. By the 1890s most Mississippi communities had recovered from the devastation of the Civil War and were once again bustling with economic activity. Courtesy, Mississippi Department of Archives and History

cally eliminating most black voters and many poor white ones.

1902 The Mississippi legislature approves a primary system for nominating political candidates, the first state in the nation to adopt this reform; the following year, Democratic officials declare their party's primary a whites-only election.

1906 Governor James K. Vardaman ends the convict leasing system, establishing in its stead Parchman Farm.

1907 The boll weevil arrives in Mississippi, damaging the state's primary agricultural commodity, cotton.

1908 Mississippi passes a state prohibition of liquor law, eleven years before the beginning of federal prohibition.

1918 The Great Migration of blacks from Mississippi to the North begins; the exodus continues for the next 50 years.

1924 Mississippi enacts an ineffective severance tax, which provides for a tax on timber when severed from the land. A similar, but strengthened, measure passes in 1940 and helps encourage the widespread reforestation of the cut-over pine forests of south Mississippi.

1927 A major flood of the Mississippi River devastates the Mississippi Delta.

1932 Governor Mike Conner convinces the state legislature to approve a sales tax to help lift Mississippi out of bankruptcy.

1936 Governor Hugh White pro-

Downtown Pass Christian was littered with debris and collapsed buildings after Hurricane Camille slammed into the Mississippi Gulf Coast on August 17, 1969. Practically the only building still standing on this street is the Pass Christian City Hall (left). Courtesy, McCain Library and Archives, University of Southern Mississippi Libraries

poses the BAWI plan (Balance Agriculture with Industry), which begins a major effort to industrialize Mississippi's economy.

1939 Geologists discover oil at Tinsley Field in Yazoo County.

1944 The Choctaw Indian reservation is established in parts of four east Mississippi counties; the following year, the Choctaw reestablish tribal government.

1948 Mississippi Governor Fielding Wright runs as the vice presidential candidate under the banner of the States' Rights Party, commonly known as Dixiecrats.

1950 William Faulkner wins the Nobel Prize for literature.

1954 The U.S. Supreme Court's *Brown v. Board of Education* decision rules that segregated schools are unconstitutional. A group of well-to-do white citizens in the Delta, calling themselves the White Citizens' Council, mobilizes to

Left: *Black and white students throughout Mississippi began to attend public school together in the early 1970s. Years of pressure from black parents and the federal government forced Mississippi to abandon its dual system of public education. Courtesy, Mississippi Department of Archives and History*

Right: *John Grisham, author of a string of legal thrillers, is a former Mississippi lawyer and state legislator. His fourteen novels have been international bestsellers.*

maintain the racial status quo by using their prestige and financial power to intimidate black supporters of civil rights.

1959–1960 Dr. Gilbert Mason leads the state's first direct-action protests against racial segregation with wade-ins on the segregated beach in Biloxi.

1961 SNCC (Student Non-Violent Coordinating Committee) comes to southwest Mississippi to help local black activists launch a voter registration project.

1962 James Meredith's effort to become the first black student to enroll at the University of Mississippi leads to a riot in which two die and over 150 are injured. Six thousand federal troops restore order in Oxford.

1963 Byron de la Beckwith assassinates Mississippi civil rights leader Medgar Evers, state field secretary for the National Association for the Advancement of Colored People. Dr. James Hardy and his team of physicians perform the world's first successful lung transplant at the University of Mississippi's Medical Center.

1964 During Freedom Summer,

thousands of northern college students come to Mississippi to help with voter registration and focus national attention on the struggle for civil rights in the state. The Civil Rights Act of 1964 outlaws racial segregation in public accommodations. The first school desegregation occurs in the state.

1965 The federal Voting Rights Act outlaws Mississippi's literacy test for voting and provides for federal registrars to oversee the voting process.

1966 Mississippi repeals liquor prohibition, the last U.S. state to do so.

1968 Women are allowed to serve on state juries for the first time.

1969 Hurricane Camille ravages the Mississippi Gulf Coast with a twenty-five foot tidal wave surge and winds in excess of 200 m.p.h.

1970 The U.S. Supreme Court forces the complete integration of Mississippi public schools. After a student protest at Jackson State College, Jackson city police and state highway patrol officers fire on a women's dormitory, killing two students.

1978 Thad Cochran is elected to the U.S. Senate—the first Republican to

win statewide office in the twentieth century.

1982 The Mississippi legislature approves the Education Reform Act, which establishes public kindergartens, creates a compulsory school attendance law, and makes other improvements in the state's public education system.

1990 State lawmakers adopt riverboat gambling; the measure sparks a multimillion dollar industry along the Mississippi River and the Gulf Coast.

1994 A Hinds County jury convicts Byron de la Beckwith of the murder of Medgar Evers.

1998 A Forrest County jury convicts Ku Klux Klan leader Sam Bowers of the 1966 murder of Vernon Dahmer, a local civil rights leader.

2000 In the 1999 gubernatorial race, neither Democrat Ronnie Musgrove or Republican Mike Parker receives a majority of the popular or electoral votes, so the largely-Democratic Mississippi House decides the election and picks Musgrove. Mississippi voters choose to retain the state flag with its Confederate emblem—in use since the 1890s.

SELECTED BIBLIOGRAPHY

The following listing is not meant to be comprehensive. It merely serves as a beginning guide for study of Mississippi history.

General Works

Claiborne, John F. H. *Mississippi, as a Province, Territory and State, with Biographical Notices of Eminent Citizens*. Jackson: Power & Barksdale, 1880. Reprint, 1978.

Doyle, Don H. *Faulkner's County: The Historical Roots of Yoknapatawpha, 1540-1962*. Chapel Hill: University of North Carolina Press, 2001.

Fickle, James E. *Mississippi Forests and Forestry*. Jackson: University Press of Mississippi, 2001.

McLemore, Richard Aubrey, ed. *A History of Mississippi*. 2 vols. Hattiesburg: University & College Press of Mississippi, 1973.

Rowland, Dunbar. *History of Mississippi, the Heart of the South*. 4 vols. Chicago: The S. J. Clarke Publishing Co., 1925. Vols. 3 and 4 contain biographies.

Sparks, Randy J. *Religion in Mississippi*. Jackson: University Press of Mississippi, 2001.

Skates, John Ray. *Mississippi: A Bicentennial History*. New York: Norton, 1979.

Mississippi to 1865

Baldwin, Joseph G. *The Flush Times of Alabama and Mississippi: A Series of Sketches*. New York: D. Appleton & Company, 1853.

Ballard, Michael B. *Pemberton: The General Who Lost Vicksburg*. Jackson: University Press of Mississippi, 1999.

Bettersworth, John K. *Confederate Mississippi: The People and Policies of a Cotton State in Wartime*. Baton Rouge: Louisiana State University Press, 1943.

Bolton, Charles C. *Poor Whites of the Antebellum South: Tenants and Laborers in Central North Carolina and Northeast Mississippi*. Durham: Duke University Press, 1994.

Bond, Bradley G. *Political Culture in the Nineteenth-Century South: Mississippi, 1830-1900*. Baton Rouge: Louisiana State University Press, 1995.

Bynum, Victoria E. *The Free State of Jones:*

Mississippi's Longest Civil War. Chapel Hill: University of North Carolina Press, 2001.

Galloway, Patricia Kay. *Choctaw Genesis, 1500-1700*. Lincoln: University of Nebraska Press, 1995.

Jordan, Winthrop D. *Tumult and Silence at Second Creek: An Inquiry into a Civil War Slave Conspiracy*. Baton Rouge: Louisiana State University Press, 1995.

May, Robert E. *John A Quitman: Old South Crusader*. Baton Rouge: Louisiana State University Press, 1985.

Moore, John Hebron. *The Emergence of the Cotton Kingdom in the Old Southwest: Mississippi, 1770-1860*. Baton Rouge: Louisiana State University Press, 1988.

Morris, Christopher. *Becoming Southern: The Evolution of a Way of Life, Warren County and Vicksburg, Mississippi, 1770-1860*. Oxford: Oxford University Press, 1995.

Olsen, Christopher J. *Political Culture and Secession in Mississippi: Masculinity, Honor, and the Antiparty Tradition, 1830-1860*. Oxford: Oxford University Press, 2000.

Usner, Daniel H. *Indians, Settlers, and Slaves in a Frontier Exchange Economy: The Lower Mississippi Valley Before 1783*. Chapel Hill: University of North Carolina Press, 1992.

Wells, Mary Ann. *Native Land: Mississippi, 1540-1798*. Jackson: University Press of Mississippi, 1994.

Mississippi, 1865 to the Present

Barry, John M. *Rising Tide: The Great Mississippi Flood of 1927 and How It Changed America*. New York: Simon & Schuster, 1997.

Cobb, James C. *The Most Southern Place on Earth: The Mississippi Delta and the Roots of Regional Identity*. Oxford: Oxford University Press, 1992.

Cresswell, Stephen E. *Multiparty Politics in Mississippi, 1877-1902*. Jackson: University Press of Mississippi, 1995.

Davis, Jack E. *Race Against Time: Culture and Separation in Natchez Since 1930*. Baton Rouge: Louisiana State University Press, 2001.

Dittmer, John. *Local People: The Struggle for Civil Rights in Mississippi*. Urbana:

University of Illinois Press, 1994.

Harris, William C. *Presidential Reconstruction in Mississippi*. Baton Rouge: Louisiana State University Press, 1967.

Harris, William C. *The Day of the Carpetbagger: Republican Reconstruction in Mississippi*. Baton Rouge: Louisiana State University Press, 1979.

Holmes, William F. *The White Chief: James Kimble Vardaman*. Baton Rouge: Louisiana State University Press, 1970.

Kirwan, Albert D. *Revolt of the Rednecks: Mississippi Politics, 1876-1925*. Lexington: University of Kentucky Press, 1951.

Lomax, Alan. *The Land Where the Blues Began*. New York: Pantheon Books, 1993.

McMillen, Neil R. *Dark Journey: Black Mississippians in the Age of Jim Crow*. Urbana: University of Illinois Press, 1989.

McMillen, Neil R. *The Citizens' Council: Organized Resistance to the Second Reconstruction*. Urbana: University of Illinois Press, 1971.

Morgan, Chester. *Redneck Liberal: Theodore G. Bilbo and the New Deal*. Baton Rouge: Louisiana State University Press, 1985.

Oshinsky, David M. *Worse Than Slavery: Parchman Farm and the Ordeal of Jim Crow Justice*. New York: Free Press, 1996.

Ownby, Ted. *American Dreams in Mississippi: Consumers, Poverty, and Culture, 1830-1998*. Chapel Hill: University of North Carolina Press, 1999.

Payne, Charles. *I've Got the Light of Freedom: The Organizing Tradition and the Mississippi Freedom Struggle*. Berkeley: University of California Press, 1995.

Wayne, Michael. *The Reshaping of Plantation Society: The Natchez District, 1860-1880*. Baton Rouge: Louisiana State University Press, 1983.

INDEX